Urban Waterfront Promenac

Some cities have long-treasured waterfront promenades, many cities have recently built ones, and others have plans to create them as opportunities arise. Beyond connecting people with urban water bodies, waterfront promenades offer many social and ecological benefits. They are places for social gathering, for physical activity, for relief from the stresses of urban life, and where the unique transition from water to land eco-systems can be nurtured and celebrated. The best are inclusive places, welcoming and accessible to diverse users. This book explores urban waterfront promenades worldwide. It presents 38 promenade case studies—as varied as Vancouver's extensive network that has been built over the last century, the classic promenades in Rio de Janeiro, the promenades in Stockholm's recently built Hammarby Sjöstad eco-district, and the Ma On Shan promenade in the Hong Kong New Territories—analyzing their physical form, social use, the circumstances under which they were built, the public policies that brought them into being, and the threats from sea level rise and the responses that have been made.

Based on wide research, *Urban Waterfront Promenades* examines the possibilities for these public spaces and offers design and planning approaches useful for professionals, community decision-makers, and scholars. Extensive plans, cross sections, and photographs permit visual comparison.

Elizabeth Macdonald, Ph.D., is Associate Professor of Urban Design in the Departments of City and Regional Planning and Landscape Architecture/Environmental Planning at the University of California, Berkeley. She is author of *Pleasure Drives and Promenades: A History of Frederick Law Olmsted's Brooklyn Parkways* (2012), co-author of *The Boulevard Book: History, Evolution, Design of Multiway Boulevards* (2002), and co-editor of *The Urban Design Reader* (2013).

Urban Waterfront Promenades

Elizabeth Macdonald

Routledge
Taylor & Francis Group

NEW YORK AND LONDON

First published 2018
by Routledge
711 Third Avenue, New York, NY 10017

and by Routledge
2 Park Square, Milton Park, Abingdon, Oxon, OX14 4RN

Routledge is an imprint of the Taylor & Francis Group, an informa business

Library of Congress Cataloging-in-Publication Data
Names: Macdonald, Elizabeth, 1959- author.
Title: Urban waterfront promenades / Elizabeth Macdonald.
Description: New York: Routledge, 2017. | Includes bibliographical
references and index.
Identifiers: LCCN 2016047545| ISBN 9781138824195 (hardback) | ISBN
9781138824218 (pbk.) | ISBN 9781315740836 (ebook)
Subjects: LCSH: Waterfronts. | Promenades (Pedestrian areas) | Public spaces.
Classification: LCC NA9053.W38 M33 2017 | DDC 711/.4--dc23
LC record available at https://lccn.loc.gov/2016047545

ISBN: 978-1-138-82419-5 (hbk)
ISBN: 978-1-138-82421-8 (pbk)
ISBN: 978-1-315-74083-6 (ebk)

Typeset in Adobe Caslon
by Servis Filmsetting Ltd, Stockport, Cheshire

MIX
Paper from
responsible sources
FSC® C014174
www.fsc.org

Printed and bound in the United States of America by Sheridan

To Georgia and Dick Bassett
To Allan Jacobs

Contents

Acknowledgements

This book was inspired by the joys of walking and biking Vancouver's waterfront promenades every year since 2001, while sketching and painting along the way. I came to know the "seawall" and fell in love with Vancouver when I taught for an all too short year in the School of Community and Regional Planning at the University of British Columbia. The public life I have experienced on the seawall, along with the sheer beauty of the waterfront setting, has greatly enriched my life. This personal experience started me on a quest to learn about waterfront promenades elsewhere.

There are many people to thank. First, I would like to thank my students at the University of California at Berkeley, whose inquisitiveness, passion, creativity, and dedication make my teaching life so rewarding.

Most particularly I give thanks to two students who made invaluable contributions to the development of the book manuscript. Tamar Nativ helped create all the 1:400,000 and 1:40,000 plans included in the case study chapters and the 1:12,000 plans included in Part 2. She worked with amazing skill and diligence and I cannot thank her enough. Hyokyung Ryu helped with the process of creating a draft graphic layout of the manuscript for my use in communicating with my publisher, refined several of the 1:12,000 maps, and created the one for Seoul. His skill and humor under deadline pressure were and are much appreciated.

I am indebted to people who helped me conduct the research by hosting me in various different cities. My good friends Tony and Plu Dorcey introduced me to Gruissan, where I have enjoyed many pleasant days in their company on their canal boat, *Tempus Fugit*. They have also for several years generously let me housesit their Granville Island home in Vancouver while they travel, and this was an immense help to me in completing the Vancouver case study. Patricia Frithiof and the Jacobs-Frithiof family, Janet, Niko, Björn, Anders, and Johan, helped host me during my visit to Stockholm, making that trip very special. José María Ureña and Paloma Álvarez de Lara hosted me in Bilbao and guided me around the city. José María Ureña, Borja Ruiz Apilánez, and Eloy Solis Trapero helped me gather GIS data for San Sebastián and Bilbao. Amy Jacobs-Colas and Dominique Colas hosted me in Paris, and have guided me around the city many times. Kathy and Rolf Wolter helped host me in Hamburg, and Judith Stilgenbauer helped me gather GIS data for that city. Jaime Lerner and Ilana Lerner helped make arrangements for my visit to Rio de Janeiro, and also hosted me in Curitiba. Hyungkyoo Kim helped make arrangements for my Singapore visit, guided me around the city, and helped me obtain GIS data. Sunjin Park helped make arrangements for my Seoul visit, helped me obtain GIS data, hosted me nightly with amazing dinners, and provided me with students who guided me around the city. These students included Hyokyung Ryu, Daehee Kim, Namhyun Kim, Hwi-seo Yoon, Dongwook Moon, and HongJun Yang. They were particularly resourceful at finding vegetarian restaurants for me to eat in and provided much welcomed laughter.

I would also like to thank the professionals and academic colleagues who generously gave of their time to talk about the waterfront promenades in their cities or issues related to promenades more generally. Particular thanks go to Joyce Drohan, Roland Kupfer, Scot Hein, Julia Hein, Frank Ducote, Susan Taylor, Larry Beasley, John Ellis, Joe McBride, and Kristina Hill.

A number of academic colleagues have provided me with mentorship through the course of my academic life, which has helped immeasurably. I would particularly like to thank Karen Chapple, Stephen Wheeler, Annette Kim, Betty Deakin, Louise Mozingo, Renee Chow, Michael Southworth, Peter Bosselmann, and Paul Waddell.

I need to thank the institutions that provided financial and other support for this project. During the research and book preparation, I was assisted by grants from the Committee on Research of the University of California at Berkeley, from generous research funds made available to me by Berkeley's Department of City & Regional Planning, and by a faculty research grant from Berkeley's Department of Landscape Architecture & Environmental Planning.

At Routledge, I am grateful for editor Nicole Solano who believed in this project from the start and to editor Kate Schell who saw it through to completion. I appreciate as well the help of others who helped shepherd the book through its publication, including editorial assistant Krystal LaDuc, copy editor Mary Dalton, and production editor Cathy Hurren. The *Journal of Planning History* originally published some parts of the Vancouver case study chapter, and I appreciate the editorial advice given at that time.

My biggest thanks go to my husband, Allan Jacobs. He has been a constant companion, my inspiration, and my joy. I am amazed at how generous he has been with his support and good advice, and I have been constantly buoyed by his wonderful sense of humor. My thanks also go to members of my extended family and to dear friends for lending me their support and encouragement while I focused on this all-consuming project. You know who you are and you have my gratitude. Particular thanks go to Georgia and Dick Bassett for their encouragement all these many years to travel and see the world, to my mother Edy Macdonald, who has always been there for me and helped with the Florida case studies, and to Cheryl Parker, who always provides good insights on everything and much laughter. I am also grateful for the mindfulness, laughter, and healing provided by my restorative yoga teacher, Britt Fohrman, and the support of all my yoga buddies.

Introduction

Waterfronts draw people to them. The attraction has to do with the open space they provide but also with the sheer joy of looking at water. Water may be calm and restful or roaring and dramatic, but it is always moving through the action of currents, waves, or wind and the play of light and reflection, and this is part of why it is so fascinating: its movement keeps the eye moving and people's eyes like to move. Placing a public promenade along an urban waterfront gives one of the best places in the city, this special water place, to everyone.

Some cities have long had treasured waterfront promenades that serve as focal areas for public life, many other cities have recently built them, and still others are considering doing so. The recent proliferation of waterfront promenades has come with de-industrialization. Many urban central waterfronts were long used for shipping and industrial uses, but over the last 40 or so years these activities have in many cities declined or shifted elsewhere. People see new social and environmental opportunities for water edges after the industrial uses diminish or leave, and walking and biking promenades are often deemed a good way to re-connect the city with the waterfront. Depending upon a city's circumstances and predilections, promenades may be built incrementally over time as waterfront land and funding become available, or all at once as part of a major waterfront transformation.

At the same time that urban waterfronts are being re-envisioned and embraced as places for people, their future prospects, and the prospects of the old or new precincts near them, are threatened by the impacts of global warming induced climate change, sea level rise, and elevated storm surge risk, raising a host of challenges. The Intergovernmental Panel on Climate Change has recently projected a global sea level rise of up to 98 cm (or 38 inches) by 2100, and acknowledges that this rise could be much greater if the Greenland and Antarctic ice sheets melt more quickly than expected. The questions are: What is the threat to existing waterfront promenades? How are cities responding? And, perhaps most important, how might urban waterfront promenades be designed to create a resilient urban water's edge that can help cities adapt to future sea level rise and increased storm surge?

This book is about urban waterfront promenades worldwide. More specifically, it is about the physical and social qualities of such promenades, their urban contexts, the processes through which they were created, the challenges they face related to climate change, and the opportunities they provide for sea level rise adaptation.

A major purpose is to provide knowledge that may be helpful to concerned citizens, public policy makers, city planners, urban designers, and landscape architects grappling with the opportunities and constraints of transforming urban waterfronts. There will be many more waterfront promenades built in the years to come, and so it is important to study what has been done and is being done, to comparatively analyze issues and opportunities, and to develop design guidance for future promenades.

The Roles of Waterfront Promenades

Waterfront promenades have a number of roles in urban life, both social and ecological. First and foremost, they are spaces for the unfolding of public life. They are gathering spaces where people go to see and be seen by others, to be a part of the social life of the city. Water bodies create abrupt edges to urban development and this edge condition offers the possibility of creating a linear public open space, often one of some length. A waterfront promenade within this linear open space can connect city neighborhoods with each other, offering the possibility for people to come together.

It could be argued that waterfront promenades are not inclusive public spaces. The word "promenade," which derives from the French *se promener*, meaning 'to walk,' connotes both a generous walkway and the act of strolling leisurely in the company of others. The term was first associated with gatherings of fine people, finely dressed, strolling along a grand avenue—a parade of high society with "everyone who's anyone" coming out to see and be seen. But today, promenades are understood to be much more egalitarian: walkways open to anyone and everyone, where people can move at their leisure amongst others.

The best waterfront promenades are designed to be welcoming to diverse users. The main physical conditions that can work against waterfront promenades being inclusive public spaces are if they are located in exclusive parts of the city, if the land uses along them cater only to a wealthy clientele, if they do not provide free places to sit, or if they are not easily accessible by public transit. These potential problems can be overcome through thoughtful planning and design, and perhaps also through programming. Waterfront promenades may also feel exclusive if local people are not involved in their design or if the needs and desires of diverse people are not taken into account. Creating an inclusive planning process can address these problems. Programming a promenade with activities appealing to a range of different people can also help make them feel and be welcoming and inclusive.

Along with being social spaces, urban waterfront promenades are also recreational spaces that offer people the opportunity for active living. Their linearity encourages people to move along them, and their edge condition makes movement on foot and bike particularly enjoyable because intersections with vehicle roadways do not interrupt the flow. In many cities, this possibility of uninterrupted linear flow stands in stark contrast to the continually interrupted flow that pedestrians and bicyclists encounter on city streets.

Most waterfront promenades are particularly inclusive places for doing physical activity. They are open to everyone because they are free. Most feel safe because they tend to be very visible public open spaces with many eyes on them, and so they are attractive to women walking or biking alone who might feel unsafe on less frequented or visible paths, such as walking trails in parks. Most also feel safe because they tend to be separated from vehicle traffic, and so are attractive to families with small children. Bicycle promenades along urban waterfronts are likely to attract people of all ages and abilities to them, unlike bicycle routes on city streets, because they can be completely separated from vehicle traffic.

Beyond their contribution to physical health, it is also possible for urban waterfront promenades to contribute to mental health because they can be designed as restorative spaces. Research has shown that people find views of open space and greenery restorative, conducive to an "unbending of the faculties" and providing relief from the stresses of urban life. Waterfronts provide open views and promenades can be designed with greenery and to have a calm ambience. The land uses fronting a promenade have much to do with how it feels. Parkland along it helps create a contemplative environment, although certainly parks can also be used for vigorous activities. Commercial or entertainment uses along a promenade tinge it with an air of consumption, and if there is too much of it or if it caters to boisterous activity, it may take away from a promenade's restorative possibilities. Likewise, nearby major roadways usually detract from restorative qualities because of the noise created by vehicle traffic and the visual disturbance created by its constant motion. Of course, there are situations where if there is going to be a waterfront promenade at all it has to be close to a major roadway. In these cases, the promenade usually provides a somewhat more restorative environment than there would otherwise be, especially if design steps are taken to mitigate the roadway's impact.

In addition to the social and health opportunities they afford, waterfront promenades also offer ecological opportunities. Urban water edges are many-faceted interface zones: between land and water, between city and nature, between built and un-built landscapes. This offers many possibilities for creative design. Water to land interface zones are naturally ecologically rich, but in urban areas these zones have all too often been severely damaged. The water's edge of a promenade can be designed to help restore the natural richness, and perhaps also to allow people to get close to the water where they can see the natural processes occurring there.

Research Approach

A central issue with this research was choosing which promenades to study. It was deemed important to be able to speak from firsthand knowledge, to have directly seen, experienced, and measured the promenades, to have counted the flows of people and watched what people were doing. This placed limits on how many promenades could be studied and so those included represent but a small sampling of all that exist worldwide. Choices were made based upon personal experience, advice from professional and academic colleagues, and by reviewing literature about waterfront development. Inevitably, many fine promenades are not here.

An attempt was made to cover a variety of different promenade types. One clear distinction is the type of water body a promenade runs along, and so an effort was made to include some along oceans, bays, rivers, and lakes. It would have been good to include some along canals as well, but for various reasons it was not possible to do so. There are many other contrasts between the promenades studied. Some have been around for a long time and others are recently built. Many are in big cities, but several are in small towns or suburban areas. Some are part of large waterfront promenade networks, and others are singular promenades, some quite small. Some are highly commercialized and others purposefully bucolic. Some are tourist oriented and some locally oriented. Some are grand in their design and others modest. All have things to teach.

Readers will notice that many of the promenades are located in North America or Europe, with a handful in Asia and one in South America. The geographic focus reflects where in the world it was easiest to travel given the constraints of time and available funding, and the opportunities afforded to piggyback the research onto travel undertaken for other reasons. It was hoped to include examples from elsewhere, in particular Australia, Africa, the Middle East, and Mexico, but the constraints, combined with the need to bring some closure to this research project, did not allow this.

In the end, 38 promenade case studies have been completed. Some focus on a single promenade and others on multiple promenade segments that are part of a connected system. A number of tasks were undertaken for each case study. A literature review was conducted to learn the promenade's history, the social context and circumstances in which it was conceived, the planning process used to develop its design, and the implementation approach used to create it. For some promenades, information on these things was also gathered through informal interviews with knowledgeable people, including professional urban designers and academics. Research was also undertaken to learn something of the challenges each promenade faces from climate change and sea level rise.

A series of empirical observations were conducted in the field. Measurements of the promenade's physical form were taken and recorded in notebooks. Photos were taken to record elements of physical form, the character of the water views and landside frontage, and the ways in which the promenades were being used. Time was spent watching the social activity taking place and also directly participating in it, by walking, biking, and sitting along the promenades. User counts were taken and analyzed. Because of the large number of case studies involved and the limited field work that could be conducted given time constraints, it was not possible to do systematic sampling, covering all times of the day, week, and year. Instead, the count data collected provides a snapshot of particular moments that give a sense of how each promenade is used. In some cases it was only possible to conduct single counts, and elsewhere there was time to do more. In general, an attempt was made to conduct counts at the busiest times of day and week, and during weather conducive to being outside.

The counts recorded the number of people passing a given point on the promenade. In most cases, information was also recorded about the people observed and what they were doing. This included gender, age range, whether they were with others or alone, and their mode of movement. When possible, in other words when the numbers were low enough, notes were made on the numbers of people using mobile phones or wearing headphones. The idea was to see how engaged people were with their immediate environment.

It would have added to the study to interview people about their perceptions and use of the promenades, but this was not possible, again because of the large number of case studies. Surveys of people using Vancouver's waterfront promenades were conducted as part of an earlier study, which was focused on the use of waterfront promenades by older adults, and understandings gained from that work, including that people deemed the promenades very important and used them frequently, served as inspiration for this larger research study.

Spatial data was collected from Geographic Information System (GIS) and map sources. This data along with the physical measurements taken in the field was used to create graphics that allow comparative analysis across the promenades. These graphics include city location maps, at a scale of 1:400,000, local context maps showing street and block and open space patterns, at a scale of 1:40,000, and cross sections representative of typical or unique conditions, at a scale of 1:2,400 (1 inch equals 20 feet). For select promenades, more detailed local context maps showing building footprints were also created, at a scale of 1:12,000 (1 inch equals 1,000 feet), in order to analyze patterns of connectivity and access. All plan graphics are oriented with north to the top of the page.

Analysis of the relative crowdedness of each promenade during the snapshot observation period was undertaken by combining the cross sectional information and the user counts.

What Follows

Part 1 of this book presents the case studies. The promenades are grouped into 12 chapters based upon their most salient physical or social features, understanding that readers will think of them as they wish. Deciding on these groupings was challenging because the promenades all have multiple qualities. Of course, there is no mistaking a bridge promenade! All the chapters contain multiple case studies except the first, which focuses solely on Vancouver. This is to pay homage to Vancouver because its extensive waterfront promenade network provided the initial inspiration for this research study. It is also to highlight what can be achieved when a city implements a simple idea over the long term through public-sector-led planning efforts, most recently using participatory planning processes.

Each case study includes a brief summary of when and how the promenade or promenades came into being, the formative ideas behind them, and the public policies instrumental to their creation. The design characteristics of each promenade are discussed, along with findings about their use and analysis of their connectivity. The challenges presented by climate change and future sea level rise particular to each promenade's situation are also analyzed, along with discussion of any efforts being made to address these issues. Ecological issues are both distinct from sea level rise and go hand in hand with it, and so any ecologically inspired design characteristics are also highlighted.

Part 2 of the book is devoted to analysis of the physical patterns of urban areas adjacent to and encompassing select promenades. The case studies selected for this analysis were chosen in order to show a range of urban context conditions. The analysis focuses on how different patterns contribute to or work against access to the promenades, and the connectivity between the promenade and adjacent neighborhoods. This analysis might have been included within the individual case study chapters but instead is gathered together in order to facilitate comparison across different promenades. Different built forms result in different patterns of access to waterfront promenades and may make them more or less inviting and inclusionary. The fine grain of residential streets abutting the Venice Beach Boardwalk, in Los Angeles, gives easy and regular access to it. A major roadway parallel to a promenade, as in Rio de Janeiro, gives visual access to those driving by but may cause barriers to pedestrians.

Part 3 reflects on the lessons learned from the promenades studied and also provides comparative analysis of key similarities and differences between the promenades. The first chapter provides observations about the physical, designable qualities of waterfront promenades that contribute to them being inviting and inclusive social places, observations on special qualities that take advantage of the possibilities afforded by their unique water's edge location, and a summary of key planning concepts that have proved useful. A second chapter reflects on the challenges to urban waterfront promenades posed by sea level rise, summarizes what cities with waterfront promenades are doing to address these challenges, and highlights some adaptive designs that have been implemented or proposed. Finally, a third chapter provides some brief summarizing reflections.

As writing of this book was nearing completion, a tragic event occurred on the Promenade des Anglais, in Nice, France, which is the lead case study in Chapter 2. On July 14, 2016, Bastille Day, a man purposefully drove a truck into crowds of people gathered there for a fireworks display, killing over 80 people and wounding scores more. The joyful gathering of people that night was exactly the sort of public activity waterfront promenades are made for. The tragedy lends an aura of sorrow to this long-standing and well-loved promenade that will now always be there, but no doubt people will continue to embrace the promenade for public life because it will remain the city's main public open space and because it is so treasured. The case study write-up that had already been completed when the event occurred was left unchanged in order to keep the focus on the promenade's everyday qualities and its contributions to public life, rather than on this one sad event, as shattering as it may be.

Part 1 | An Assembly of Waterfront Promenades

Chapter 1

Vancouver's Waterfront Promenade Network

Waterfront Promenade Network, Vancouver, British Columbia, Canada

Scale: 1:400,000

Vancouver is widely known for the beauty of its natural setting and for its waterfront parks. Situated along English Bay and the southern shore of the Burrard Inlet, the central city has a stunning waterfront backdrop made the more dramatic by tall mountains rising steeply from the north shore. The downtown's compactly grouped towers glitter against the mountains, Stanley Park seemingly floats in the bay, and everywhere the city meets the water's edge with greenery. Within the greenery lies one of the world's best and longest connected system of pedestrian and bicycle promenades.

Vancouver's 44-square-mile land mass is surrounded by water on three sides and much of the water's edge is public. The bucolic mouth of the Burrard Inlet and English Bay lies to the northwest, the partly de-industrialized Coal Harbour lies to the northeast, the largely industrialized Fraser River lies to the south, and the broad Salish Sea—the arm of the Pacific Ocean that lies between Vancouver Island and the mainland—lies to the west. The craggy peninsula on which the downtown and Stanley Park are located is carved out from the rest by the narrow False Creek inlet, once completely industrialized but now largely residential. In all, Vancouver has over 29 miles of shoreline, plus six more miles that lie along the unincorporated University of British Columbia (UBC) endowment lands at the western tip of the city. Waterfront walkways and bikeways, some rustic and others highly designed, line almost 60 percent of the city's part of the shoreline. They, and the park spaces and beaches in which they're situated or run along, are the city's main public open spaces. They are used daily by many people, residents and visitors alike, for promenading and other social activities, no matter what the weather.

Vancouver has been building waterfront promenades for more than 90 years, beginning with those in Stanley Park, and now has one of the longest connected networks anywhere in the world. They came about because early in its history the city embraced a vision to create them and has consistently held that vision and implemented it ever since. The promenades are today a major part of the urban design vocabulary of the city and a reflection of the city's sense of self. They speak to what can be achieved when a city steadily claims its waterfront for public uses and public life.

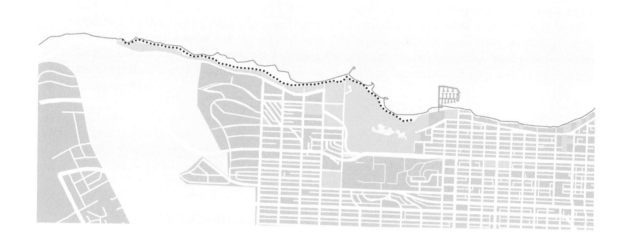

Scale: 1:40,000

Public Policy Related to Waterfront Promenades

Vancouver is Canada's premier west coast city—really the only one, other than much smaller Victoria on Vancouver Island, which is the provincial capital—and has always had big ambitions for itself and charted its own progressive course. It is a small big city, with a population of about 575,000 people, but it is the main city of a vast, largely suburbanized metropolitan region that spreads east along the Fraser River Valley for hundreds of miles and south to the American border. It has its own charter, rather than being a creature of the province as are most Canadian cities, which gives it a good deal of political autonomy.[1] In a bold move running counter to virtually all other North American cities as well as its own metropolitan neighbors, Vancouver never built any freeways. They were stopped in the 1960s before they were ever begun by a coalition of progressive citizens, bold politicians, and visionary planners.[2] Over the last three decades, driven by concerns for sustainability and livability, this coalition has helped enact public policies that support public transit and encourage high density residential development in and around the downtown and near major transit stops. A Vancouver neighborhood model has emerged, led by the public sector, which emphasizes the building of complete, walkable neighborhoods and is accomplished through comprehensive design guidelines and a sophisticated

Scale: 1:40,000

community planning process.[3] Perhaps best known for the unique "point tower over podium town-house base" building form that resulted, which provides density but also human-scaled street-facing frontage, the model also includes neighborhood community centers, schools, childcare facilities, public libraries, integrated social housing, traffic-calmed streets, and greenery. Open space is an important part of the package and the city requires that new shoreline neighborhoods have public waterfront parks and be lined with continuous waterfront walking and biking paths of generous design that link up with each other and with the seawall paths around Stanley Park and English Bay that have existed for some time. The goal is to create a connected system of public paths along the whole waterfront, building on a legacy from earlier times.

The vision of creating a public waterfront dates from the city's first comprehensive plan of 1929, and the design ideas contained in the plan planted the seeds for the pedestrian-oriented waterfront seen today. The well-known American city planner Harland Bartholomew prepared the plan at the behest of a citizens' group. While it was never formally adopted as policy it was looked to for guidance for many years and is still remembered fondly by many. The Bartholomew plan strongly emphasized preserving the waterfront for public uses, which at the time meant for the port and harbor operations that supported the city's economy but equally for recreation. "The recreational waterfront of Vancouver is as closely linked with the progress and development of the city as the harbour and commercial water frontage."[4] While the plan envisioned maintaining the Coal Harbour waterfront for port uses and the False Creek waterfront and part of the Fraser River waterfront for industrial uses, the rest of the city's shoreline was to be devoted to public bathing beaches, walks, parks, and pleasure drives.[5]

The plan recommended focusing first on the beach-lined English Bay waterfront, both the north side that fronted the city's West End apartment district, and the south side that stretched along Point Grey's affluent suburbs. Bartholomew's survey of existing conditions found that just 30 percent of this 5.4-mile beach frontage was public, and that it was in danger of being privatized through housing development. The city was urged to act immediately to secure the whole English Bay shoreline and foreshore for public recreation. Included in the plan was a schematic design for a waterfront park along the east side of English Bay showing wide lawns, picturesque tree planting, waterfront promenades, overlooks, bathhouses, and a swimming pool, plus parking areas and an adjacent pleasure drive.[6] Also included was a schematic design for parks along the Point Grey Beaches with similar lawns and promenades, a series of refreshment stands and restrooms, buffered parking lots for over one thousand cars, and a flanking boulevard.[7]

Another proposal was an "around the city" waterfront pleasure drive. While the drive was for automobilists, pedestrian access to the waterfront was given highest priority. Roadways were to be held back some distance from the shore while pedestrian paths would edge it. This was a pattern that had already been established by the Parks Board in its development of Stanley Park, which Bartholomew pointed out, congratulating the city:

> The Parks Board has done extremely well in building a drive and promenade around Stanley Park. The Board has not made the common mistake of giving the automobile riders first position along the sea wall. There is a disposition in park circles to make too many concessions to the motorist. The fact is overlooked that few elements of natural scenery are seen to advantage from a moving vehicle. The pedestrian deserves primary consideration, for he is willing to exert himself to see the landscape under advantageous conditions.[8]

Vancouver took Bartholomew's advice and over the next 50 years succeeded in creating parks along the English Bay beachfronts with walking paths at the water's edge, and also completed a continuous seawall walk around Stanley Park. In the 1970s, the city also built waterfront walking and bicycling paths along the southwest side of False Creek as part of the South False Creek redevelopment project that reclaimed former industrial lands for residential uses and created the well-known Granville Island marketplace. Only a few segments of the proposed around-the-city pleasure drive were built, in the West End and Point Grey, and they were modest in scale. The emphasis was clearly on pedestrians.

Walking and biking on the Point Grey, West End, Stanley Park, and South False Creek waterfront paths became a cherished activity of residents, which helped embed within the city's culture the idea that the water's edge should be public and this eventually led to adoption of the idea as public policy. The surveying done in conjunction with the City Planning Commission's 1980 city goal setting exercise indicated that citizens placed a high importance on the city's natural setting and access to natural areas and outdoor activities. One of the goals developed was: "Maintain access to and enjoyment of the natural setting and environment which is perceived as one of the principal components of the quality of life of Vancouver."[9] Implications of this policy were articulated as including preservation of water edges and public access, extension of seawalls, and increasing waterfront access where it was restricted. In 1989, a report entitled *Vancouver's Future: Toward the Next Million Futures* identified waterfronts to be one of the clearest manifestations of Vancouver's setting (the other being streets) and first spelled out the dream of a continuous publicly accessible recreational waterfront around the whole city.[10] Three years later, the Urban Landscapes Task Force's report noted that public opinion surveying had ascertained that access to the waterfront was very important and that the waterfront parks and waterfront views were considered sacred.[11] In keeping with this, the Park Board adopted a long-term strategy of maximizing waterfront parks and public access around the entire city.[12] These sentiments and findings helped spur the city to enact policies that would ensure the city's other waterfronts would be publicly accessible as they were de-industrialized and turned into residential neighborhoods. Considering the value of waterfront properties, the city's insistence on continuous additions to the waterfront public realm is no small achievement and speaks to the staying power of the idea contained in the original plan.

Promenade Design Characteristics

Starting at Coal Harbour at the northwest edge of the downtown, it is today possible to walk or bike along the water's edge on a continuous network of waterfront paths that go around Stanley Park, along English Bay, all around False Creek, around Kitsilano Point, and along the Kitsilano waterfront. After a short break, where very expensive houses occupy waterfront land along a bluff and the walking and bike paths are along designated city streets, the public waterfront paths pick up again at Jericho Park and continue the length of the Locarno and Spanish Banks beaches. From end to end, this "Seaside Route and Seawall" is about fifteen and a half miles long. In addition, walking and biking paths line several sections of the Fraser River shoreline at the city's southern edge, including the 1½-mile-long Fraser River Trail toward the middle section of this shoreline adjacent to a golf course and long established neighborhoods, and the almost 1½-mile-long path near Vancouver's eastern city limit adjacent to an area called the West Fraser Lands that was developed about 25 years ago with low density housing. Plans are in place to extend the later path for another mile to the city limit as the adjacent East Fraser Lands are developed over the next decade with medium density housing.[13]

The promenades along Coal Harbour and the north side of False Creek were mostly built during the 1990s and 2000s in conjunction with the new high density residential neighborhoods lying adjacent to them, with some segments, such as around the Vancouver Trade and Convention Centre completed in 2009 in advance of the Winter Olympic Games that Vancouver hosted in 2010.[14] Those along Southeast False Creek and the Science Centre at the eastern end of the creek were also completed for the Olympics and indeed Southeast False Creek served as the athletes' Olympic Village. The path along the Fraser River has been built in successive stages over the last several decades.

Whereas the earliest promenades are rustic and run along wide parks, the more recent ones are highly designed and lined with dense residential buildings along with some narrower parks. A few places have commercial uses, mostly cafés, and several neighborhood community centers face directly onto promenades. The design differences create delightful variability within the overall sense of continuity of the waterfront path system. A characteristic of the whole system is that the promenades are all well removed from traffic streets, with only a few exceptions, and major traffic streets never have to be crossed.

Let's look more closely at the design details of the promenades, starting with the older ones. The promenades along the Point Grey beaches are simple dirt paths ranging from 10 to 25 feet wide, shared by walkers and bikers alike, sometimes with only a narrow grass strip denoting different zones. There are a few random benches and picnic tables near the paths, and also randomly planted trees that sometimes shade the path but mostly do not.

Around Kitsilano Point, the promenades are simple concrete paths, usually just 10 feet wide and shared by walkers and bikers, though bikers are encouraged to use the nearby traffic-calmed residential street for through movement and many do so because this promenade gets very crowded where it passes by a highly used beach and park. The walking path is lined with benches, many situated at the best viewing spots. Continuing east around Vanier Park the shared path widens out and is of dirt. Here there are many pairs of benches, spread all along the waterside of the path. They are favorite places for couples to sit and watch the sunset.

Along the South False Creek/Granville Island neighborhood, pedestrians and bicyclists mostly share a paved path, typically about 15 feet wide, that wends through parks and past low- to medium-scale condominium buildings. In some places, bollards mark off pedestrian-only places, but otherwise walkers and bikers mix it up. Things work because most people follow the unwritten rule of keeping to the right and passing to the left whichever way they're moving, most bikers go relatively slow and are vigilant, and walkers are generally acceded the water's edge of the path.

Along the West End neighborhood, which was built with high-rise multi-family buildings in the 1960s replacing the bungalows that had been there before, the relatively narrow, asphalt or concrete paved bicycle and pedestrian paths are in a few places adjacent to each other but mostly widely

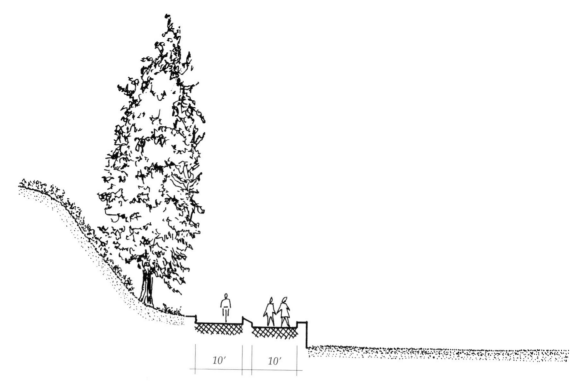

Section: Stanley Park seawall
Scale: 1" = 20'

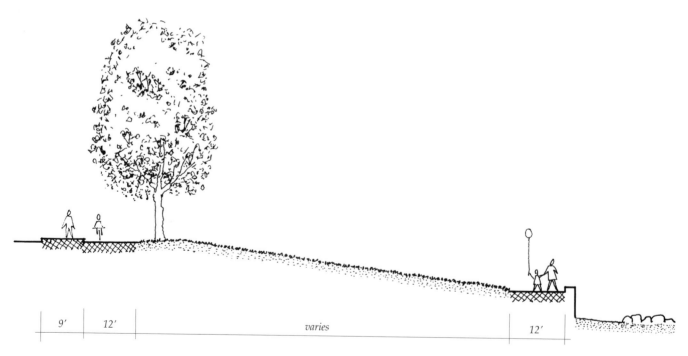

Section: West End
Scale: 1" = 20'

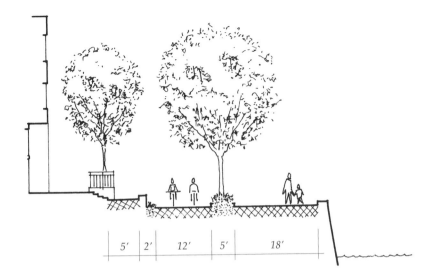

Section: False Creek North,
along townhouses
Scale: 1" = 20'

5' 2' 12' 5' 18'

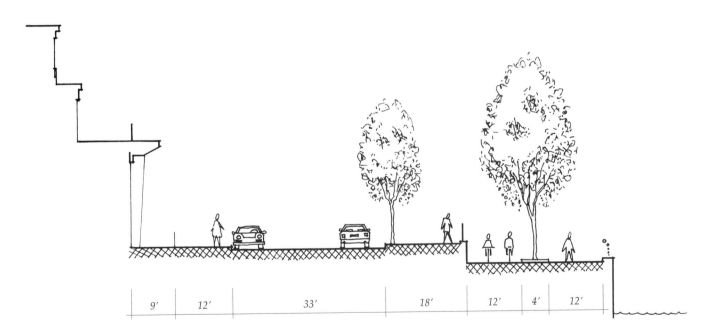

9' 12' 33' 18' 12' 4' 12'

Section: False Creek North,
along Marinaside Crescent
Scale: 1" = 20'

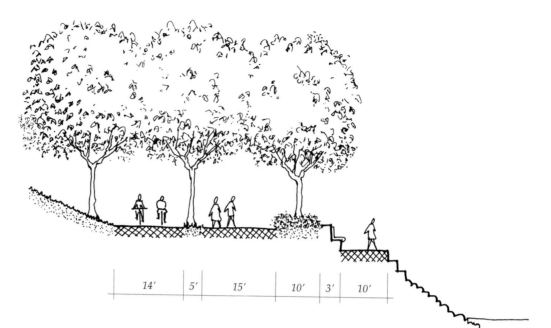

Section: False Creek North, near
David Lam Park
Scale: 1" = 20'

14' 5' 15' 10' 3' 10'

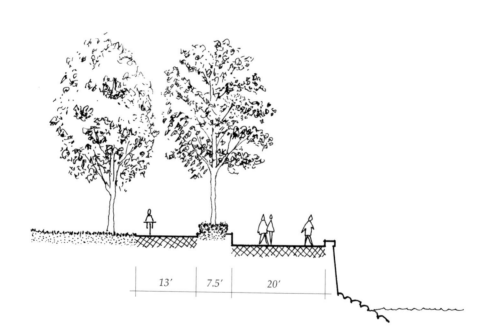

Section: Coal Harbour
Scale: 1" = 20'

13' 7.5' 20'

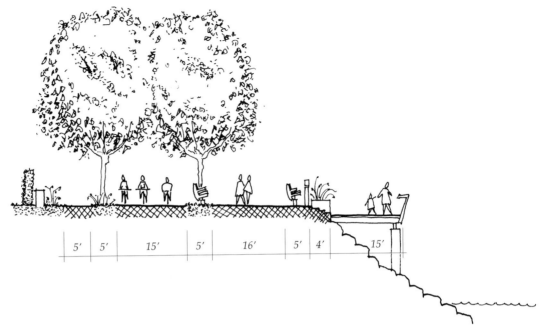

Section: Southeast False Creek,
near Hinge Park
Scale: 1" = 20'

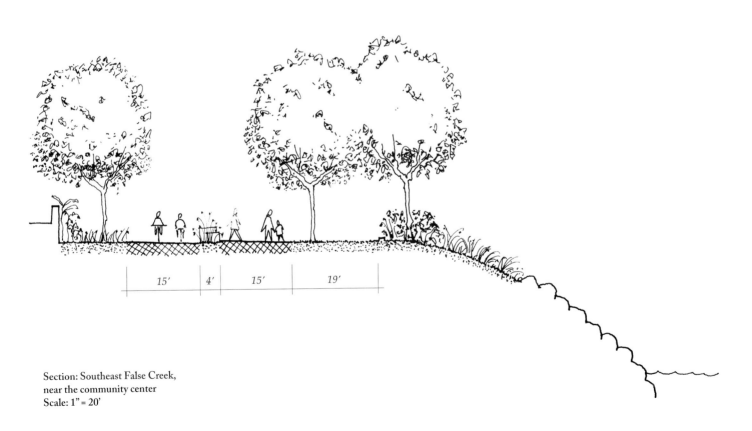

Section: Southeast False Creek,
near the community center
Scale: 1" = 20'

Stanley Park Seawall

False Creek North, along
townhouses

separated by park space. The pedestrian paths are always near the water, but the bicycle paths for the most part move through or at the top of sloping grass areas, in some places running on sidewalks at the edge of the two- to four-lane wide Beach Boulevard.

Around Stanley Park, the asphalt-paved seawall is typically about 20 feet wide and divided in half by a 6-inch rounded curb. The inner, upper area is for one-way travel by bikers, roller skaters, and skateboarders, and the lower half, nearer the water, is for pedestrians. The seawall itself is 4 to 8 feet tall and topped, in most places, with a wide granite curb. Along the northwestern edge of the seawall, massive rock walls rise steeply from the edge of the bike path while elsewhere rise gentle or steep slopes lined with tall trees.

The promenades around the new Coal Harbour, False Creek North, and Southeast False Creek neighborhoods all have a similar overall form: a 15-foot-wide pedestrian path near the water's edge, then a planted median, then a 15-foot-wide two-way bicycle path. Pedestrian paths are paved with

Fraser River Boardwalk

unit pavers while bicycle paths are asphalt or concrete. Beyond this, each promenade has its own detailing, tree and planting design, bench and lighting designs, railing designs where they occur and ways of allowing people to interact with the water, such as via steps or overlooks. Common features are two to three rows of closely spaced trees, pedestrian scale lighting, and many places to sit. The high-end condominiums that face the water look over the promenades, but are carefully set back so as to not dominate them.

The promenades along the Fraser River are for the most part simple dirt paths although there are short sections of boardwalk in some places.

Promenade Use and Connectivity

Goodly numbers of people use the Seaside Route and Seawall promenades throughout the year. They are particularly popular in the summer when it is warm and sunny, but people also enjoy them when it is cold and even when it is raining, as it often is. Notable is how easily accessible and connected with the urban fabric they all are. Many local streets lead into those along both older and newer neighborhoods and the Stanley Park seawall is relatively easy to get to from a traffic-calmed drive circling through the park. Vancouver has a great public transit system and all the promenades have nearby bus stops and some are close to Skytrain rapid transit stations.

Observations reveal that there is some variability in how the different promenades are used but that there are some commonalities: most people use them for strolling; most people are with others but there are also many people on their own; they attract both women and men; and they attract people of all ages, though young and middle-aged people predominate. Notably, relatively few people wear earphones or talk on their phones while moving along a promenade, suggesting most people are tuned in to and enjoying the immediate physical and social environments.

The number of people using the promenades varies from place to place with the highest numbers occurring on the promenades edging recently developed high density neighborhoods. In those areas, the numbers are toward the higher end of all promenades studied but well below the very highest numbers. (See the Appendix for a summary of promenade usage.)

The following snapshots give a sense of how alive with public life the promenades are and the diversity of activity and people on them.

The Southeast False Creek promenade is highly used on weekends. By way of example, on a sunny Sunday afternoon in early September, 1,062 people per hour were observed moving along it, overwhelmingly in groups (79%) rather than alone. Most were strolling (58%), many were biking (38%), and relatively few (4%) were jogging or fast-walking. There were slightly more women (55%) than men; most were young (56%) or middle-aged (32%) but there were also some children (7%) and some elderly (5%); very few were using phones or listening to music (3%).

A similar number of people, 1,044 people per hour, were observed moving along the promenade on another September Sunday afternoon, with the differences being that the percentages of people strolling (36%) versus biking (57%) were essentially flipped, slightly fewer people were in groups (66%), and this time there were more men (58%) than women. The promenade is somewhat less used on weekdays, but still draws many people to it. For example, on a sunny Tuesday late afternoon in early September, 788 people per hour were observed moving along the promenade. Relatively similar numbers of people were strolling (46%) and biking (41%) and the rest were jogging or fast-walking (13%). Men and women were almost equally divided and again people were overwhelmingly in groups (70%).

The Coal Harbour promenade is particularly well used on weekdays around the noon hour, a reflection of its close proximity to the city's downtown and nearby office employment. On a warm and sunny day in mid-September, 1,086 people per hour were observed moving along the promenade during the lunch hour. There were slightly more men (52%) than women, more were in groups (61%) than were alone, and as might be expected for office workers they were overwhelming strolling (73%) rather than biking (12%) or jogging (13%). Most people were middle-aged (52%), many were young (42%), a few were elderly (4%), and fewer were children (2%). Only a handful of people were talking on phones (3%) or listening to music (3%).

Southeast False Creek, near the community center

Coal Harbour

Kitsilano Point

The promenade on the Stanley Park seawall is attractive to tourists and residents alike. People get to it from the park or walk to it from the West End neighborhood. While experience suggests that the numbers of users is highest on weekends, it also attracts many people to it at other times. By way of example, on a warm and sunny Monday mid-afternoon, 495 people per hour were observed moving along its southern end, near the Stanley Park swimming pool. Most were biking (47%), many were strolling (42%), and the rest were jogging or fast-walking (11%). Most people were with others (57%) but many were also on their own (43%). While most people were young (44%) or middle-aged (41%), there were also a number of elderly people (14%) although only a few children (1%).

The Kitsilano Point promenade is a favored place for early evening activity. On a sunny Thursday early evening in early September, 474 people per hour were observed moving along it. Most were strolling (49%), many were jogging (35%), and the rest (16%) were biking. The low number of bikers is because of the constrained nature of the shared path; many bikers use instead the signed bike route on a nearby neighborhood street. Many people (55%) were with others, but many people were also on their own (45%). Many were young adults (61%) or middle-aged (28%) but some were elderly (6%) and a few were children (4%).

False Creek North, near
Marinaside Crescent

False Creek North, near David
Lam Park

West End, along English Bay

All this suggests the social nature of the promenades. The number of people on their own is particularly interesting, suggesting that the promenades feel safe and provide a place where people can be part of the social life of the city while also being alone.

The numbers of people walking and biking suggest that the promenades make an important contribution to public health by offering an attractive place for people to partake of physical activity. The research didn't track the distances people were walking or biking, but casual observation and personal experience suggest that many people go for long distances. It seems possible that seeing people walking or biking along the promenades inspires other people to do likewise. Vancouver is well known as having a culture of physical activity and it is plausible that the waterfront promenades have contributed to the establishment of that culture. It is also plausible that the culture contributed to the creation of the promenades. Likely it went, and goes, both ways.

Climate Change and Sea Level Rise Concerns

As important as the waterfront promenades are for the people of Vancouver and for many visitors to the city, they are threatened by sea level rise. The seawalls behind which the promenades lie, except the promenades along the Kitsilano and Point Grey beaches where there is no sea wall, have a geodetic datum height of approximately 3 meters (9.8 feet), some a little higher and some recently built ones on False Creek a little lower.[15] These heights have been sufficient to protect the promenades and areas inland of them from flooding except when major storm events with high winds have coincided with King Tide events, such as happened in December 2012 when water overtopped the Stanley Park seawall and also flooded Kits Beach.[16] The City of Vancouver has recently been studying the implications for flooding of future climate change and sea level rise and is in the process of developing mitigation strategies. A study initiated by the city released in December 2014, which modeled the city's coastal flooding for a range of sea level rise and storm event scenarios, found that a one-meter sea level rise coupled with a 500-year storm event could produce high water levels within the Burrard Inlet of geodetic datum 4.6 to 4.9 meters (15 to 16 feet).[17] While Vancouver has been experiencing slightly lower relative sea level rise in recent years than the global average due to land uplift from glacial rebound,[18] the city has decided to use a one-meter rise in sea level by 2100 as the scenario to use for long-term planning and is establishing policy based on this.[19] This scenario is in line with the upper range of projections for 2100 recently released by the Intergovernmental Panel on Climate Change (IPCC),[20] but less than the recent upper end projections of other climate assessment bodies, which are as high as 2 meters. (See Part 3, Chapter 14 for more about projections of future sea level rise.) Flood modeling did not include increases in storm severity or frequency because these effects of climatic change on the local environment have not yet been fully studied.[21]

The city has mapped new flood boundaries based on the one-meter sea level rise and 500-year storm scenario, and the maps show inundation of most of the city's waterfront promenades as well as large parts of some of the new neighborhoods that have been built around False Creek.[22] The city has taken the immediate action of requiring that all new buildings within the newly mapped flood zones have a ground floor elevation of geodetic datum 4.6 meters[23] but has yet to adopt any other mitigation strategies. Given the understood importance of the city's waterfront promenades, it is highly probable that the city will develop strategies that will keep them in place and protect their cherished qualities at the same time that they protect inland properties. This would likely mean not raising walls seaward of the promenades but raising the sea walls and the promenades themselves, although other strategies, such as building a flood control barrier at the mouth of False Creek have also been floated in the media.

Vancouver's extensive waterfront promenade system is testimony to what can be achieved by implementing a simple but visionary planning idea—creating a public waterfront and prioritizing pedestrians—over many years. If the past stick-to-it-ness is any indication of the future, no doubt the city will develop creative redesign strategies for the promenades as needed to address sea level rise and will find the wherewithal and political will to implement them.

Notes

1   John Punter, *The Vancouver Achievement: Urban Planning and Design* (Vancouver: UBC Press, 2003), 13–14.

2   Ibid., 24–26.

3   Punter, *The Vancouver Achievement*.

4   Vancouver (B.C.), ed., *A Plan for the City of Vancouver, British Columbia, Including Point Grey and South Vancouver and a General Plan of the Region* (Vancouver: Wrigley Printing Company, Ltd, 1929), 206.

5   Ibid., 200.

6   Ibid., 205–206.

7   Ibid.

8   Ibid., 237.

9   Vancouver City Planning Commission, "Goals for Vancouver" (Vancouver City Planning Commission, February 1980), 6.

10 Vancouver City Planning Commission, "Vancouver's Future: Toward the Next Million" (Vancouver City Planning Commission, 1989), 6.

11 City of Vancouver Urban Landscape Task Force, "Greenways, Public Ways," 1992, 10–11.

12 Vancouver Board of Parks and Recreation, "Management Plan," 1992, 44.

13 City of Vancouver Planning Department, "East Fraserlands: Phase One Design Guidelines, Section A – Public Realm Plan," June 12, 2008, accessed October 4, 2015, http://former.vancouver.ca/commsvcs/currentplanning/current_projects/east_fraserlands/phase1guidelines/sectionA.pdf.

14 City of Vancouver, "Vancouver's New Neighborhoods: Achievements in Planning and Urban Design," 2003.

15 David Suzuki Foundation, "Hot Properties: How Global Warming Could Transform B.C.'s Real Estate Sector," November 2007, 6, accessed September 25, 2015, www.davidsuzuki.org/publications/downloads/2007/DSF_HotProperties_final1.pdf.

16 Northwest Hydraulics Consulting, "City of Vancouver Coastal Flood Risk Assessment," December 2014, 8.

17 Ibid., 70.

18 Ibid., 17.

19 Ibid., 19.

20 J. A. Church et al., "2013: Sea Level Change," in *Climate Change 2013: The Physical Science Basis. Contribution of Working Group I to the Fifth Assessment Report of the Intergovernmental Panel on Climate Change* [Stocker, T.F., D. Qin, G.-K. Plattner, M. Tignor, S.K. Allen, J. Boschung, A. Nauels, Y. Xia, V. Bex, and P.M. Midgley (eds)]. (Cambridge, United Kingdom and New York, NY, USA: Cambridge University Press, 2013), 1182.

21 Ibid., 11.

22 City of Vancouver, "Designing and Protecting Buildings to Withstand Floods," text/xml, (July 9, 2014), http://vancouver.ca/green-vancouver/flood-proofing-buildings.aspx.

23 "Minutes of the Regular Meeting of Council Held in the Council Chamber, City Hall, 141 West 14th Street, North Vancouver, B.C., on Monday, June 17, 2013; Item 4-Interim Flood Construction Levels," June 17, 2013, accessed September 25, 2015, www.cnv.org/attach/2013%2007%2015%20item%2004.pdf.

Chapter 2

Classic Grand Promenades

People have been building walkways along city waterfronts for a long time, celebrating the water's edge as a place for people to gather and to stroll. The walks range from simple paths to grand promenades designed to be major public spaces. Generously proportioned and often formally designed, grand waterfront promenades quite often come to represent the public face of their city. Some have long drawn visitors to them and their cities are famous for them. Questions about these long-standing and well-known promenades come to mind. How did they come to be? Why are they celebrated? Why have they been so enduring? What are their design qualities? Are they as wonderful now as they have been held to be in the past or does their reputation rest on past laurels? There are many things to be learned from the grand waterfront promenade stalwarts.

Grand waterfront promenades are often ambitious in both scale and scope, qualities that contribute to their sense of grandeur. Wide promenades are visually impressive and have room on them for many people to congregate and move. Long promenades are also visually impressive, especially if their length, or a good part of it, can be seen in a glance; if well designed, they connect with a long swath of the adjacent city, thereby inviting many people to them, or at least giving many people the ready option to visit them. A promenade that is both wide and long speaks of the community commitment to it, which is not to imply that smaller promenades reflect lesser community concern, but simply that the ambition and marshaled resources are greater. The dedication of a sizable piece of highly valuable waterfront land to a public promenade reflects a community ambition to create something special and make it stand out.

Of the grand waterfront promenades that exist worldwide, why do some become famous? Why are some widely thought to be among the best? Promenades become classics because there is something about their context, something about their design, something about how these variables interact, that is particularly memorable. A striking natural context contributes much to memorability: a perfectly curving bay, crystal clear or deeply colored water, the juxtaposition of tall mountains or jagged outcroppings with the water's horizontal expanse. Likewise, a striking urban backdrop of visually engaging buildings also contributes: red tile rooftops climbing a hillside, ornate rococo facades, buildings all of similar height. The actual promenades themselves are usually most memorable if they have a signature style. Many of the best known grand promenades have a sense of formality to them, a regularity of design that makes them feel all of a piece, an elegant style, sometimes simple and sometimes more complex, that makes them immediately graspable.

The three promenades that follow—or in the case of Rio de Janeiro the system of multiple linked promenades—have all been in place for a long time and are among the best known. They are all classics. Interestingly, they are all beachfront promenades in cities known for their magnificent beaches, and where early development along them happened because of the beach and was oriented toward it. For each city the beach is both part of residents' everyday life and a draw for tourists. These promenades and the beaches they front are their city's primary public open spaces and they represent the image of the city to outsiders. Looking at them closely helps us understand the ways in which the classic waterfront promenades work and also some ways in which they have difficulties.

Promenade des Anglais, Nice, France

Scale: 1:400,000

The Promenade des Anglais along the Mediterranean Sea in Nice, in southeastern France near the Italian border, is perhaps the most iconic waterfront promenade in the world, the one that comes to mind for many people as the classic example. Dating from the 1820s, when it was built as a narrow dirt path that allowed wintering wealthy English visitors to walk along the seaside, and widened into a 50-foot-wide promenade in the 1860s,[1] it has long been *the* place to stroll in the city. Today, the promenade lines the full length of the gently sweeping arc of the Baie des Anges, running some four and half miles (7 kilometers) from the old city center at its eastern end to the airport at its western end, which sits on land that used to be an automobile racetrack.

The promenade has long been and remains the middle ground feature of the standout picture postcard view of Nice: beyond the promenade, the buildings of the city climb hills that rise into the Ligurian Alps; in front of it is the sparkling blue water of the Mediterranean and a narrow beach; along it are large buildings with elegant facades. There have been many changes to the Promenade des Anglais and its surrounds over the last 150 years to accommodate different clienteles and different ways of promenading, so it is a different place than it once was but it has always been grand.

Promenade Design Characteristics

The Promenade des Anglais is for the most part all of a piece and relatively simple in design. Its most prominent features are the dark pink tarmac surface, the tall three-globed *belle époque* styled light fixtures that line its outer edge, the clusters of several dozen blue metal chairs, welded together back to back so that some face the sea and others the promenade, that occur every so often along its length, and the line of palm trees planted along the adjacent thoroughfare. This basic palette continues along three distinct promenade sections that are differentiated primarily by width and planting arrangements.

Scale: 1:40,000

A beach club to the left and a public area of beach to the right

The central section of the promenade and the beach along it are major destinations and often crowded. From the promenade, the view is as much of the beach activity as of the water. The beach is covered with small pebbles rather than sand, making for a tricky walking surface, but this doesn't stop it from being much enjoyed. Much of the beach is public but some stretches are controlled by beach clubs and set up with rows of densely packed chaises longues and umbrellas that can be rented by the day. At some of the clubs, the lounges are backed by wooden platforms on which sit tables and padded chairs, where people can sit to eat and drink items served from a kiosk café.

The promenade itself is 50 feet wide, extending from the 10-foot-high (3 meters) breakwater that lines the beach to the curb that lines the roadway. Within this width, toward the roadway side, runs a 7-foot-wide two-way bike lane, marked with painted dashed lines. A knee-high white painted rail protects the seawall edge.

There are no trees along the promenade but shade is created in three locations by trellised pergolas that span the walkway. These simply designed structures are made of wood, painted white, and draped overhead with beige canvas awnings. They are quite large, one is almost 180 feet in length and the others are almost 140 feet, and are lined with four rows of continuous white slat benches, including two rows that are back to back at the edge of the breakwater. This bench arrangement gives people the choice of sitting where they can look over the water or where they can watch the steady stream of people walking by, although since the benches are often full, people usually take a seat wherever they can get it. People of all ages use the benches: middle-aged and older couples sitting quietly, groups of older men talking, young men sprawled out.

The eastern section of the promenade, called the Quai des Etats-Unis, begins with a quarter-mile-long segment that is about 100 feet wide and then narrows to about 42 feet wide. It is lined on its roadway side by a row of tall palm trees, between which are placed white painted wood slat benches. At its far end, the palm trees end and the promenade narrows and curves around a point of land, widening into plazas at two overlooks along the way, ending at a ferry dock. The western section of the promenade narrows down to about 16 feet wide and here there are no trees and only occasional benches facing the water.

Some of the visual grandness of the Promenade des Anglais comes from the elegant buildings and parks that face onto it across the roadway. Along the central section of the promenade are six- to ten-story buildings in a mix of architectural styles, ranging from ornate *belle époque* to modern. A number of the buildings are hotels, including the famous and very expensive Hotel Negresco, built in 1913, which stands out for its domed pink rotundas adorned with greened copper fittings. Others

Section: Promenade des Anglais
Scale: 1" = 20'

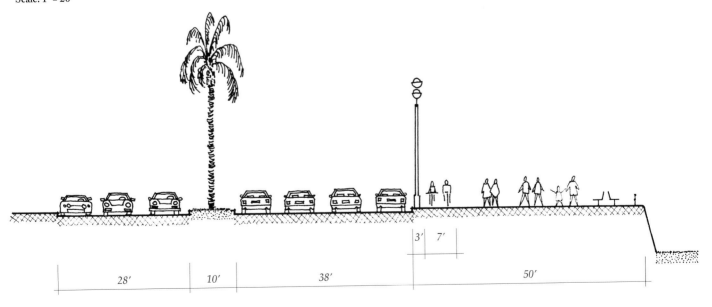

3'   7'

28'   10'   38'   50'

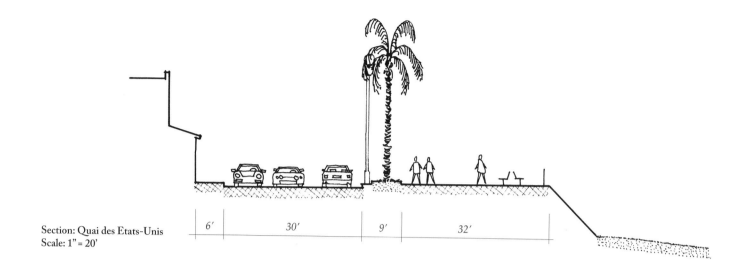

Section: Quai des Etats-Unis
Scale: 1" = 20'

6'   30'   9'   32'

The central section of the Promande des Anglais, with one of the trellis shelters in the background

The famous blue benches

The wide throughfare that runs along the central section of the Promenade des Anglais

buildings contain high-end apartments. An elegant public garden faces the promenade just south of the central area.

The wide and well-planted thoroughfare running adjacent to the central section of the promenade likewise contributes something to the promenade's overall sense of grandeur, but it also adversely impacts the promenade's ambience and accessibility. The thoroughfare serves as a main traffic artery of the city and is part of the continuous coastal highway that connects Nice with Antibes, Cannes, and a host of other well- and lesser-known Mediterranean destinations. The 76-foot-wide roadway carries three lanes of traffic heading southwest and four lanes of traffic heading northeast, with the outside lanes dedicated to buses. Northeast-bound curb lanes in places lead into and out of the underground parking garages that lie beneath stretches of the roadway. Raised planting beds protect the level change where these ramps occur adjacent to the promenade. A grassy median, typically 10 feet wide and planted with tall palm trees and a mix of other lower trees, separates the directional flows. The roadway carries upwards of 65,000 vehicles per day[2] and so traffic movement and noise are a constant presence along the promenade, but the impact is buffered by the promenade's width because it is easy to get far away from the moving traffic. The bigger impact is on the promenade's accessibility. Pedestrians and bicyclists can get across the thoroughfare on the crosswalks at the many signalized intersections, but must often wait through long signal phases for the lights to turn in their favor.

The thoroughfare narrows along the Quai des Etats-Unis after intersecting with two wide boulevards that serve as feeders to and from the regional highway that parallels the coast a short distance inland. Here different sections of the roadway have either one traffic lane in each direction or two southwest-bound lanes and one northeast-bound lane. In some areas there is also a parking lane.

Promenade Use and Connectivity

Promenading along the Promenade des Anglais is a casual affair

Aside from the street crossing issues, the Promenade des Anglais is well connected with the city because many streets lead into it, intersecting the coastal highway at 200 to 500-foot intervals. The promenade is just over half a mile from the train station making it readily accessible by day-trippers and others. The city's tram/streetcar line, which loops through both the old and expanded city from an inland highway where there are park-and-ride stations, stops two blocks away from a central part of the promenade. Along the promenade itself are several public bike share stations.

Walking along the Promenade des Anglais these days is very much an informal stroll. People are overwhelmingly casually dressed, many, maybe most, in shorts and t-shirts or light dresses. Bare chested young men are common. The ambience is distinctly different from the images of elegantly dressed ladies with parasols and dogs and bow-tied gentlemen walking along the promenade in the late 1800s and early 1900s. Once a formal promenade for the well-to-do, today it is an informal promenade for everyone. The daytime walking experience can be somewhat chaotic. In some places young men set up lines of cones and skate through them, often at speed in zigzag patterns. Walking toward the street one must be careful to avoid bikers moving at various speeds along the not-too-well-defined bike path. The evening stroll is more genteel. On some Sundays, part of the roadway is closed to traffic and people on foot, bicycles, and skates have more room to spread out.

Climate Change and Sea Level Rise Concerns

A typical summer afternoon on the Promenade des Anglais

It is unclear what the impact of future sea level rise will be on the Promenade des Anglais. Experts are debating how the rise of the relatively isolated Mediterranean Sea will vary from global sea level rise and consensus has not been reached, but there is some agreement that the rise will be close to the global average.[3] Well protected as it is by its 3-meter-high seawall, the promenade would remain above the maximum global rise of .98 meters (3.2 feet) that has been projected for 2100 by the Intergovernmental Panel on Climate Change.[4] However, as the sea rises the city will face increased flooding from storm surge and the seawall and promenade will face increased damage from wave action. The south of France, along with much of Europe, has in the last decades been experiencing increased winter storm severity and this pattern could continue and get worse with climate change. In May 2010, a storm sent waves crashing over the seawall and onto the promenade, causing considerable damage and washing away part of the beach.[5] As yet the city hasn't adopted an adaptation plan to address the coming sea level rise problem.

As timeless and relatively unchanging in physical form as the Promenade des Anglais has been, sea level rise may well require a redesign in the future. It is hard to imagine Nice without the Promenade des Anglais, which has long been the city's icon, so it seems likely that that the promenade will be maintained in some form no matter what.

Copacabana, Ipanema, Leme, Arpoador, and Leblon Promenades, Rio de Janeiro, Brazil

Scale: 1:400,000

Rio de Janeiro is famous for its picturesquely situated white sand beaches and the colorful promenades that line them. The legendary Copacabana and Ipanema beaches and promenades, plus the lesser-known ones of Leme, Arpoador and Leblon, are in the southern part of the city, some distance from the downtown, in an area of dramatic topography. Picture a long gently curving beach arcing southwest until it meets a rocky promontory that juts into the sea, then another long arcing beach continuing westerly from the promontory until ending at another, taller, outcropping. Together, the five beaches and the promenades that line them run continuously for about 5 miles, interrupted only by the promontory around which people must walk on city streets. The beaches and promenades are named for the neighborhoods that back them: from east to west, the sequence starts with Leme and Copacabana, Arpoador lies at the promontory hinge, and then come Ipanema and Leblon. The neighborhoods sit on relatively narrow strips of flat land backed by steep hills and punctuated with several enormous rocky outcroppings. Tunnels through the hills make the only connections between this part of the city and other parts.

The dramatic natural landscape contributes to the grandness of the promenades, but they are also designed to have a dramatic flair of their own. The Copacabana and Leme promenades are surfaced with black and white cobblestones laid in a wave pattern, the design of Brazil's most famous landscape architect Roberto Burle Marx. The Ipanema, Leblon, and Arpoador promenades are also paved with black and white cobblestones, laid in a different though equally distinctive large-scale pattern. The paving patterns continue on the medians and sidewalks of the wide thoroughfares that run almost the entire length of the promenades, creating a striking visual ensemble when seen from above. The only place a thoroughfare doesn't run adjacent to the promenade is along a short stretch of Arpoador, where the roadway turns inland to avoid the promontory and only a single narrow lane, controlled by a guarded gate, continues on to give access to adjacent properties.

Scale: 1:40,000

Arpoador promenade

The neighborhoods backing the beaches have both similarities and differences. The thoroughfares along Leme and Copacabana are wider than those along Ipanema and Leblon, but all carry heavy traffic and are fronted with mid-rise to high-rise hotels and high-income housing. In all neighborhoods, dense, mid-rise middle-class housing occupies the rest of the flat land and favelas lived in by poorer residents climb the steep hills. The differences between the neighborhoods lie in their orientation: Copacabana and Leme are very tourist oriented, Leblon is locally oriented, and Ipanema and Arpoador lie somewhere in between. The ground floors of many buildings facing the Copacabana and Leme promenades, across the thoroughfare, are filled with bars and restaurants, whereas there are fewer such establishments along the thoroughfare facing the other promenades. Likewise, there are many kiosks serving food and drink directly on the Copacabana and Leme promenades, and considerably fewer of these along the others.

Promenade Design Characteristics

In contrast with a sense of being removed from the adjacent traffic roadway experienced on the 50-foot-wide Promenade des Anglais in Nice, the experience on Rio's promenades is of ever-present traffic. The adjacent thoroughfares carry three lanes of traffic in each direction, with directional flows separated by palm tree-lined medians that are very wide along Copacabana and Leme and narrow along Ipanema and Leblon. Many buses, large and small, use the curb lanes. During morning and evening commute hours directional flows are shifted so that all lanes serve the dominant traffic direction, further contributing to the sense of being on a highway.

In many ways, the promenades feel like elegantly surfaced boulevard sidewalks, perhaps because of their relative narrowness compared to the wide roadways. The promenades are 27 feet wide at Copacabana and Leme, 33 feet wide at Arpoador and just 13 feet wide at Ipanema and Leblon. The

| 43' | 32' | 2' | 9' | 26' |

Section: Copacabana and Leme
Scale: 1" = 20'

Section: Arpoador
Scale: 1" = 20'

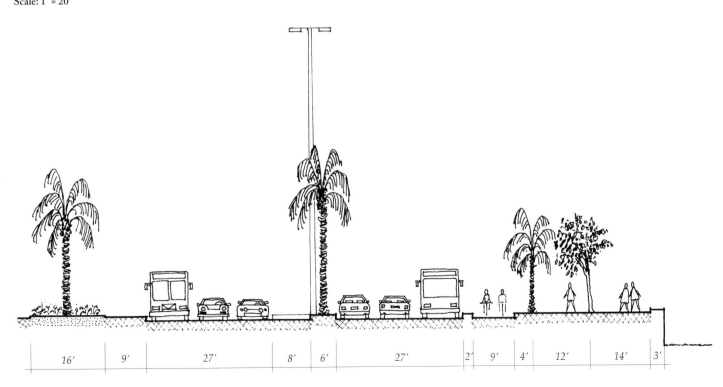

| 16' | 9' | 27' | 8' | 6' | 27' | 2' | 9' | 4' | 12' | 14' | 3' |

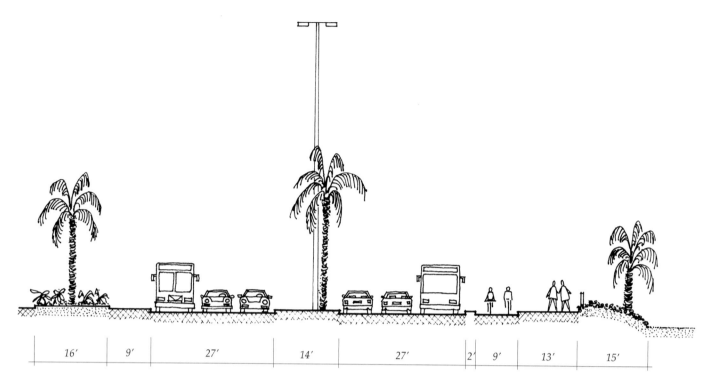

| 16' | 9' | 27' | 14' | 27' | 2' | 9' | 13' | 15' |

Section: Ipanema and Leblon
Scale: 1" = 20'

immediately adjacent two-way cycle tracks, which are at street level but separated from the roadway by a 2-foot-wide curb, are a narrow 9 feet wide. Including the promenades within the overall right-of-way, at Copacabana and Leme the pedestrian promenade and bike lane together comprise just 16 percent of the 220-foot-wide right-of-way; at Ipanema and Leblon they comprise just 18 percent of the 125-foot-wide right-of-way.

Promenade Use and Connectivity

The beaches and promenades constitute *the* major public open space of the city, heavily used by residents and tourists alike and alive with activity. On the beaches, people soak up the sun playing volleyball and soccer, lying on towels or sitting in rented beach chairs to be had from the many vendors that stake out claims on different sections of beach. Other vendors walk the beach offering fruit, drinks, and snacks of all kinds or colorful trinkets and beachwear. The promenades themselves are full of people walking and jogging and there is usually a steady flow of bicyclists on the bicycle paths.

Observations taken during summer weekday mornings and afternoons reveal that at least at those times Rio's promenades are used somewhat differently than the other promenades studied. Of the approximately 900 people per hour passing any given point during the daytime, there were considerably more men (above 60%) than women, particularly at Copacabana and Ipanema, whereas on most promenades there tend to be roughly equal numbers of men and women. Also, many people, almost 20 percent, had earplugs in and were listening to music, a considerably higher percentage than that observed elsewhere. It may be a cultural thing or it may be that people felt the need to block out the traffic noise. There were also many more people alone (60%–75%) than was typical elsewhere. It's unclear why this is the case but it may be that the traffic noise works against socializing.

Activity along the promenades continues into the evening but after dark it varies by location. Only a modest number of people stroll the Leblon and Ipanema promenades, while the Copacabana promenade, which is lined by tall stadium lights that illuminate the beach, can be very active and many

Leblon promenade

of the food and drink kiosks remain open until late. Tourists are warned to not walk the beaches at night because of possible muggings but the promenade is considered safe.

On weekends and during special events, all the promenades get mobbed with people. On weekends, the roadway closest to the beach is closed to vehicle traffic, giving a much wider promenade space. On New Year's Eve, Copacabana beach hosts a major fireworks display and concert and revelers from all over the city come to party.

Rio's promenades are both compelling and problematic. Their beach settings are extremely attractive, especially for the many people who live in the dense housing areas behind them. The Burle Marx designed pavements undeniably set a high standard and contribute a strong sense of place. At the same time, the promenades aren't particularly comfortable. Because of the vehicle traffic, they are very noisy and the air is polluted. There are very few public benches so virtually the only way to sit along the promenade is to buy an expensive tropical fruit drink at one of the kiosks that provide chairs. Also, except at Arpoador where the promenade is lined with two rows of trees, there is no shade other than that provided by the kiosk table umbrellas. Riding on the cycle track is challenging, because of their narrow width, the close proximity to traffic, and conflicts with bus stops. The cycle track is separated from the adjacent traffic lane by a less than 2-foot-wide curb that serves as the bus loading and off-loading zone. Especially along Ipanema and Leblon, buses and jitney vans flow along the curb lane almost non-stop and riders are constantly loading and unloading at the relatively frequent bus stops. Getting to the promenades is difficult, in spite of the many streets that feed into the roadways that run along the water, because traffic moves quickly and there are few signalized crosswalks. Crossing is particularly difficult during morning commute hours when all the lanes are dedicated to the inbound flow.

A bus stop on Leblon promenade

Copacabana promenade

Climate Change and Sea Level Rise Concerns

Biking next to buses along the Arpoador promenade

Rio de Janeiro's beaches and promenades are in many ways the cultural heart of the city, and yet they face constant environmental challenges. The ocean water is often fouled with sewage because of the city's inadequate drainage system. The beaches can experience intense erosion during major storm events, with sand subsequently replenished by city efforts and natural deposition. Future sea level rise coupled with a predicted increase in storm severity due to climate change could lead to greater beach erosion. Although the sea level rise prospects for Rio's coast have not been well studied, the city's land is neither uplifting nor subsiding so future sea level rise is likely to be close to the global average. While future flood levels have not been modeled, experts have concluded that buildings along Copacabana and Ipanema would not be impacted by a .5-meter (1.6 feet) sea level rise and so presumably the promenades would also be safe.[6] However, the Intergovernmental Panel on Climate Change projects that the average global sea level rise by 2100 could be up to .98 meters (3.2 feet).[7] Clearly more study needs to be done, but for now efforts are focusing elsewhere. The major climate change threat anticipated is more frequent and severe storm events leading to increased flooding of the city's hillside favela neighborhoods, and the city has responded to this threat by creating an operations center that allows agencies to coordinate flood monitoring and warning efforts.[8] As of now, no sea level rise adaptation strategies are being considered.

Paseo de la Concha, San Sebastián (Donostia), Spain

Scale: 1:400,000

The Paseo de la Concha (Kontxa Pasealekua) in San Sebastián, Spain is the elegant front face of this well-to-do provincial city, which is located in the Basque region of northeastern Spain along the Atlantic Ocean's Bay of Biscay. The promenade lines the southeastern end of the Playa de la Concha, the broad sandy beach that embraces the southern side of the small clamshell shaped bay around which San Sebastián is built. Rocky promontories and a small island, Isla Santa Clara, pinch the mouth of the bay, almost to visual closure. Immediately to the west of the Paseo de la Concha, beyond a short tunnel bored through a rocky outcrop, lies the lovely but less grand Paseo de Ondarreta (Ondarreta Pasealekua), lining a smaller stretch of beach. To the east, beyond a small grid of city streets and the mouth of the Rio Urumea, a modest promenade lines the city's other beach, the Playa de la Zurriola, which faces directly on the Atlantic Ocean. While all three promenades are popular places to stroll, the Paseo de la Concha is where most people gather and is the promenade for which San Sebastián is world famous.

The turquoise waters of San Sebastián's bay and the city's salubrious climate have long drawn summer visitors and the Paseo de la Concha was built for their enjoyment. In the late 1800s a royal palace was built overlooking the bay and the city became the summer home of the Spanish court and central government, and also a fashionable destination for well-to-do visitors from Spain and other countries, particularly England. The elegant Hotel de Londres, which anchors the promenade and caters to this clientele, dates from the turn of the twentieth century, replacing an earlier casino.

Promenade Design Characteristics

The Paseo de la Concha has a strong architectural presence because it sits on an artfully designed seawall. At the level of nearby city streets, it stands some 12 feet above the beach atop a columned arcade that rings much of the bay. The arcade makes an impressive backdrop for the beach and

Scale: 1:40,000

The Arcade below and promenade above, with the Hotel de Londres on the right

foreground for the city. It also serves functional uses, being lined in some areas by public changing rooms and restroom facilities and in other areas by private beach clubs. Expansive views can be had from the promenade's elevated vantage point and this contributes to the overall sense of grandness.

The promenade has three distinct sections that have different widths and frontage conditions, but repeated design elements draw the sections together into a unified visual ensemble. Buildings directly front the central part of the promenade, a fast-moving four-lane road borders the western section, and the eastern section runs along a park.

The central section is perhaps the most elegant. The fronting buildings give a sense of enclosure to this part of the promenade, and also protect it from traffic noise. They contribute to the elegance even though most, with the exception of the ornate Hotel de Londres, are eight- to ten-story slab residential buildings of modern design, whose ground floors, while of good materials, typically have very little interface with the promenade. The promenade's outer edge is lined with an elaborately designed iron rail, painted white, into which globe-topped lampposts are integrated at approximately 135-foot intervals, lining up with columns below, which have a 15-foot spacing. Elaborate sculptural light fixtures mark the several broad stairways and ramps leading to the beach, some including clock towers.

The promenade itself is about 68 feet wide and divided into various channels. A main walkway occupies the 20 feet closest to the railings. This is bordered by two rows of tamarind trees under which are situated rows of double-sided benches with light blue stanchions that add splashes of color. The trees in the outer row are closely spaced at 17 feet on center, whereas those in the row furthest from the beach are more widely spaced at 25 to 35 feet. The trees are less than 15 feet high and their canopies are tightly trimmed, so they are not big shade givers but the feathery leaves and pink flowers lend a sense of graciousness. A secondary walk hugs the building line; it is half as wide as the main walk and lined with globed light fixtures at 60-foot spacing. Outside of it runs a 6-foot-wide two-way bike

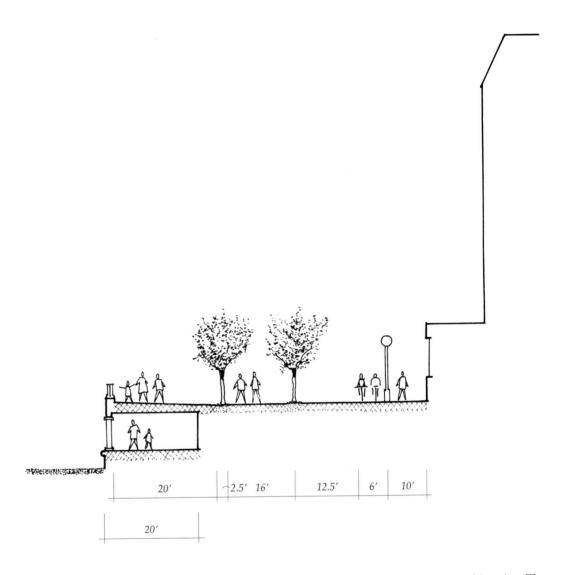

| 20' | 2.5' | 16' | 12.5' | 6' | 10' |

| 20' |

Section: Paseo de la Concha
Scale: 1" = 20'

path; bike parking occurs in line with the inner row of trees, situated between trees and benches. The various movement channels are set off with different surfacing. The main promenade and the building edge walk are paved with white hexagonal tiles outlined with square gray tiles, the area under the trees is paved with concrete aggregate pavers, and the bike lane is asphalt.

The white railings and globe light fixtures that are such prominent features of the central part of the promenade continue along the other parts to either side, but the rest of the cross section differs. On the eastern part, the main walk continues, backed by four or more rows of tamarind trees, through which the bike path runs and under which many benches are placed. On the western part, the main walk, the bike lanes, and a single row of tamarind trees continue. Here, a number of small one-story structures line the outer edge of the promenade. Within them are either high quality restaurants, with outdoor terraces overlooking the beach below, or the upper levels of private sports clubs, which control stretches of the beach below.

A notable characteristic of the Paseo de la Concha is how easily graspable it is. The promenade's curving form makes it easy to take in much—even most—of it in a glance and the regularity of its design, including the arcade's rhythm, makes the whole seem all of a piece. Likewise, the bay itself is easily graspable because of its curve and the sense of enclosure created by the promontories and island at its mouth. The curving wall of uniformly high buildings accentuates the ornate specialness of the promenade and gives definition to the public space. Up close, the promenade retains its sense of wholeness, in large part because of the regularity of the design but also because of the fine quality materials, good detailing, and the overall sense of graciousness.

Tamarind trees and benches

Hotel de Londres Café

Promenade Use

The central section of the promenade is the most highly used. People move along it in great numbers, especially during the summer. For example, on a warm, sunny Thursday in late June, just before the lunch hour, about 3,000 people per hour passed the Hotel de Londres, more than 80 percent strolling and about 15 percent biking. The overall tally is a high number compared with most of the other promenades studied. Sixty percent of the people strolling did so on the main promenade, while the rest walked where there was more shade. Bikers overwhelmingly kept to the bike lanes. The very few joggers observed mostly kept off the main promenade, preferring to use the path along the buildings, where there was shade, or to run between the trees. People of all ages use the promenade; there are

The bicycle path along
the interior of the promenade

People sitting along the busy
central section of the Paseo de la
Concha

often many groups of young people strolling along but there are also usually a fair number of older people, many carrying folding chairs to and from the beach.

Café service directly on the promenade, between the trees, happens at the Hotel de Londres and one other place. People also gather in small groups on the many benches. On hot, sunny days they seek small bits of benches that happen to be shaded by the tamarinds.

Climate Change and Sea Level Rise Concerns

What of future prospects?

The Paseo de la Concha, because it is elevated so high above the bay, would seem relatively protected against sea level rise, but it is surprisingly vulnerable. Local threats have not yet been firmly established, but the European Environment Agency projects that relative local sea level rise along Spain's northern coast will be similar or slightly less than average global sea level rise,[9] which according to recent projections of the Intergovernmental Panel on Climate Change would be a maximum of .98 meters (3.2 feet) by 2100.[10] With such a rise the beach would be narrowed and the water would get closer to the floor of the lower arcade, unless the beach were to be built up. The biggest risk will come from storm surge combined with wave action because very high waves often hit this part of the Atlantic coast. In the past, high waves have at times overtopped the hard vertical seawalls at the mouth of the Rio Urumea, destroying its railings and flooding parts of the central city. A study modeling 50-year extreme wave events coupled with a .49-meter sea level rise shows that the Paseo de la Concha itself could be overtopped and likely damaged.[11]

The city has not yet adopted a sea level rise adaptation plan, but the Paseo de la Concha has been such a defining feature of San Sebastián for so long that it is hard to imagine the city doing anything other than what is needed to ensure its preservation.

Notes

1   Alice M. Barker, "Nice: An Unexpected Jewel," *AMB Cote d'Azur*, September 22, 2004, accessed June 16, 2016, www.amb-cotedazur.com/nice-an-unexpected-jewel/.
2   Ibid.

3 "Global and European Sea-Level Rise (CLIM 012) - Assessment Published Sep 2014" (European Environment Agency, 2014), accessed June 16, 2016, www.eea.europa.eu/data-and-maps/indicators/sea-level-rise-2/assessment.

4 J. A. Church et al., "2013: Sea Level Change," in *Climate Change 2013: The Physical Science Basis. Contribution of Working Group I to the Fifth Assessment Report of the Intergovernmental Panel on Climate Change* [Stocker, T.F., D. Qin, G.-K. Plattner, M. Tignor, S.K. Allen, J. Boschung, A. Nauels, Y. Xia, V. Bex, and P.M. Midgley (eds)]. (Cambridge, United Kingdom and New York, NY, USA: Cambridge University Press, 2013), 1182.

5 "France–Freak Waves Smash French Riviera," *France 24*, accessed July 21, 2015, www.france24.com/en/20100505-freak-waves-smash-french-riviera-storm-cannes-nice-disaster-destruction-beach-croisette/.

6 Alex De Sherbinin, Andrew Schiller, and Alex Pulsipher, "The Vulnerability of Global Cities to Climate Hazards," *Environment and Urbanization* 19, no. 1 (April 1, 2007): 39–64, doi:10.1177/0956247807076725.

7 J. A. Church et al., "2013: Sea Level Change," 1182.

8 Lourdes Garcia-Navarro Facebook Twitter Instagram, "Rio Goes High-Tech, With An Eye Toward Olympics, World Cup," *NPR.org*, accessed October 13, 2015, www.npr.org/sections/parallels/2013/05/31/187316703/Rio-Goes-High-Tech-With-An-Eye-Toward-Olympics-World-Cup.

9 "Global and European Sea-Level Rise (CLIM 012) – Assessment Published Sep 2014."

10 J. A. Church et al., "2013: Sea Level Change," 1182.

11 P. Liria et al., "Extreme Wave Flood-Risk Mapping Within the Basque Coast," *Journal of Coastal Research*, Special Issue 64 (2011): 228.

Chapter 3

Beachfront Boardwalks and Promenades

Beach boardwalks come in many different flavors just like the ice cream always somewhere to be had on them or that one imagines can always be found. Some boardwalks are wide, others narrow; most are long but some are short; some boardwalks are made of wood as the name implies, but others are paved; some wooden boardwalks are elevated high above the sand, some raised a little, others hardly raised at all; some walks locally known as boardwalks are not formally named boardwalks but are called promenades or simply walks; some boardwalks are lined with entertainment venues, be they glittering casinos or light-splashed amusement parks, while others are lined with parks, or apartment buildings, or houses, or beach cottages, or motels, or hotels, or resorts, or retail stores, or myriad combinations of these. The designs and situations of beach boardwalks are all over the map.

What unites many beach boardwalks is their immediate relationship to a beach, their creation of a linear social space along the beach, their sense of relaxed informality, and a certain sense of romance. In beachfront communities the beach is usually a main public gathering place, but since walking on soft sand is not easy most people stay in one place once they get to the sand. A boardwalk along the sand invites people to move, to walk along a shared linear path, perhaps for some distance, bringing people together. When boardwalks are located in cold climes, they speak of the anticipated and cherished moments of summertime, in warmer climes, of endless summertime. Perhaps this is why they seem so romantic. Indeed, American beach boardwalks are the stuff of amorous songs from bygone eras. The very idea of a boardwalk seems intertwined with the idea of taking a leisurely stroll, hand in hand, with a special someone.

Another characteristic of many boardwalks is that they are well removed from streets and have uses fronting directly onto them; they are for pedestrians and perhaps also for cyclists and skaters, but not for cars. This doesn't hold true for all boardwalks, but it is the usual situation.

The classic old-time beach boardwalk is a wooden structure raised over the sand at the edge of a beach and surfaced with planks. Wooden boardwalks were built in many North American seaside communities in the late nineteenth and early twentieth century, particularly in cities and towns along the east coast of the United States. They were conceived as a practical solution to keep sand out of beachfront commercial establishments and out of the railroad cars that brought people to the beach. Some of these wooden boardwalks remain and are cherished, having been rebuilt over the years as necessary, while others were taken down and replaced with paved walks.

Modern boardwalks tend to be paved, are usually close to level with the sand, and are often of simple design.

The six beachfront boardwalks that follow are all very different. Brooklyn's Coney Island Boardwalk and Toronto's Beach Boardwalk are classic old boardwalks that were initially built in conjunction with amusement parks. The Long Beach Boardwalk, in Washington, is in a resort town that has a carnival-like nature, but the boardwalk is set away from the attractions within a broad expanse of windswept dunes. The Venice Beach Ocean Front Walk is a classic Southern California boardwalk and the Hollywood Beach Boardwalk is a classic Florida boardwalk: both have been in place for a long time and have mythic reputations. The Fort Lauderdale Beachfront Promenade and Miami Beach Boardwalk are both relatively recently created and are more elaborate in their design than the classic examples. Barcelona's Passeig Marítim is an unprecedented example of a city that once almost completely turned its back on its waterfront, recreating itself as a beachfront city by creating a long stretch of beaches, starting near the city center, and connecting them with a continuous promenade.

Coney Island Boardwalk, New York City, New York, USA

Scale: 1:400,000

New Yorkers may well think of Coney Island as being home to the most famous and noteworthy of all American beach boardwalks. To the south, the people of New Jersey might well argue in favor of Atlantic City's boardwalk and people living in Southern California, especially the Los Angeles area, might vote for one of theirs as being as good or better, although much newer. But few would argue that Brooklyn's Coney Island Boardwalk, long and wide and built of wood, is an icon of a particular kind of beach boardwalk associated with amusement park entertainment and also a cherished local place for afternoon and evening strolls and solitary morning walks. It has been a grand oceanfront promenade for almost a hundred years, and while the amusement park uses along it are not as robust and dazzling as they once were, it nonetheless remains a magnificent public space. Above all, the Coney Island boardwalk is a place for everyman.

Coney Island's beach has long drawn urbanites to it, all the more so as transportation routes were extended to it and amusements were built along it. Located some eight and a half miles from the center of Brooklyn, Coney Island first became easily accessible to city residents in the 1860s when a steam railroad line was extended to it from downtown Brooklyn. In the 1870s, wealthy people started coming to it in horse-drawn carriages after Frederick Law Olmsted's famous Ocean Parkway was built and connected the beach with Brooklyn's Prospect Park; the route down Ocean Parkway to the beach and back became a favorite weekend promenade route.[1] The 1870s also saw the building of the first carousel and the first rollercoaster near the beach. Meanwhile, Coney Island became known as Sodom by the Sea because many houses of prostitution also located in the area.[2] Around the turn of the twentieth century, a number of large amusement parks—Tilyou Park, Luna Park, Dreamland, and Sea Lion Park, which later became Steeplechase Park—were built along the beach. These were places of spectacle: rides big and small, tall towers giving views of the ocean, and lights galore. By the 1920s, Coney Island was home to 11 rollercoasters, 20 shooting galleries, wax museums, freak shows, and countless carnival games.[3] A newly built subway line allowed people from all over New York City to easily get to Coney Island, and they came in droves.

Scale: 1:40,000

The boardwalk itself was built in the 1920s in conjunction with a beach expansion. Between 1921 and 1923, under the leadership of Brooklyn Borough President Edward Riegelmann, the city gained title to the beachfront and added 1.7 million cubic yards of sand to it, making it considerably wider than it had been in its natural state. The whole boardwalk was built at once, 80 feet wide and 1.7 miles long, stretching from West 37th Street east to Ocean Parkway.[4] In 1941, a 50-foot-wide boardwalk was extended another mile eastward along the adjacent Brighton Beach waterfront.

Coney Island had its heyday in the 1920s and 1930s, has had its ups and downs since then, but still draws crowds. According to Fortune Magazine, in 1938 over 1.3 million visitors came there to celebrate the 4th of July holiday.[5] Through the 1940s the boardwalk, beach, and amusement parks together made Coney Island a pre-eminent summer entertainment place, but things were starting to decline, helped along by New York City Park Commissioner Robert Moses who in 1940 started enforcing regulations on public behavior, including requiring shirts on the boardwalk.[6] By the 1950s, the most spectacular amusement park, Luna Park, had closed.[7] The other amusement parks—declining over the years, closing, and then some re-opening—have somewhat less shine today and occupy a much smaller footprint than they once did, but they and a re-opened smaller Luna Park are still a drawing card. Other attractions and events also draw people to the Coney Island waterfront: the New York Aquarium, built in the late 1950s; the minor league Brooklyn Cyclones baseball stadium, built in 2001; the Nathan's Famous Hot Dogs eating contest that takes place every 4th of July. The beach, of course, remains the major draw and on warm summer days can get packed to almost standing room only. Throughout the years, while the land uses along Coney Island changed, the boardwalk has remained a constant, relatively unchanging fixture.

Promenade Design Characteristics

The boardwalk gives elegant form to Coney Island's foreshore. It is a spectacular 80-foot-wide wooden structure: an enormous single-level deck raised about 2 feet above the level of the sand and surfaced with two by four hardwood planks laid in continual lines of various patterns, some herringbone and some lineal. The tactile quality of the wood makes walking on the boardwalk very pleasant. The handmade quality of the boardwalk and the sheer scale of its construction—all the wood planks, all the screws and all the maintenance that must be required to keep things in good shape—cannot help but impress.

Although the boardwalk has endured in the same form for almost 100 years, change may be coming. The wooden structure is susceptible to constant weathering not to mention damage from water and sand inundation during storm events, such as occurred during Hurricane Sandy, which hit New York City and much of the east coast in October 2012. The New York City Department of Parks and Recreation, which has responsibility for the boardwalk, has a plan to reconstruct it with recycled plastic lumber planks interrupted by a 10-foot-wide concrete path to accommodate emergency vehicles.[8] The environmentally based rationale is to save the cutting of tropical hardwood.

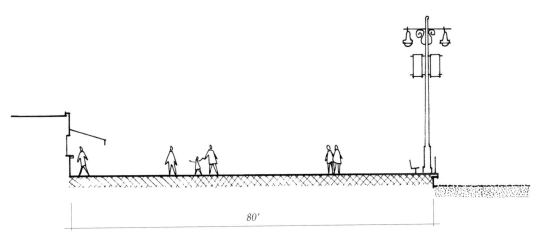

Section: Coney Island Boardwalk
Scale: 1" = 20'

80'

Strolling along the Coney Island Boardwalk on a cool Monday morning in November

Elevated lifeguard station and public restrooms

Reconstruction of the adjacent Brighton Beach Boardwalk started in 2014 and has met with considerable community protest.[9] The jury is still out as to whether the plan will be carried out on the Coney Island Boardwalk.

Beyond the impressiveness of the wooden boardwalk structure, most of the boardwalk's other design elements are simple. Tall black-painted iron light fixtures, reminders of an earlier age, line the beach edge of the boardwalk just back of the simple tubular metal railing that protects the drop-off. Also at the beach edge is a line of widely spaced wooden benches of traditional design, some with backs, which are oriented toward looking out at the water, and some without backs, which afford a choice of looking either toward the water or the boardwalk. A new design feature is the pair of sleek

Steeplechase Pier

Trellis structure on Steeplechase
Pier

pre-fabricated modular structures, constructed of galvanized steel and wood siding, that jut over the beach off the boardwalk, raised well above the sand on concrete pilings, and house restrooms, a lifeguard station, and park offices. They were installed in 2013 as part of the city's post-Sandy reconstruction efforts and are of the same design as used on other city beachfronts.[10]

The central part of the boardwalk is the most commercially active. The amusement parks are clustered here and they come right up to its edge. The sizable structures of the most spectacular rides are colorful and eye-catching, not only the aging Cyclone Roller Coaster, Parachute Jump, and Wonder Wheel Ferris Wheel but also the recently built Thunderbolt Roller Coaster. Nearby are many eateries, places where one can buy fun and inexpensive food for kids as well as for oneself: Nathan's famous hot dogs, lemonade, clam chowder, cotton candy, and popcorn, to a name but a few of the delights.

In spite of the towering rollercoasters and other rides, the feeling one gets on the boardwalk, especially when it is not crowded with people, is a sense of expansiveness. This feeling comes from the wide beach and the low scale of the buildings along the boardwalk, most just one story high. After the intensity of building height and traffic noise experienced in so much of New York City this expansiveness can feel like quite a relief and may be one reason why so many people like to come here.

A long pier called Steeplechase Pier extends over the beach and water just west of the amusement park area, offering another place for people to walk. Twenty-four feet wide and 800 feet long, it is solely for pedestrians. The pier was heavily damaged by Hurricane Sandy and was rebuilt. It is surfaced with the recycled plastic lumber proposed for the boardwalk. The pier is lined on both sides with closely spaced wooden benches of modern design that allow people to sit facing either the water or toward people passing by. Somewhat further than mid-way along the pier, a cross pier structure with overhead trellises that offer some sun protection extends at right angles to either side. People come to the pier to walk, to sit, and to fish. The ambience is more tranquil than on the boardwalk.

Promenade Use

The boardwalk is largely a pedestrian environment. Bicycling and rollerblading are allowed from 5 am to 10 am daily, but other than that all movement is on foot. Motorized vehicles are hardly to be seen because Surf Avenue, the main street of Coney Island, is a long block away and the only nearby roadways are the cul-de-sac ends of the relatively widely spaced streets that run between Surf Avenue and the boardwalk.

The experience of walking along the boardwalk is different at different times. On summer evenings it is a place to walk amongst many others and be part of the action, perhaps walking hand in hand with your sweetheart or strolling with your kids and very likely eating ice cream. On winter weekday afternoons it is a place to stroll or walk briskly either alone or with some friends to get some exercise and see others who might be out and about. On nice but off-season days older men sit in small groups near the eateries, at assorted picnic tables or on their own portable beach chairs, talking and maybe playing cards. There is a sense that they will be there again the next day and also the next.

Climate Change and Sea Level Rise Concerns

The Coney Island Boardwalk seems timeless, like it will never change, but as we have seen it has changed and more change must come. The 2015 report of the New York City Panel on Climate Change predicts that sea levels around New York City could rise as much as 6 feet by 2100.[11] Maps prepared by Climate Central's Surging Seas project indicate that with this much rise half of Coney Island's beach will be gone and much of the city will be flooded, with water coming in from the backside of the island rather than from the beach side.[12] Coney Island lies on very low land, much of it on fill over former marshes and creeks. City streets often flood from storm surge during major storm events and these occurrences will become more and more frequent. One rationale the parks department gives for rebuilding the boardwalk with plastic lumber is that it will be more resistant to storm damage. Because of the community protest, is uncertain whether the reconstruction of the whole boardwalk will happen or not, but this argument plus the argument against using tropical hardwoods is compelling.

In 2013 the city issued a comprehensive plan for making its coastal areas more resilient to climate change, which focuses on areas impacted by Hurricane Sandy. For Coney Island the plan envisions creating protective dunes along the beach.[13] Dunes would change the fundamental relationship between the boardwalk and the ocean because the water would no longer be visible from the boardwalk. In any case, given the boardwalk's history, to say nothing of its continuing popularity, it seems a good bet that some form of boardwalk will remain for some time.

Beach Boardwalk, Toronto, Canada

Scale: 1:400,000

The boardwalk in the Beach neighborhood of Toronto is small and humble compared to the Coney Island boardwalk, but no less delightful. Toronto sits on the north side of Lake Ontario, and the Beach neighborhood, at the far eastern edge of the pre-amalgamation old city of Toronto, is one of the few places in the city where a neighborhood comes right up to the lake's shore without the barrier of an elevated freeway or at-grade expressway. The beaches here—from east to west: Balmy Beach, Kew Beach, and Woodbine Beach—comprise the longest stretch of beach in the city, almost a mile and a half. The boardwalk that lines these beaches is very much a neighborhood affair but it draws people from all of Toronto because it is such a special place.

The Beach neighborhood has a colorful history. In the 1800s several small villages, from which the beaches get their names, occupied the area. By the 1880s, after the opening of the Woodbine Racetrack, the Kew Gardens pleasure grounds, and the Victoria Park amusement park, people began flocking to the area in droves, especially during the summer, arriving by steamer or trams from downtown Toronto. A second and more raucous amusement park, the Scarboro' Beach Amusement Park, fashioned on Coney Island, opened in 1907, drawing even more people. By the turn of the twentieth century many hotels and summer cottages had been built in the area along with fancy summer homes for the wealthy. By 1930, during the lean years following the end of World War I, the amusement parks had closed, Kew Gardens had become a public park and the Beach neighborhood had been largely sub-divided and built with houses.[14] In 1932 a narrow boardwalk was built along the beach in conjunction with the creation of a continuous public waterfront park.[15] Over the years it was expanded and widened, with reconstruction often following its destruction during winter storms.[16]

Promenade Design Characteristics

The boardwalk that exists today is a simple affair with a relaxed, bucolic character. It runs along about a mile of the beach and is generally about 15 feet wide. The 2 x 8 planks of the boardwalk, laid crossways, sit atop joists that have settled and so the boardwalk is almost flush with the sand. The boardwalk is

Scale: 1:40,000

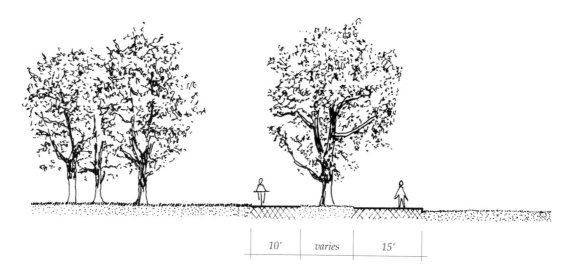

Section: Beach Boardwalk
Scale: 1" = 20'

10'   varies   15'

The boardwalk on a cold October morning

tucked up against a linear park that fronts the beach, beyond which sits a dense but low-scale fabric of single-family and duplex bungalows and small apartment buildings on narrow tree-lined streets. Large trees of many species overhang the northern side of the boardwalk, emerging from grassy slopes and lawns. A line of traditionally designed metal light fixtures, painted light blue in reference to the waterside location, run along the backside of the boardwalk, spaced at 80 feet on center. Benches of simple design, wooden slats over concrete or metal supports, are set randomly along the park edge of the boardwalk.

The boardwalk is for pedestrians but bicyclists are not forgotten. A paved path parallels the boardwalk, tucked into the trees of the park, and people on bicycles, skates, and scooters stick to it, respecting the boardwalk as a place for walking. The separate paths allow people in close proximity to each other to move at different speeds.

The bike path meandering along the edge of Kew Gardens

Promenade Use and Connectivity

People stroll along the boardwalk all year long: in large numbers during the warm summer and early fall months and in lesser but still sizable numbers during the cold winter and spring months. Temperatures in Toronto drop below freezing during the winter and while Lake Ontario doesn't usually completely freeze over its edges do ice up; walking along the boardwalk in winter the experience is full of sound—the squishy crunch of boots on the frozen boardwalk planks and the musical clinking of the lake ice being stirred by any winds or currents. The boardwalk faces south and so when there is sun to be had this is a good place to find it.

Late morning on a Sunday in early April, the first real day of spring, over 600 passersby per hour were observed moving along the beach. Most were strolling on the boardwalk but about a quarter were biking, skating, or scootering on the adjacent paved path and a handful were walking on the sand near the water's edge. Most people were in pairs or groups and there were quite a few children, babies in strollers, and dogs on leashes. Many people were stopping to chat and dogs were stopping to sniff other dogs. Exclamations of "we knew we'd see you here" were heard. Looking down the boardwalk in either direction there seemed to be a sea of walkers.

Throughout the year, no matter what the weather, the boardwalk is where residents of the Beach community come together. It is where people come for exercise or to walk the dog. It is where families come to be outside together. It is where elderly people come to sit and watch people walking by. It is where couples come to walk together and where people on their own come to walk among others. On weekends many people stroll the whole length of the boardwalk and back. Others stroll along the boardwalk, walk through Kew Gardens up to Queen Street, the shopping street that parallels the boardwalk a long block to the north, and then stroll along it, window shopping and maybe stopping for something to eat or drink. On some weekends the boardwalk is used for sporting activities that everyone comes out to see such as short running events for little kids. During a 2-kilometer run on a Saturday in early spring a father was overhead to say: "Look, Michael, I can almost see the finish line. Pretty soon the people will be clapping."

The boardwalk is easily accessible and most people, it seems, arrive on foot. Residents can easily walk to the boardwalk because the block pattern of the neighborhood is structured such that many streets lead into it. People living elsewhere in the city or visiting the city can get to the boardwalk via the Queen Street streetcar, which runs the whole three and a half mile length of Queen Street, passing through many successive neighborhoods as well as the downtown. When the streetcar enters the

People strolling with leisure along the boardwalk, and biking and jogging along the bike path

Beach neighborhood riders on it are for the first time in their journey connected with Lake Ontario because at every intersecting street on the south side, which means about every 200 feet or so, glimpses can be had of the lake. Most of the time, it is also possible to see a steady stream of people walking along the boardwalk.

Many beach boardwalks started in association with public amusements and if the amusements leave transitions are not always easy or graceful, witness the decline of Asbury Park in New Jersey.[17] After amusements left Toronto's Beach Boardwalk it was elegantly transitioned into a bucolic neighborhood amenity while remaining an occasional destination for city residents who live elsewhere.

Climate Change and Sea Level Rise Concerns

Being situated on a lake, albeit one connected with the Gulf of Saint Lawrence via the long Saint Lawrence River, Toronto's Beach Boardwalk is not immediately vulnerable to sea level rise, but it may nonetheless be impacted by climate change. The jury is out on whether climate change will raise or lower water levels in the Great Lakes. Along with water withdrawal by local communities, lake water levels vary seasonally, impacted by rainfall, snowmelt, and evaporation, and different studies project different climate change impacts on these variables. Nonetheless, the Great Lakes Environmental Research Laboratory concludes there is "little evidence that future water level variability will greatly exceed the historical range."[18]

The bigger threat to the boardwalk is from storm events because of the large waves they can bring to the Toronto shoreline. Storms have in the past caused major damage to the boardwalk, but the damage has always been repaired. Presumably any future storm damage will also be repaired.

Long Beach Boardwalk, Long Beach, Washington, USA

Scale: 1:400,000

The small resort town of Long Beach, Washington, with fewer than 1,500 residents, has aspirations to be a major tourist destination that takes advantage of what is locally claimed to be the longest beach in the world. The beach is in reality one of the longest continuous beaches on North America's west coast, some 28 miles, and that is impressive enough. The town also has a half-mile long wooden boardwalk and it likes to proudly boast that *Travel + Leisure* Magazine deems it one of the best boardwalks in the United States. The boardwalk is notable for being located within dunes and for its rustic design.

The boardwalk is but one of many attractions Long Beach offers visitors. The city hosts regular "fun beach" events, some 79 in 2015 alone. There are kite festivals galore, crab festivals, firework shows, and hot-rod auto processions on the town's main street, to name but a few. The wide sand beach is open to motorized vehicles much of the year, except from mid-April to Labor Day, and is posted with a 25-mile-per-hour speed limit. A walk up and down the town's main street, Pacific Avenue, is akin to a walk in an amusement park because of the many entertainments for kids and their parents, including carnival rides and go-carts, and the many purveyors of t-shirts, ice cream, and cotton candy. Visitors can also partake of zip-line tours at a nearby lake, rent mopeds and surreys, ride horses on the beach, or walk on the boardwalk.

Long Beach's unusual geography contributes to the beach focus of the community. The city is situated in the southwest corner of Washington on a narrow peninsula that starts north of the mouth of the Columbia River and juts between the Pacific Ocean and Willapa Bay. One of several sequential small towns that line the peninsula, it parallels the beach for about 2¼ miles, set some distance back behind expansive grass-covered dunes. The urbanized area of the town is only four to five blocks wide; the beach and dunes combined are much wider. The boardwalk traverses the section of dunes lying west of the town center. Running roughly parallel to it is an 8½-mile-long biking and walking trail, called the Discovery Trail in homage to the Lewis and Clark Expedition that reached the Pacific Ocean via the Columbia River Discovery Trail.

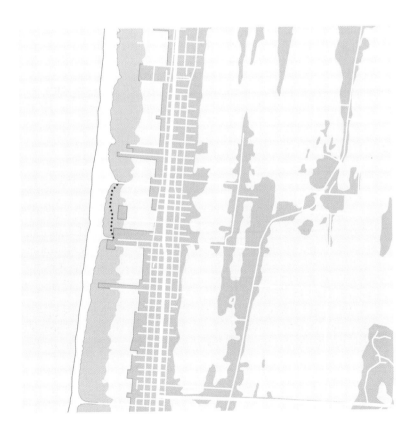

Scale: 1:40,000

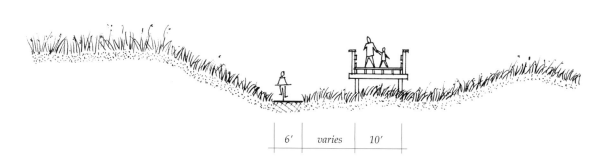

Section: Long Beach
Boardwalk
Scale: 1" = 20'

6'   *varies*   10'

Promenade Design Characteristics

The boardwalk is of simple rustic construction and informal design. Only 10 feet wide, it has weathered 2 x 6 planks for the walking surface and horizontally laid boards for railings. It is formed of multiple segments set at different, seemingly random, angles. The walking surface slopes up and down in a cadence suggestive of the dunes below. Set several feet above the top of the grasses, the boardwalk is just high enough to provide glimpses of the ocean beyond the outermost dunes. At three places along its length the boardwalk widens out into picnic areas, roughly 35 feet wide by 62 feet long, where there are benches and tables, as well as displays that describe the ecology and maritime history of the area and have barcodes that can be scanned by smartphones to access more information. Steps lead down from the picnic areas to sandy paths that wend through the grasses.

Promenade Use

During special events the boardwalk can become crowded but on normal days it sees only light use. On an overcast and cool non-beach festival Sunday in September, just 25 people per hour were seen on the boardwalk and Discovery Trail combined. Most people on the boardwalk were strolling and most of the people on the trail were biking. On kite festival days, when the sky above the beach and dunes is aflutter with kites of all shapes, sizes, and colors, many people of all ages take to the boardwalk, promenading back and forth. It is the perfect place to enjoy the show.

Climate Change and Sea Level Rise Concerns and Other Challenges

Relative local sea level rise along the Washington coast is expected to be slightly less than the global sea level rise average due to on-going land uplift. A 2012 report prepared by the National Research

The rustic boardwalk zigzags above the dunes

Bicycling along the Discovery
Trail next to the boardwalk

Council projects that by 2100 relative local sea level rise will be between .1 to 1.4 meters (.33 to 4.6 feet).[19] The high end of this range is considerably higher than the maximum global sea level rise in 2100 projected by the Intergovernmental Panel on Climate Change in its 2013 report (.98 meters),[20] because the National Research Council's assessment includes a larger possible contribution from the melting of the Antarctica ice shelf. Long Beach and its boardwalk will be relatively well protected from this level of rise by the dune system that lines the entire western shore of the Long Beach peninsula. As seas rise the wide beach will gradually become narrower, but the boardwalk will be protected from wave action by the dunes. Maps prepared by Climate Central's Surging Seas project show that rising water will first begin to encroach on the Long Beach peninsula from the eastern bay side, with the town center impacted only after 7 or 8 feet of sea level rise.[21]

A much larger concern for Long Beach, indeed for all of the coastal Pacific Northwest, is the threat posed by earthquakes and giant tsunamis. Recent research suggests tsunamis have struck the Washington coast on a regular basis in the past, generated by both distant and nearby earthquakes. Along with being located on the notorious "Ring of Fire," the horseshoe shaped string of active faults and volcanoes banding the Pacific Ocean along which 90 percent of the world's earthquakes occur,[22] it is within the Cascadia Subduction Zone, where the Juan de Fuca oceanic plate is subducting under the North American continental plate. The plates have long been stuck, building up massive pressures that have been uplifting the edge of the continental plate. When the plates unstick the resulting megathrust earthquake will be large, generating massive coastal heaving and a huge tsunami that will hit the Washington coast within 15 minutes. The historical record, only recently understood by researchers, suggests that a big earthquake is overdue. The entire Pacific Northwest coast will be reconfigured when the event happens. Long Beach residents, and visitors caught there will be lucky to escape with their lives. Coastal Washington is also at risk of being hit by tsunamis generated by earthquakes in Japan, Alaska, and elsewhere, but there would be more of a lag time. Warning systems in place in the deep ocean would detect the oncoming waves and send alerts, giving people time to flee.[23]

The town of Long Beach was established before people understood the tsunami danger. Now that the risk is clear, the state and town have made efforts to disseminate risk and evacuation information. The town also plans to build a "safe haven vertical evacuation structure" within the tsunami zone, where people could go to get above the wave height and be safe if they are unable to flee.

Long Beach's boardwalk is not a typical beach boardwalk but it does help connect the town with its waterfront. Given the tall dunes and the low-scale town buildings, it is not possible to see the ocean from the town's streets or from most buildings. The beach is the city's claim to fame but it is not visible from the town. The boardwalk is a place where people can go to get glimpses of it and of the ocean.

A glimpse of the ocean, and
a path through the dunes

Venice Beach Ocean Front Walk, Los Angeles, California, USA

Scale: 1:400,000

Over a span of 110 years, the Venice Beach Ocean Front Walk has gone from being part of a grand and imaginative real estate venture to being a counterculture homeland embedded within an upscale part of the City of Los Angeles. Today, it and the wide beach it fronts upon draw some six million people annually.[24] These numbers make it an impressive boardwalk even though the walk itself is of simple design.

The community of Venice has had its ups and downs. Today a neighborhood of Los Angeles, it dates from 1905 when its wealthy developer, Abbot Kinney, envisioned turning what was then marshland into a seaside village modeled on Venice, Italy, complete with canals, imported gondolas, and roving gondoliers.[25] Kinney built the canals, sold property along them, and built the beginnings of today's Ocean Front Walk along the new community's relatively narrow beach. For entertainment beyond the gondolas he built a pier extending over the beach into the ocean and filled it with amusements including an aquarium, a carousel, a Ferris wheel, and a nautically themed restaurant. By all accounts the community was an early success but people seemed to care mostly about the amusements and less about replicating the real Venice. Kinney died in 1920 and a few years later residents voted for annexation to Los Angeles, whose public works department promptly filled many of the canals for what they deemed to be transportation improvements. In 1930 oil was discovered in the Venice area and almost 150 oil wells were set up in the community. In short order the beaches became soiled and Venice became run-down and seedy.[26] Extensive nourishment of Santa Monica Bay beaches was undertaken in the late 1930s, substantially increasing the width of Venice's beach.[27] In spite of this effort, Venice continued to decline and Kinney's amusement pier was removed in 1946.[28]

The Ocean Front Walk remained intact throughout the community's travails and it and Venice were eventually rediscovered. In the 1960s it became a magnet for the "Beats" and then the "Flower Children" of the times. A bike path wending through the sand was built in 1972 as part of a long beachfront route stretching from Santa Monica to Torrance. It and the Ocean Front Walk, which became known as the Venice Boardwalk, became favored places for skating. A section of the beach was

Scale: 1:40,000

used for bodybuilding and became famous as Muscle Beach. In the late 1970s the boardwalk started being used by street performers, artists selling their creations, and political activists declaiming their views.[29] The atmosphere became carnival-like and it remains so today. Meanwhile, the community itself became more and more upscale, with many houses and condominium units now valued in the millions of dollars.

Promenade Design Characteristics

The boardwalk runs along most of Venice's 2½-mile-long beach front and consists of two distinct sections. The northern mile and a half, beyond the Venice Pier, is wider than the southern part and more commercially oriented; it is the section that people gravitate to. Fronting on it are one- to four-story buildings, most with small shops and restaurants on the ground floor. Fronting on the narrower southern section is a mix of single-family and multi-family three- to five-story buildings.

The northern part is generally 40 feet wide and surfaced with concrete. In one area, where shops are set back, it widens to 50 feet. For a long stretch just north of Venice Boulevard, vendors and street performers occupy the 10 feet closest to the beach, operating from card tables in 205 designated spaces. The marked vendor spaces are allocated on a first come first serve basis and vendors must take down their setups every evening.[30] Along the same stretch and also further to the north, wares from adjacent stores and tables and chairs from adjacent restaurants spill out onto the 10 feet of the walk nearest the buildings. There have long been tensions between homeowners and local merchants and the boardwalk vendors. Strict rules for vending have been established to keep it to its traditional forms—free speech, performance, and artists selling their wares.[31] Tensions have recently increased because of homeless encampments along the beach and vendors not following the rules.[32]

From Venice Boulevard south to Washington Avenue, which leads to the Venice Pier, the boardwalk narrows to 20 feet wide and is partially asphalted. Further south it narrows to 10 feet wide and there are gaps in its continuity.

The boardwalk is lined with a variety of beach edge conditions. North of Venice Pier the walk and the beach are separated by a raised grassy mound, planted with palm trees, and by the bicycle path. The mound is sometimes as narrow as 10 feet wide and elsewhere more than 50 feet wide, with its outer edge undulating in and out. The two-way bicycle path, surfaced with concrete and typically 14 feet wide, curves along the edge of the mound. South of Venice Pier the raised mound and separated bike path end and bicyclists share the narrow sidewalk with pedestrians. For two blocks to either side of Windward Avenue, a commercial street that feeds into the busiest central part of the boardwalk,

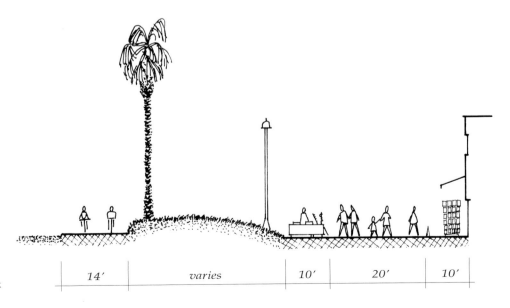

Section: Venice Beach Boardwalk
Scale: 1" = 20'

14'   varies   10'   20'   10'

The central commercial area on the northern part of the boardwalk

The southern section of the boardwalk

The southern section of the boardwalk

The bicycle path meanders at the edge of the beach

the boardwalk is edged with a park that occupies half the width of the beach. Here there are grassy lawns, wide concrete paths, a community center, and a skate park. Just to the south other recreational spaces front the boardwalk, including an open-air weight lifting arena (Muscle Beach), a cluster of tennis and paddleball courts, and a basketball court. Three large public parking lots are also carved out of the beach, one to the north, one to the south, and one near the center.

Promenade Use and Connectivity

People come to the boardwalk to see and be a part of its carnival-like atmosphere as much as they come for the water views, perhaps more so, and they come in big numbers. On a Sunday morning in early November 2015, counting just the people moving on the main walk and not on the bicycle path, 1,245 people per hour were moving along the central part of the boardwalk. There were slightly more men (56%) than women, people were overwhelmingly in groups (80%) rather than alone, and most were young. Most were strolling (87%) and the rest were biking or skating. The daytime number pales in comparison with the number that same evening when over 3,200 people per hour passed the same location. This tally is among the highest observed on all the promenades studied (see the Appendix). Most people (95%) were strolling.

It is relatively easy to get to the main northern part of the boardwalk by car because of the three big parking lots and also relatively easy to get to it on foot from the immediately adjacent neighborhood, but it is somewhat difficult to get to it on foot from inland parts of the community. From the Venice Pier north to the city limits, 33 public streets lead directly to the boardwalk. Most of these streets are very narrow and easy for pedestrians to walk along. A narrow one-way alley, incongruously named Speedway, runs along the backside of the blocks that face the boardwalk. Here there are no sidewalks, so pedestrians mix with occasional slow-moving cars, whose drivers are often looking to find a parking space. Attendants at the handful of privately owned parking lots along the alley wave flags to draw attention to available spaces. The next parallel street to the east is narrow but busy Pacific Avenue, along which vehicles tend to be fast moving except during the traffic jams that can occur during commute hours or on weekends when lots of people head to the beach. Pacific Avenue can be challenging for pedestrians to cross because not all intersections are signalized. Multi-family

People throng the boardwalk
in the early evening

residential buildings fill the blocks between Pacific Avenue and Speedway, along with a number of former industrial buildings that have been inconspicuously turned into tech office space, so there is a density of people living and working very close to the boardwalk who can walk to it.

It is more difficult to reach the southern part of the boardwalk. South of the pier Venice becomes a narrow peninsula, just two to three blocks wide plus the beach, backed by the marinas and inwardly oriented development of Marina del Rey. Not many people try to get to the boardwalk from here, except for local residents, because although 25 streets lead directly to the beach there is almost no public parking. While the one-way alley continues along the back of the beach-facing blocks, many of the street segments between it and Pacific Avenue are closed off to through traffic. It makes a very pleasant pedestrian-oriented environment for local residents but also creates an exclusive enclave. Some of the condominium buildings facing the beach have a unique design feature. They are designed with a parking garage on the ground floor, so units facing the beach start one story up. All the beach-fronting residential units have balconies across their width, and the balconies on the first residential floor are equipped with ladders leading down to the Ocean Front Walk.

Climate Change and Sea Level Rise Concerns

Venice has seen many changes since its beginnings and it may in the future see more, tied to climate change. The city is extremely vulnerable to sea level rise because it sits on former marshland and is very low-lying, but the boardwalk is less vulnerable than land inland along the canals. With climate change, sea level rise along the Southern California coast is expected to be just slightly higher than the global average. If one accepts the projections of the Intergovernmental Panel on Climate Change, this could mean up to slightly more than .98 meters (3.2 feet) by 2100;[33] if one accepts the projections of the National Research Council it could mean up to 1.67 meters (5.5 feet).[34] Maps prepared by Climate Central's Surging Seas project show Venice's canal neighborhoods beginning to flood with one foot of sea level rise and inundated with 3 feet, with water entering from the Marina del Rey entrance channel to which the canals connect at the community's southern boundary.[35] Three feet of sea level rise would reduce beach width somewhat but a wide beach would still remain and the boardwalk would not be impacted. However, given the devastation of the rest of the community, who knows where the boardwalk vendors would be. The good news is that all of this information is known locally and local policy makers and technicians have some time to do something about it. Marina del Rey, which is also low-lying, faces sea level rise issues as well, so in all likelihood some kind of a barrier will be installed within the entrance channel, perhaps a lock structure that would allow Marina del Rey's marinas to keep operating. But this is only speculation because as yet no climate change plan has been adopted.

South Florida Boardwalks

The beach communities on the barrier islands along South Florida's Atlantic Coast are famous destinations for visitors and retirees from cooler northern climates and their long sandy beaches function as the main public open spaces for local residents and visitors alike. Some communities have built pedestrian and bicycle promenades along parts of their beachfronts to create a public way of some specialness that enhances people's ability to move along the beach and also encourages more connections between adjacent private and public development and the beach experience. The small city of Hollywood built a beachfront promenade in the 1920s and the larger cities of Fort Lauderdale and Miami Beach built them in the 1980s. The design and character of each city's promenade is different as are the uses that front them. All the cities face considerable sea level rise threats because of their geomorphological conditions but local community situations and responses differ. Ominously, maps prepared by National Geographic showing coastlines worldwide should all the world's sea ice disappear indicate that the entire state of Florida would be gone.[36]

Beaches are the primary public open spaces of Florida's coastal communities

Hollywood Beach Boardwalk, Hollywood, Florida, USA

Scale: 1:400,000

Hollywood's Beach Boardwalk is a classic example of a paved boardwalk. It is in some ways similar to the Venice Boardwalk but has a sleepier ambience. It has been in existence for almost 90 years and has a timeless quality, but changes may be coming.

Hollywood, located just south of Fort Lauderdale but separated from it by the wide inlet that serves the massive Port Everglades cruise ship terminal, is both a beach city and not a beach city because its downtown is far inland, but the boardwalk is what it is best known for. The city was envisioned as a "Florida dream city" by its founder and developer Joseph Wesley Young, who had plans to build a broad boulevard lined with lakes extending from the coast to the everglades. Development was begun in 1921 and for five years the city grew rapidly, becoming home to 18,000 people and also the grand 500-room Hollywood Beach Hotel and an elaborate bathing pavilion. Construction of a 30-foot-wide concrete promenade along the beach was underway in 1926 when a hurricane devastated the community. The city lost much of its population and grew slowly through the depression and world wars until the 1960s, when Florida coastal communities starting booming.[37] Today, Hollywood covers an area of about 30 square miles and has a population of just over 140,000 people. Its coastline is approximately 7 miles long, about 4 miles of which is developed. A continuous 1.8-mile-long boardwalk lines the central part of this coastline.

Promenade Design Characteristics and Connectivity

The boardwalk is easily accessible and almost all of the commercial activity on Hollywood's coast centers on it. The barrier island on which the coastal strip lies averages somewhat less than 1,000 feet wide. Two north-south roadways run its length, highway A1A along the west side and Surf Road toward the middle. The boardwalk forms a third north-south route for pedestrians and bicyclists only. Numerous streets run east-west across the island and 44 of them end at the boardwalk. Along the boardwalk's length, either fronting on it or a block away, are some 50 restaurants,

Scale: 1:40,000

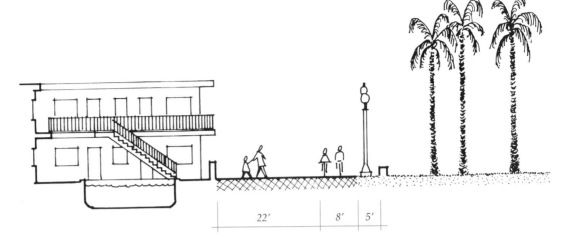

Section: Hollywood Beach
Boardwalk
Scale: 1" = 20'

22'   8'   5'

Leisurely strolling and biking on
the boardwalk

Entry portals in the undulating
wall at the edge of the sand give
entry to the beach at regular
intervals

A long line of people promending along the boardwalk in the morning

30 shops, and 30 small motels, mostly housed in small-scale two- to four-story buildings. There are also several recently built large resorts and condominiums in taller buildings, plus a handful of single story homes.

The boardwalk was recently given a facelift that reflects the community's growth aspirations. In 2007, the Hollywood Community Redevelopment Agency prepared a Hollywood Beach Masterplan that is "guided by the view that there is a tremendous opportunity for the redevelopment of Hollywood Beach." The plan declares that the two guiding principles are preserving the scale and character of Hollywood Beach and making Hollywood Beach a model green community.[38] A first action, in 2008, was the reconstruction of the boardwalk. It remains 30 feet wide but has new surfacing and design detailing. The 22 feet closest to the buildings is for pedestrians and is surfaced with concrete pavers of different sizes and brick-like hues. The outer 8 feet is designated as a two-way bike path and is surfaced with concrete. Beyond this lies a 5-foot-wide zone that is in places sandy and in other places paved. A modestly undulating sitting-height wall lines the beachside of the promenade. Entries to the beach through the wall, marked with columns and fanciful scrolls, line up with abutting cross streets. Clusters of palm trees line the beach just beyond the wall. A line of triple-globe light fixtures runs just outside the bike path, spaced at 80 feet on center. Each abutting street ends in an individually designed palm tree-lined mini-plaza. Pairs of single-globed light fixtures and pairs of benches mark the transition between these plazas and the promenade, and street names are inlaid on the ground surface with mosaic tiles.

Mini-plazas cap the end of each street leading into the boardwalk

Promenade Use

The boardwalk seldom gets very crowded and the atmosphere along it is usually calm and relaxed: people populate it but don't throng it. On a hot and sunny weekend afternoon in early May, 420 people per hour moved along the boardwalk. Most people were strolling, a few were jogging, and many were

Biking along the boardwalk

biking (36%). The high number of cyclists is influenced by the ease with which visitors can find a bike to use. The city has a public bike share program that allows people to cheaply rent bikes for short periods of time and stations are located in several places along the boardwalk. There are also several private bike rental shops where all kinds of bikes can be rented, including recumbent bikes that are very popular.

Challenges

The leisurely, laid-back feel of the boardwalk goes hand-in-hand with the simple, relaxed nature of the small motel and cottage accommodations along it, but things may get more crowded and active in the future. The large new resorts and condominiums give a message that physical change is already coming to Hollywood Beach as predicted and encouraged by the Masterplan, and these projects may help change the boardwalk's character. Whether the new projects are in keeping with the traditional character and scale of Hollywood Beach is a matter of some contention. The Villas of Positano condominium complex, which opened at the northern end of the boardwalk in 2009, has 62 units. The Margaritaville resort hotel, which opened in 2015, has 349 rooms and the Melia Costa Hollywood Beach Resort condominium hotel, which opened in 2016, has 304 units. All of these buildings occupy large parcels that interrupt the fine grain division of the blocks along the boardwalk. A long-time manager of an older motel on the boardwalk sums the changes up as follows: "Hollywood Beach has been a mom-and-pop resort for years and now it's becoming corporate."[39] Local residents and business owners are concerned that elsewhere along the boardwalk building rents and restaurant and shop prices will rise.

The Masterplan identifies a major challenge to maintaining the character of the boardwalk as development occurs along it. The Florida Building Code requires that habitable floors in new construction or substantially renovated existing buildings be located 19 feet above the National Geodetic Vertical Datum (NGVD), to protect against storm surge flooding. Most of Hollywood Beach is at +8 to +10 feet NGVD, which means habitable uses, including restaurants, shops, and motel rooms, could only be on the second floor and above. If many buildings along the boardwalk were rebuilt in this way it would radically change the feel of the boardwalk. The city is considering creating an historic district along the boardwalk, which would help circumvent the code, but this would mean not addressing the storm surge vulnerability. The large new resorts have been designed to somewhat withstand storm surges. Outdoor facilities at the Margaritaville resort within 45 feet of the beach were built with materials that will easily break away and planted with native trees that can withstand storm winds.[40]

Large resort under construction

Climate Change and Sea Level Rise Concerns

The building code requirement, however draconian it may seem, reflects the serious environmental issues that Florida communities face. The state's coastal areas are at extreme risk from sea level rise because they are low-lying, made of porous limestone into which water will infiltrate as the seas rise, and often hit by hurricanes that bring considerable rain and storm surge. A 2015 report of the Southeast Florida Regional Compact, which was formed by a consortium of Florida counties to advance regional sea level rise adaptation strategies, projects that by 2100 Southeast Florida sea levels will have risen between 2.6 and 6.75 feet above the 1992 mean sea level.[41] These projections of relative local sea level rise derive from an amalgamation of recent global sea level rise projections made by the Intergovernmental Panel on Climate Change, the National Oceanic and Atmospheric Administration, and the United States Army Corps of Engineers. The Hollywood Beach Boardwalk and the whole Hollywood Beach community will be in serious trouble if the sea level reaches even the lower range of these projections. As yet, no adaptation plan has been prepared.

Beachfront Promenade, Fort Lauderdale, Florida, USA

Scale: 1:400,000

Fort Lauderdale's beachfront promenade is of relatively recent vintage and was built to help change the city's image. Fort Lauderdale has long been known as a place for college student revelry during spring break and its central beachfront has long had many places to eat and drink along it, some of them with a raucous character. In the mid-1980s the city decided it would prefer to be known as a year-round family destination. An ordinance was passed against public drinking and citizens approved a redevelopment bond measure that included $26 million for renovating the city's central beach area, which is where highway A1A runs along the waterfront and where commercial uses front it and the beach. Diagonal parking was removed from the highway and a 2-mile-long pedestrian promenade was built along the beachfront.

The promenade is edged with a "wave wall" that undulates up and down as well as in and out and has sculptural elements along it. It is the signature feature that now gives identity to the central beach area, helping draw together the disparate urban fabric on the other side of the roadway which consists of one- and two-story commercial buildings of different ages, parking lots, scattered hotel towers and an area of single-family houses.

Promenade Design Characteristics

The beach promenade has four different sections distinguished by varying designs, different adjacent roadway configurations, and different fronting land uses. Starting in the south, the promenade first runs between a parking lot and a beach park planted with many trees that give shade to numerous picnic tables. The walk is a minimum of 12 feet wide along the undulating wall, and cyclists mix with pedestrians. The promenade next runs through the heart of the central commercial area where A1A splits into two one-way streets flanking commercial blocks. Northbound traffic runs adjacent to the beach on a 27-foot-wide roadway that includes two travel lanes and a 5-foot-wide northbound bike lane next to the promenade. Here the promenade varies from 16 to 22 feet wide and is randomly planted with palm trees. The wave wall varies in width from 28 to 42 inches and in height from 14 to 20 inches. Entries through it to the beach, opposite connecting streets, are marked with sculptural spiral gateways with steps down to the sand. Traditionally designed light fixtures with banners run in a line just inside the wave wall and there are clusters of palm trees on the beach side of the wall.

Further north, still in the commercial area but where A1A is not split, the roadway is 70 feet wide with two vehicle lanes and a curbside bike lane in each direction, separated by a palm tree planted median. The promenade is just 10 feet wide, has no palm trees on it, and is edged with a straight wall.

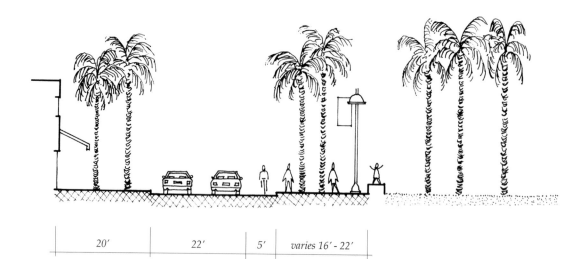

Section: Fort Lauderdale
Beachfront Promenade
Scale: 1" = 20'

| 20' | 22' | 5' | varies 16' - 22' |

Scale: 1:40,000

North of Sunrise Boulevard, where A1A runs along a park and a residential area, the roadway and beach promenade are under reconstruction. The severe erosion caused by storm surge associated with Hurricane Sandy, which put a foot of water over A1A and toppled the beach promenade, necessitated this $11.8 million undertaking.[42] A1A has been reduced to one lane in each direction, the beachfront has been reinforced with constructed dunes planted with native vegetation, and a sheet pile sea wall was driven deep into the sand at the edge of the promenade.[43]

Promenade Use

The central commercial part of the promenade is the most highly used. Children like to walk atop the wave wall enjoying its varying height and direction changes. For others, walking along the promenade requires weaving among the palm trees and avoiding the many southbound cyclists who choose to travel on the walk rather than on the dedicated bike path provided on southbound A1A one block to the west. Numbers are not particularly high and are often greater in the evening than during the day. On a hot sunny Saturday morning in early May, 345 people per hour were observed moving along the

The promenade along the central commercial area

Cafes and restaurants line the far side of A1A where it passes through the central area

promenade as compared with 513 that same evening. While during the daytime few people moved along the sidewalk on the opposite side of A1A in front of the businesses, in the evening it hosted the greater flow: over 1,600 people per hour. During the day most of the activity comes from the constant flow of vehicles on the roadway. Things pick up in the evening. Many people sit along the wave wall, sidewalk café tables on the west side of A1A are full, and there are lots of sparkling and moving lights. Integral to the wave wall is a strip of lights that constantly changes colors, restaurants are lit up, and slowly moving cars fill the roadway with headlights and taillights.

Climate Change and Sea Level Rise Concerns

Fort Lauderdale plans to improve its central beach area but has not yet addressed the issue of future sea level rise. Since 2008, the city has been working on a Central Beach Masterplan. While not yet

Children enjoy walking on the wave wall

Dunes lie between the promenade and the beach along the northern part of the promenade

finalized, the draft plan envisions creating "a more comfortable, pedestrian-oriented beach environment, framed with appropriately-scaled, mixed use buildings that help create a vibrant, active resort and residential community."[44] Development aspirations aside, the city faces enormous challenges related to projected sea level rise because most of the city is less than 10 feet above sea level and sits on porous limestone. Rising water and storm surge will affect not only the coastline but also the city's 135 miles of inland canals, and saltwater will infiltrate the aquifers that the city relies on for fresh water. In 2013, the city adopted a *2035 Vision Plan* that envisions the city having successfully implemented adaptive strategies, but what those strategies will be has yet to be determined.[45] The 2015 assessment released by the Southeast Florida Regional Compact may encourage the community to feel some urgency about preparing a plan because it projects that by 2060 the sea level will have risen between 1.2 and 2.8 feet above the 1992 mean sea level, and between 2.6 and 6.75 feet by 2100.[46]

Miami Beach Boardwalk, Miami Beach, Florida, USA

Scale: 1:400,000

The Miami Beach Boardwalk has a different feel than most classic boardwalks because it runs behind tall dunes rather than along flat sand.

Miami Beach sits on a narrow barrier island, just 900 feet to one and a half miles wide. Its eastern side faces the Atlantic Ocean and its western side faces Biscayne Bay, which separates Miami Beach from the separate city of Miami. A dune system was constructed along the ocean shoreline in the late 1970s as part of a Beach Erosion Control and Hurricane Protection Project and the dunes were vegetated in the mid-1980s.[47] The boardwalk dates from the mid-1980s when a 1.75-mile-long, 12-foot-wide elevated wooden structure for pedestrians was built along a stretch of beachfront resorts and, further south, a half-mile-long paved promenade for pedestrians and bicyclists was built along another stretch of resorts and through Lummus Park, which fronts the city's famed Art Deco hotel district.

The boardwalk and the dunes have recently seen changes. In 2013 the dunes were restored with native vegetation to fortify them and also eliminate overgrowth that had become a place for vagrants. The elevated boardwalk structure, under which feral cats apparently reside and where homeless people apparently sometimes sleep, is slowly being replaced with an on-grade path. The goal is to solve the perceived social problems and also realize the city's vision of creating a continuous pedestrian and bicycle path along its entire Atlantic Ocean coastline.[48] Since 2007, city policy has required that when resorts are redeveloped property owners must take down the elevated boardwalk along their land and build an on-grade multi-use path. Some segments have been completed but the future of the effort is in doubt because some residents see the wooden structure as an historic feature to be protected, and many don't want to lose the water views it affords.[49] From the paved walk, glimpses of the water can only be had from the widely spaced beach entryway points through the dunes.

Promenade Design Characteristics and Connectivity

The existing paved walk gives a sense of what the entire promenade might someday be like. It varies from 20 feet wide in Lummus Park to 15 feet wide behind the resorts and is shared by pedestrians and cyclists. It takes a loosely meandering path through the park where it is lined with a sitting-height wall and occasionally shaded by palm trees. The path meanders more tightly where it runs behind the resorts and is bordered with high vegetation on both sides, often hedges along the resorts and palm trees and grasses on the dunes. Along some stretches a sitting-height wall edges the walk. The street pattern of the adjacent blocks is such that street ends abut the path

Section: Miami Beach
Boardwalk
Scale: 1" = 20'

15'   varies 75' - 150'

Scale: 1:40,000

every 200 to 500 feet, with high-rise resort buildings occupying the intervening blocks. At these intersections the path widens into plazas of various circular shapes and trails lead over the dunes to the beach. Craft and food and drink vendors ply their wares at some of the plazas, but for the most part the walk is free of commercial uses. At night, the walk is lit by a string of lights along its dune side edge and by the array of lights emanating from the restaurants and poolside venues of the resorts.

The boardwalk as it transitions from Lummus Park to behind the resorts

Promenade Use

The boardwalk is usually relatively uncrowded and the pace of movement is slow and relaxed. People mostly stroll along it but many people also bike the paved section. Miami Beach has a public bike share program that allows people to cheaply rent bikes for short periods of time and there are several stations in Lummus Park where bikes can be picked up. Many tourists take advantage of this program to bike the promenade. Around mid-day on a hot, humid, and sunny Sunday in early May, 333 people per hour were observed moving along the Lummus Park part of the boardwalk. Of these 46 percent were walking, 42 percent were biking, 11 percent were jogging, and the remaining few were skating or skateboarding.

Climate Change and Sea Level Rise Concerns

Strolling along the promenade in Lummus Park

Miami Beach faces serious challenges from sea level rise. Even now, the city is seeing severe flooding from just high-tide events.[50] When flooding happens it is acute because the city sits on porous limestone, which means that water intrudes from below ground as well as above and floodwaters have nowhere to drain. Things will only get worse as the city experiences a sea level rise that is expected to be much greater than average global rise. The rise by 2100 is projected to be 2.6 to 6.75 feet above the 1992 level.[51] The coastal dunes make land along the Atlantic shore less vulnerable to flooding than land along the western side of the barrier island. Maps showing the inundation that would occur with 3 feet of sea level rise show the western two-thirds of the island under water and the ocean side still above water.[52] Maintaining the beach and dunes will be a constant undertaking because according to a factsheet prepared by the World Resources Institute the beach can be expected to erode at a rate of 100,000 cubic yards per year from regular wave action coupled with the sudden erosion that often happens during storms, when there can be considerable storm surge and big waves.[53] With climate change it is predicted that storm events will become more frequent and intense. For instance, the 7-foot storm surge that happened in 2005 as a result of Hurricane Wilma, which when it occurred had the likelihood of happening every 76 years, would have the likelihood of happening every five years if sea levels were 2 feet higher.

In spite of the future risk the city has not yet prepared a sea level rise adaptation plan, perhaps because the situation is so daunting or because politicians prefer to ignore the scientific consensus that sea level rise will happen. To handle immediate flooding problems the city is in the process of installing a pumping system that will catch storm waters in underground concrete vaults, purify them, and pump them into Biscayne Bay.[54] The city is apparently also considering raising the height of the 3-mile-long seawall running along Biscayne Bay and raising the level of some city streets.

The promenade in Lummus Park

Pedestrians and bicyclists mix
on the boardwalk that meanders
through heavy planting between
the resorts and the beach

A small plaza along the
boardwalk and a path leading
through the dunes

Passeig Marítim, Barcelona, Spain

Scale: 1:400,000

Until 30 years ago Barcelona was known best for its exuberant Catalan Modernist architecture, its famous Guell Park, and its engaging street life. Now it is also known for its long and very active beachfront and promenade created as part of a major redevelopment project done in conjunction with the city's hosting of the 1992 Olympic Games. The 3-mile-long promenade, called the Passeig Marítim (Marine Walk) with the names of local beaches appended to different sections, has become the Mediterranean front face of the city and a highly used public space.

Barcelona, which is the capital city of the autonomous Catalan region of Spain and has been a port city since the late Middle Ages,[55] has long had an ambiguous relationship with its waterfront. The city lies on a lowland plain that fronts the Mediterranean Sea and is hemmed in by mountains to the south and west. The harbor was initially wedged haphazardly into a small natural cove and constructed breakwater that lay immediately south of the city's walled core. In the fifteenth century the walled city was expanded and a boulevard called the Ramblas was extended to the waterfront.[56] In the seventeenth century, Barcelona formalized its relation to the sea by building a high rampart along the waterfront backed by a wide street along which merchant palaces were built. This embrace of

Scale: 1:40,000

the waterfront was curtailed in the eighteenth century when, following a Catalan rebellion, the central government constrained the city to remain inside its walls, building a citadel near the waterfront from which this edict could be enforced.[57] At the same time, the central government built a new district of tight housing blocks near the harbor and relocated most of the rebels there. This district, called Barceloneta, remained a working-class district and until the 1980s it was the only place where the general public could get to the shore.

During the twentieth century the city did a number of things that cut it off from the waterfront: the harbor area was expanded into a large industrial port; a broad quay, the Moll de la Fusta, was constructed along the waterfront north of the Ramblas and built with a solid mass of large harbor buildings;[58] and a railroad station was built north of Barceloneta and tracks serving it were run along the northern waterfront.[59] And so, Barcelona largely turned its back on the waterfront except at Barceloneta.

As with many other big cities, change came with the relocation of industrial uses, the demolition of the industrial buildings that dominated the waterfront, and the creation of new public spaces. In Barcelona, the change followed the city's adoption in the early 1980s of policies aimed at improving urban neighborhoods and creating more public spaces.[60] The port was moved south and public spaces along the water started to be opened up. Redevelopment of the waterfront accelerated after Barcelona won the 1992 Olympic Games: beachfront shanties along the Barceloneta beach were removed, a gas-works north of Barceloneta and a major sewer outfall were relocated, a string of beaches was created and promenades were built along them, a leisure port (used for the Olympic Games) and a hospital extension were built at the waterfront, and a partially below-grade coastal ring road, an athletes' village, and other residential blocks were built just inland. Public investment along the waterfront decreased after the Olympics and so the northernmost beachfront promenades, farthest away from Barceloneta, are less developed than the others.[61]

Promenade Design Characteristics

Section: Passeig Marítim at Barceloneta Beach
Scale: 1" = 20'

The Passeig Marítim has different physical characteristics, design qualities and fronting land uses along its 3-mile journey. Going south to north, it starts at Sant Sebastia Beach where it is fronted at

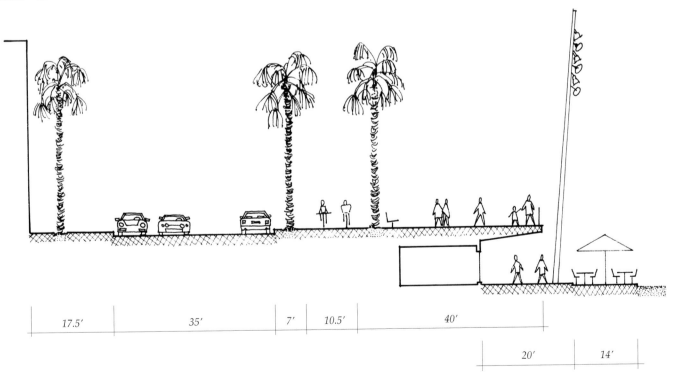

17.5'   35'   7'   10.5'   40'

20'   14'

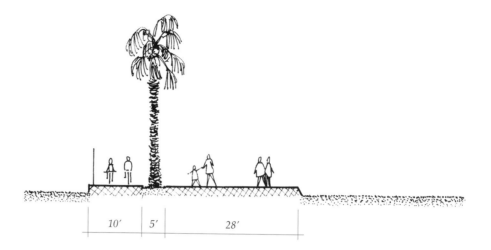

Section: Passeig Maritìm at Sant
Sebastia Beach
Scale: 1" = 20'

10' 5' 28'

first by recently built high-rise resort hotels and then by a number of private sport clubs. Along the resorts the promenade consists of a wide walk backed by a lawn that is lined with a double row of palm trees. Along the sport clubs the walk widens to 28 feet and is lined by a single row of palm trees beyond which runs a 10-foot-wide two-way bike path. The spacing of palm trees varies, ranging from about 13 feet to 35 feet. Set in line with the trees are benches, spaced 50 to 70 feet apart, and light fixtures, set in an alternating pattern: two low, then one high. The high fixtures have multiple floodlights on them to light the beach at night. Located at several places along the beach side of the promenade are food-serving kiosks with awning-covered seating areas.

The promenade changes character when it reaches Barceloneta, where neighborhood streets run at an acute angle to Sant Miquel Beach. It first merges into the wide space of the Plaça del Mar and then runs between the beach and a series of saw-tooth plazas fronted by residential buildings, many

Passeig Maritìm at the northern
end of Barceloneta Beach

Passeig Marìtim is lined with restaurants and palm trees along the Port Olimpic

of which contain ground-floor restaurants. Here the walking path becomes an 18-foot-wide wooden boardwalk that is bordered by a line of low bollards containing downlights. Outside of this is a zone that contains bike parking racks and a line of the tall floodlight fixtures, along which runs a two-way cycle track. Tall palm trees and lower tamarind trees loosely define another place to walk along the edge of the staggered plazas.

North of Barceloneta, along Barceloneta Beach, the promenade splits in two with one path continuing at beach level and the other rising up about 12 feet and partially cantilevering over the lower one. The 20-foot-wide lower walk is edged in places with a wooden deck on which sit tables and chairs that are served by restaurants tucked into the cantilevered structure. Elsewhere, this space houses public toilets, sports clubs, and small police sub-stations. The 40-foot-wide upper walk is lined on its inland side by a double row of palm trees (with 24-foot spacing) and light fixtures through which runs a two-way bike track. Benches face the promenade, in front of every other palm tree. Beyond the bike track runs a two-lane roadway with parking along it and another row of palm trees on the far sidewalk. The buildings lining the road are mostly low-scale and include public institutions such as a school and a hospital. Approaching the rectangular basin of the Port Olimpic the dedicated bike lanes and palm trees end, and the walk is instead lined with a series of small buildings that act as portals to restaurants and nightclubs at beach level below. Inland is a shopping mall which is topped by an enormous gold-colored stainless steel fish structure that was designed by Frank Gehry—the most eye-catching landmark along the Passeig Marìtim.

The promenade changes character again as it skirts the Port Olimpic. After traversing a wooden bridge and skirting the loop road that gives drop-off access to the port, the raised level of the Passeig Marìtim continues along a row of restaurants with broad outdoor serving terraces set around a bosque of palm trees. Down below, the marina is lined with many more restaurants. Three lines of palms continue beyond the restaurants creating multiple defined and somewhat shaded linear paths, one of which is marked as a two-way bike track. The shade can be very welcome on a hot day since little is offered elsewhere along the promenade. A line of sculptural metal light posts runs in front of the palms, defining the inland side of the main promenade.

North of Port Olimpic the Passeig Marìtim runs along the Nova Icària and Bogatell beaches and its character changes again. Here, instead of being straight like the previous sections, it curves gently around two beach coves. There are upper and lower walks, separated by a 10-foot-high sloping wall. The lower walk is about 37 feet wide, narrowing at the ramps that slope down occasionally to give access. Every so often a small "beach bar" café sits along the edge of the sand.

The palm tree-lined bicycle path along the Port Olimpic segment of the Passeig Marìtim

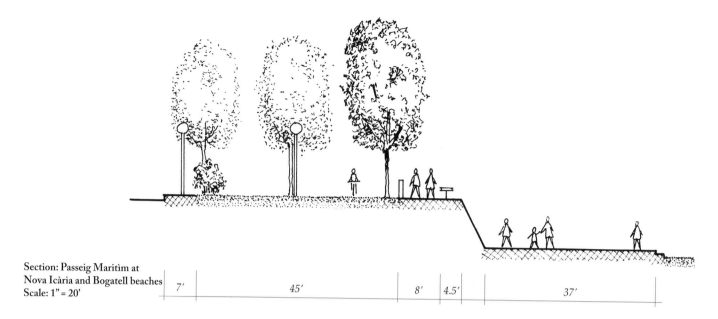

Section: Passeig Marìtìm at
Nova Icària and Bogatell beaches
Scale: 1" = 20'

| 7' | 45' | 8' | 4.5' | 37' |

Pedestrians and bicyclists mix
on the upper and lower levels of
Passeig Marìtìm where it passes
along Nova Icària and Bogatell
beaches

The 8-foot-wide upper walk is bounded on its outer edge by an almost continuous line of concrete benches and on the other side by a line of low bollards with downlights. Beyond this lies a wide open space surfaced with dirt and containing London Plane trees and benches set in various configurations, along with a scattering of food kiosks and cafés. There are no marked bike lanes so bikers mix with pedestrians.

The final stretch of the Passeig Marìtìm, along the Mar Bella and Nova Mar Bella beaches, is the least designed. In most places it consists of wide sidewalk running adjacent to a parking lot and in

Passeig Marítim runs along parking lots at the Mar Bella and Nova Mar Bella beaches

one place it runs through a parking lot. The promenade ends at the Forum sports park, an enormous mostly undeveloped waterfront space notable for its large expanses of pavement and a large concrete structure with an acutely slanted top that frames steps leading down the water. It is where the Universal Forum of Cultures event, an international gathering focused on sustainable urban development, was held in 2004.[62]

Promenade Use and Connectivity

Connections between the remade waterfront and the city remain fragmented, but this doesn't stop people from using the beaches and the Passeig Marítim. North of Barceloneta, the train station and its rail yards still create a barrier; further north, the coastal ring road creates a barrier for long stretches where it is not covered by park space. However, the working-class neighborhoods inland of the ring road now have a nearby recreational amenity that they didn't have before, and some neighborhood streets have been extended over the ring road to connect with a smaller locally oriented roadway that parallels the beaches. A number of bus routes connect the promenades with different parts of the city but there are no nearby subway stops. Clearly though, the beachfront promenades, like the beaches themselves, are used by everyone, people from all over the city as well as nearby residents; locals as well as tourists. And, on fine mid-summer days they are all crowded with people. The southernmost ones attract more international tourists than the ones farther away from the city center.

The promenades are highly used, particularly on weekends and also on weekday evenings. The number of people on the most popular segments ranks toward the higher middle range of all the promenades studied. On a Saturday afternoon in late June, 1,656 people per hour moved along the single level Barceloneta stretch, while at the same time 1,176 moved along the raised section of the promenade just to the north. In both areas most people were strolling, about 30 percent were bicycling, and 10 percent were jogging. The single-level Port Olimpic segment saw 1,828 people per hour, about

People strolling along San Sebastia Beach in the early evening

Daytime activity on Passeig Maritim at Barceloneta

20 percent of them bicycling and 2 percent jogging. Further north, the upper level promenade along Nova Icària beach saw 942 people, 36 percent bicycling and 2 percent jogging.

On a weekday evening in June, 1,761 people per hour were counted moving along San Sebastia Beach and 1,878 along the raised promenade at Barceloneta Beach. This means someone passing by about every two seconds. Most people were walking leisurely with just slightly over 20 percent cycling. More people were jogging along the Barceloneta Beach section (17%) than along the San Sebastia Beach section (8%).

All this activity is not without its downside. As evidenced by posters hanging from some apartment balconies, longtime older residents of the Barceloneta neighborhood decry the noise, partying, and even lewd behavior of some visitors. As well, some local landowners seem to be taking advantage of the economic opportunities afforded by Barceloneta's popularity and offering apartments for short-term vacation rentals, thereby removing them from the housing stock and creating conditions within buildings that are difficult for residents.

Notwithstanding the social problems of Barceloneta, which is after all the most accessible area of the waterfront, the city was thinking about social matters when it planned the waterfront redevelopment. Because of community protests, the city discarded the 1970s idea of creating a new linear waterfront district that was unrelated to existing inland neighborhoods in favor of a plan where those neighborhoods were linked with the new beachfront. This planning concept is why the promenade's design and immediate surrounds differs from place to place. What could have been a high-end residential enclave is instead an area that welcomes everyone. Whereas some cities that have built waterfront promenades in recent years have funded them by re-zoning waterfront land for expensive housing and exacting community amenity contributions from developers, Barcelona built the promenades with public funds as a public infrastructure project. The city used the opportunity created by hosting the Olympics to create a major new community amenity.

Climate Change and Sea Level Rise Concerns

Like all coastal cities, Barcelona will have to deal with the impacts climate change and sea level rise will have on its waterfront. In recent decades the Mediterranean Sea has been rising about

The Passeig Marítim creates a
linear public space that is enjoyed
by residents and visitors alike

10 millimeters per year and the European Environment Agency projects that in 2100 relative local sea level rise along Spain's Mediterranean coast will be similar or slightly less than average global sea level rise.[63] Spanish sea level rise experts have concluded that by 2100 the local sea level will have risen between .6 and .7 meters (2 to 3 feet).[64] This is somewhat lower than the high-end projection of .98 meters (3.2 feet) average global sea level rise by 2100 recently made by the Intergovernmental Panel on Climate Change.[65] While the Passeig Marítim would not be threatened by such a rise, particularly its elevated sections, the artificially created beaches fronting the promenade would no doubt be eroded unless efforts are taken to replenish them.

Notes

1   Elizabeth Macdonald, *Pleasure Drives and Promenades: The History of Frederick Law Olmsted's Brooklyn Parkways*, 1st ed (Chicago, IL: Center for American Places at Columbia College, 2012), 57, 84.
2   Jim Lilliefors, *America's Boardwalks: From Coney Island to California* (New Brunswick, NJ: Rutgers University Press, 2006), 27, 28.
3   Ibid., 31.
4   "Coney Island Beach & Boardwalk Highlights – Coney Island: NYC Parks," accessed July 29, 2015, www.nycgovparks.org/parks/coney-island-beach-and-boardwalk/highlights/204.
5   Lilliefors, *America's Boardwalks*, 2006, 31.
6   Hilary Ballon and Kenneth T. Jackson, eds., *Robert Moses and the Modern City: The Transformation of New York*, 1st ed (New York: W. W. Norton & Co, 2007), 165.
7   Lilliefors, *America's Boardwalks*, 2006, 31, 32.
8   "Reconstructing the Coney Island Boardwalk at Brighton Beach: NYC Parks," accessed July 29, 2015, www.nycgovparks.org/about/whats-happening/coney-island-boardwalk-reconstruction-at-brighton-beach.

9   "Protesters Demand City Preserve Coney Island's Boardwalk | Brooklyn Daily Eagle," accessed July 21, 2015, www.brooklyneagle.com/articles/2015/1/21/protesters-demand-city-preserve-coney-island%E2%80%99s-boardwalk.

10 "Bathroom Break: Four Sleek New Coney Island Comfort Stations on Hold - NY Daily News," accessed July 29, 2015, www.nydailynews.com/new-york/brooklyn/bathroom-break-sleek-new-coney-island-comfort-stations-hold-article-1.1332606.

11 "New York City Panel on Climate Change 2015 Report Executive Summary," *Annals of the New York Academy of Sciences* 1336, no. 1 (January 1, 2015): 11, doi:10.1111/nyas.12591.

12 "New York | Surging Seas: Sea Level Rise Analysis by Climate Central," accessed June 17, 2016, http://sealevel.climatecentral.org/ssrf/new-york.

13 The City of New York, "A Stronger, More Resilient New York" (Office of the Mayor, 2013), 363, accessed July 28, 2015, www.nyc.gov/html/sirr/html/report/report.shtml.

14 M. Jane Fairburn, *Along the Shore: Rediscovering Toronto's Waterfront Heritage* (Toronto, Ont: ECW Press, 2013), 145, 151, 153, 155, 156, 159, 167, 168, 170.

15 Ibid., 131.

16 Ibid., 117.

17 Jim Lilliefors, *America's Boardwalks*, 2006, 43–61.

18 NOAA Great Lakes Environmental Research Laboratory, "NOAA Great Lakes Environmental Research Laboratory (GLERL) Great Lakes Water Levels," accessed October 17, 2015, www.glerl.noaa.gov/data/now/wlevels/levels.html.

19 Committee on Sea Level Rise in California, Oregon, and Washington; Board on Earth Sciences and Resources; Ocean Studies Board; Division on Earth and Life Studies; National Research Council, *Sea-Level Rise for the Coasts of California, Oregon, and Washington: Past, Present, and Future* (Washington, D.C.: The National Academies Press, 2012), 107–108.

20 J. A. Church et al., "2013: Sea Level Change," in *Climate Change 2013: The Physical Science Basis. Contribution of Working Group I to the Fifth Assessment Report of the Intergovernmental Panel on Climate Change* [Stocker, T.F., D. Qin, G.-K. Plattner, M. Tignor, S.K. Allen, J. Boschung, A. Nauels, Y. Xia, V. Bex, and P.M. Midgley (eds)]. (Cambridge, United Kingdom and New York, NY, USA: Cambridge University Press, 2013), 1182.

21 "Climate Central: Surging Seas 2.0," accessed October 7, 2015, http://ss2.climatecentral.org/#8/46.3556404/-124.0556498.

22 "Ring of Fire," *National Geographic Education*, accessed October 15, 2015, http://education.nationalgeographic.com/encyclopedia/ring-fire/.

23 Jerry Thompson and Simon Winchester, *Cascadia's Fault: The Coming Earthquake and Tsunami That Could Devastate North America*, reprint edition (Berkeley, CA: Counterpoint, 2012).

24 "LAMC 42.15 Boardwalk Ordinance (Updated 2 / 2012)," accessed August 19, 2015, http://venice311.org/venice-boardwalk/boardwalk-vending-rules-information/lamc-42-15-boardwalk-ordinance/.

25 Lilliefors, *America's Boardwalks*, 2006, 176.

26 Ibid., 177.

27 Department of Boating and Waterways and State Coastal Conservancy, "California Beach Restoration Study," January 2002, 6.16, www.dbw.ca.gov/PDF/Reports/BeachReport/FUll.pdf.

28 "Venice History," accessed August 19, 2015, www.westland.net/venice/history.htm.

29 Lilliefors, *America's Boardwalks*, 2006, 181.

30 "LAMC 42.15 Boardwalk Ordinance (Updated 2 / 2012)."

31 Ibid.

32 Martha Groves, "In Venice, a Battle over the Boardwalk," *Los Angeles Times*, April 8, 2012, http://articles.latimes.com/2012/apr/08/local/la-me-venice-boardwalk-ordinance-20120409.

33 J. A. Church et al., "2013: Sea Level Change," 1182.

34 Committee on Sea Level Rise in California, Oregon, and Washington; Board on Earth Sciences and Resources; Ocean Studies Board; Division on Earth and Life Studies; National Research Council, *Sea-Level Rise for the Coasts of California, Oregon, and Washington: Past, Present, and Future*, 107–108.

35 "Sea Level Rise | Climate Central," accessed July 22, 2015, www.climatecentral.org/what-we-do/our-programs/sea-level-rise.

36 National Geographic, "Rising Seas–Interactive: If All The Ice Melted," accessed July 15, 2015, http://ngm.nationalgeographic.com/2013/09/rising-seas/if-ice-melted-map.

37 "Hollywood, FL – Official Website – History of Hollywood," accessed August 21, 2015, www.hollywoodfl.org/index.aspx?NID=187.

38 "Hollywood Beach CRA Master Plan" (Hollywood Community Redevelopment Agency, December 10, 2007), 5.

39 Miriam Valvarde, "Margaritaville Brings Change to Hollywood Beach - Sun Sentinel," *Sun Sentinel*, April 13, 2015, www.sun-sentinel.com/business/consumer/fl-margaritaville-business-impact-20150313-story.html.

40 "Addressing Rising Sea Levels in South Florida and the California Coast," *Urban Land Magazine*, accessed August 26, 2015, http://urbanland.uli.org/sustainability/south-florida-california-coast/.

41 Sea Level Rise Working Group, "Unified Sea Level Rise Projection Southeast Florida" (Southeast Florida Regional Compact Climate Change, October 2015), 4.

42 The Center for Environmental Studies, Florida Atlantic University, "Risk, Resilience and Sustainability: A Case Study of Fort Lauderdale," 2014.

43 Florida Department of Transportation, "A1A Reconstruction Project Update," July 28, 2014.

44 "City of Fort Lauderdale, FL: Central Beach Master Plan," accessed September 6, 2015, www. fortlauderdale.gov/departments/sustainable-development/urban-design-and-planning/planning-initiatives/central-beach-master-plan.

45 "Fast Forward Fort Lauderdale: Our City, Our Vision 2035" (Fort Lauderdale City Commission, 2013), 21–27, accessed September 7, 2015, www.fortlauderdale.gov/departments/city-manager-s-office/structural-innovation-division/vision-plan.

46 Sea Level Rise Working Group, "Unified Sea Level Rise Projection Southeast Florida," 4.

47 The Nature Conservancy, "Miami Beach Dune Restoration and Enhancement Project," accessed September 7, 2015, www.nature.org/ourinitiatives/regions/northamerica/unitedstates/florida/se-fl-case-studies-8-miami-beach.pdf.

48 "City of Miami Beach 2025 Comprehensive Plan" (Miami Beach Planning Department, 2011), TE–14.

49 Kathie G. Brooks, Interim City Manager, "Committee Memorandum to the Miami Beach Land Use and Development Committee," March 20, 2013.

50 Elizabeth Kolbert, "The Siege of Miami," *The New Yorker*, December 21 & 28, 2015, 42–50.

51 Sea Level Rise Working Group, "Unified Sea Level Rise Projection Southeast Florida," 4.

52 Brian McNoldy, "Water, Water, Everywhere: Sea Level Rise in Miami," *RSMAS Blog*, accessed August 21, 2015, www.rsmas.miami.edu/blog/2014/10/03/sea-level-rise-in-miami/.

53 Forbes Tompkins and Christina DeConcini, "Sea-Level Rise and Its Impact on Miami-Dade County" (World Resources Institute, 2014), accessed August 21, 2015, www.wri.org/sites/default/files/sealevelrise_miami_florida_factsheet_final.pdf.

54 "Miami Beach Shows off New Anti-Flooding Pumps," *Miamiherald*, accessed September 7, 2015, www. miamiherald.com/news/local/community/miami-dade/miami-beach/article2142718.html.

55 Han Meyer, *City and Port: Urban Planning as a Cultural Venture in London, Barcelona, New York, and Rotterdam: Changing Relations between Public Urban Space and Large-Scale Infrastructure* (Utrecht: International Books, 1999), 124.

56 Ibid., 125.

57 Ibid., 128–129.

58 Ibid., 134.

59 Ibid., 142.

60 Ibid., 148.

61 Josep Parcerisa Bundo, *Barcelona 20th Century Urbanism: Look to the Sea, Look to the Mountains*, 1st ed. (Valencia, Spain: Marge Books, 2014), 196–209.

62 Barcelona Regional S.A., "Barcelona's New Projects," in *Transforming Barcelona*, ed. Tim Marshall (London; New York: Routledge, 2004), 181.

63 "Global and European Sea-Level Rise (CLIM 012) – Assessment Published Sep 2014" (European Environment Agency, 2014), accessed July 22, 2015, www.eea.europa.eu/data-and-maps/indicators/sea-level-rise-2/assessment.

64 La Vanguardia Ediciones, "El Mar Subirá 0,7 Metros En El Mediterráneo a Final de Siglo," *LA VANGUARDIA*, accessed October 12, 2015, www.lavanguardia.com/vida/20141229/54422210716/mar-subira-mediterraneo-final-siglo.html.

65 J. A. Church et al., "2013: Sea Level Change," 1182.

Chapter 4

Riverfront Promenade Loops

Urban rivers offer the opportunity for creating a special kind of waterfront promenade: a promenade loop. Promenades can be created on both banks of the river and linked with bridges or by other means. People moving on one side can look across and see people moving on the other side. A promenade loop helps make an urban river a connector of city pieces rather than a divider.

Promenade loops have been created along both big and small urban rivers. Those along big rivers are typically well above normal river height, built atop seawalls that protect the city from high tidal flows and seasonal flooding. In cities where small or intermittent rivers or streams run through central areas, the usual course of action has been to put them into culverts, so that they can be built over or to control flood events. A few cities have chosen to keep their small rivers open (or to re-open them), manage their flooding, and build walks along them. Typically these river walks are recessed well below surrounding street levels in narrow linear corridors over which city streets cross on bridges.

The four examples that follow illustrate different design strategies and planning approaches to creating riverfront promenade loops. In Portland and Bilbao the loops are along big rivers and they cater to both walkers and bikers. San Antonio and Seoul have recessed river walks that are for the most part for pedestrians only. San Antonio's river walk has a highly commercialized area. Seoul's river walk runs through a park for its whole length. In Portland and San Antonio the promenade loops were built incrementally and are made up of segments reflecting different design opportunities that emerged over time. Seoul's river walk was created all at once and is all of a piece in its design, but different segments have somewhat different characters. Seoul's river walk and one of Portland's promenade segments replaced elevated freeways. One side of Bilbao's promenade loop was part of a major redevelopment undertaking that created a new cultural district.

Central Waterfront Promenades, Portland, Oregon, USA

Scale: 1:400,000

Portland, Oregon, has in recent decades built a marvelous waterfront promenade loop along the Willamette River where it flows through the city's central area. The loop did not happen overnight; it was carved bit by bit out of previous development and highway infrastructure over the course of 80-plus years. Part of its charm comes from being made up of multiple segments having very different design qualities: a park side promenade, a planked path across a railroad bridge, and floating docks. Bikers and walkers mix in all areas, giving a sense of informality to the whole. A southward extension of the loop is currently being created. The original promenade loop is about two and a half miles long, and the larger extended loop will be about three and a half miles long. The waterfront promenades are favored public open spaces for city residents and visitors alike. Their design reflects key aspects of Portland's urban character, a combination of genteel refinement and post-industrial grittiness.

Promenade History and Design Characteristics

Portland's connected system of waterfront promenades speaks to wonderful civic determination to create a public waterfront in the face of obstacles. Efforts began on the west bank, as recounted in the *Tom McCall Waterfront Park Masterplan*.[1] The Willamette River, a major tributary of the

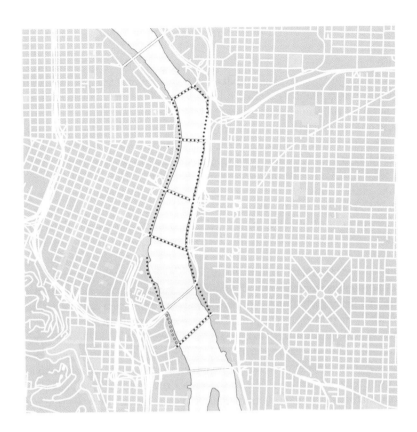

Scale: 1:40,000

Columbia River, drains a watershed more than a hundred miles long and is subject to seasonal high flows that historically caused floods along the Portland waterfront. In Portland's early days, from the 1850s through the 1920s, the Willamette's western bank was crowded with commercial wharves and warehouses serving a bustling river trade. Downtown development occurred some distance back

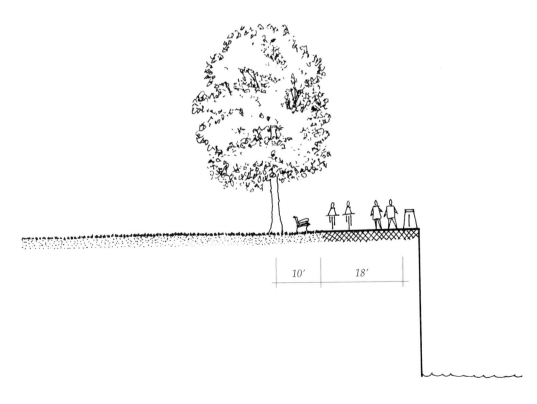

10'   18'

Section: Esplanade
Scale: 1" = 20'

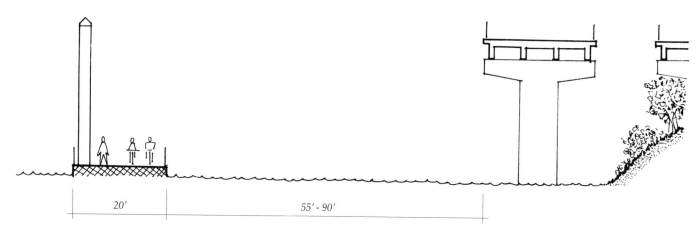

20' | 55' - 90'

Section: Vera Katz Eastbank
Esplanade
Scale: 1" = 20'

The dramatic pedestrian and
bicycle path on the Steel Bridge

from the river, out of the flood zone. Early twentieth-century planners, including the well-known Olmsted and Bartholomew firms, envisioned parks along the west bank riverfront, but this vision didn't immediately take hold. In 1927, by which time trade had shifted from ships to trucks, the city cleared the decaying wharves and warehouses and built a 31-foot-high seawall along the west bank to control flooding. In a nod to a public waterfront, a 25-foot-wide public easement was established next to the seawall, but parks weren't created. In 1943, responding to economic concerns and the emerging highway culture of the time, the city built the Harbor Drive Freeway through the cleared land, leaving just a narrow walkway along the seawall's edge. The freeway cut the downtown off from the river for 30 years, but it was taken down in 1974 under the championship of Governor Tom McCall, who envisioned a waterfront greenway. The freeway removal was made feasible, and politically possible, by the construction of another freeway, Interstate 5, on the east bank of the river, which took the bulk of through traffic. An urban renewal district was created along the west bank of the river and over the next decade tax increment financing was used to build the mile long, 36-acre Tom McCall Waterfront Park. The park was of simple design, consisting of wide lawns lined with trees, and a few plazas. A waterfront walkway called the Esplanade was built along the edge of all but the southern end of the park, within the original easement. The park lawns quickly became the city's front yard and major festival venue, and the Esplanade became a favored spot for strolling and exercise.

The Esplanade today has the same straightforward design as when it was first built. It is a simple concrete path varying from 18 to 24 feet in width and lined on the water's side with functional metal railings spanning between concrete posts. Along its landward side runs a line of classically designed light fixtures and widely spaced groups of benches set in paved alcoves carved out of the lawn. Large oak and maple trees line the walk, most set back a distance and giving it little shade. On sunny days, most of the walk gets full sun until late afternoon, making it a pleasant place to walk when it is cool, but a somewhat uncomfortable place to walk for long when it is hot and humid. But then Portlanders love the sun since the city gets so much rain.

The Esplanade's ambience is both bucolic and gritty. The park's greenery lends a sense of calm and its 200-foot width helps buffer the walk from the noise of traffic moving on Naito Parkway, the four-lane arterial street that runs next to the park. At the same time, views from the Esplanade take in the elevated freeway structure on the other side of the river and the constant motion of vehicles moving along it.

In 2001, a promenade was built on the east bank of the river opposite Tom McCall Waterfront Park. Called the Vera Katz Eastbank Esplanade in honor of a popular mayor, it is ingeniously squeezed between the Interstate 5 freeway and the river, with 1,200 feet of its length on 20-foot-wide pontoons that float on the river. The pontoons are attached to tall metal pylons, spaced at 30 feet on center, which create an impressive visual rhythm. Pairs of benches are located every third pylon space. The pontoons rise and fall with the river's tidal flows, as do the gangway ramps that connect them to the land-based sections of the promenade. Being on the floating pontoons is an exciting experience—in how many places can one traverse a long row of gently moving pontoons set atop a river? The ambience on the

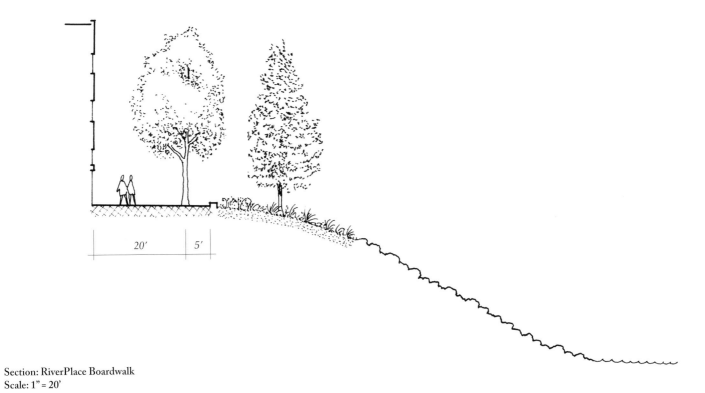

Section: RiverPlace Boardwalk
Scale: 1" = 20'

20'   5'

The west bank Esplanade along Tom McCall Waterfront Park

The Vera Katz Eastbank
Esplanade

People jogging and strolling mix
on the westbank Esplanade

pontoons is both peaceful and clamorous. The immediate environment is bucolic, but one can't help but be aware of the nearby freeway with its moving vehicles and traffic noise.

Pedestrian and bike paths on bridges spanning the river connect the two esplanades into a loop. The northern connection is on the Steel Bridge, an impressive double-decked structure that carries vehicle traffic on its upper deck and rail tracks on its lower deck, and whose central section can be lifted to allow the passage of tall watercraft underneath. The 8-foot-wide shared pedestrian and bike path cantilevers over the water from the edge of the lower deck, making for a dramatic crossing. The paths on the Hawthorne Bridge are more utilitarian.

The promenade loop is in the process of being extended to the south, making use of long-standing paths extending from the two esplanades, plus a recently completed pedestrian, bike and transit bridge, and a new path being built in a developing waterfront neighborhood. On the west bank is one older promenade segment and one recently built one. In the 1980s, a short waterfront promenade called the RiverPlace Boardwalk was built just south of Tom McCall Park, as part of a redevelopment project.[2] It sits atop a slopping revetment, rather than a seawall, and doesn't connect directly with the Esplanade but continues its line after an amphitheater-like area of sloping lawn that ends Tom McCall Waterfront Park. The northern part, approximately 1,000 feet long, is lined with four-story buildings that have cafés, restaurants, and shops on the ground floor. The water's edge is lined with pepper trees at 25-foot spacing. Light fixtures occur every fourth tree, and near each fixture is a cluster of four benches, placed back to back so that people can sit facing either the water or the walk. An assortment of café tables and picnic tables sit under the trees. The southern part of the boardwalk passes by naturalized landscaped areas and setback buildings. It ends just before Interstate 5, which soars on a bridge high overhead. Eventually this promenade will link with a greenway being

The commercial area along
the RiverPlace Boardwalk

built along the edge of a new mixed-use neighborhood being built just to the south, called the South Waterfront.

On the other side of the river, beyond the Hawthorne Bridge, the Eastbank Esplanade merges into a narrow waterfront path that continues for almost half a mile, passing beside the edge of industrial buildings and parking lots, before reaching the newly built Tilikum Crossing Bridge. People can continue south and link up with the 21-mile-long Springwater Trail, a pedestrian and bike trail paralleling the river that runs along a former rail corridor, or they can cross the bridge and loop back over to the west bank. Opened in 2015, the car-free Tilikum Crossing Bridge carries a light rail transit line and has 14-foot-wide bicycle and pedestrian paths on each side. The bridge lands toward the southern end of the South Waterfront neighborhood. Once the South Waterfront Greenway is complete, the longer loop will be complete.

Promenade Use and Connectivity

All of the promenade segments see activity, but the west bank Esplanade is the most heavily used, as might be expected given that it is closest to the downtown. On a sunny September Saturday morning, 1,176 people per hour were observed running, walking or biking along it. (These numbers are somewhat higher than those observed on the waterfront promenades along False Creek in Vancouver.) Most people were strolling (79%) and most (71%) were with others, rather than on their own. The Eastbank Esplanade gets about half as many people, generally mostly bikers and runners. On the same Saturday morning, 714 people per hour were observed on this promenade, 55 percent running and 28 percent biking. The RiverPlace Boardwalk is most active at night when people come to visit the restaurants. On a warm September weekend evening, 552 people per hour were observed moving along it, most of them strolling and in groups.

The west bank Esplanade is the most accessible promenade segment and yet access to it is somewhat constrained by roadway infrastructure. Downtown Portland is famous for its fine-grained street and block structure of 200-foot square blocks and narrow streets, which makes the city very walkable.

The 200-foot blocks are platted down to the waterfront and so streets lead toward it at regular intervals, but some streets don't give access to the waterfront because they rise to bridges or connect with bridge cloverleaf interchanges. The other streets end at the Naito Parkway, which carries two lanes of traffic in each direction, plus a left-turn lane, bike lanes, and a parking lane along the far side. Although there are marked crosswalks at most intersections, the roadway, between 64 to 95 feet wide depending on location, can be daunting for pedestrians and bicyclists to cross when traffic is heavy.

The other promenade segments are more isolated. Getting to the Eastbank Esplanade from eastside neighborhoods is no easy trick. It can only be accessed at its ends, near the bridges, and only after negotiating a couplet of one-way arterial streets, an industrial area, railroad tracks, and a freeway. This helps explain why this promenade is mostly used for long distance running and biking, rather than shorter distance strolling. Getting to the RiverPlace Boardwalk by foot is somewhat difficult because development near it takes place in large superblocks. The South Waterfront neighborhood has finer-scale blocks and so local residents and workers can more easily walk to its waterfront promenade. The South Waterfront neighborhood is largely cut off from the rest of the city by a freeway and steep grade change, but an aerial tram traversing over the freeway connects it with neighborhoods on the hill above.

The west bank promenades are relatively accessible by public transit, the east bank promenade less so. A Portland Max light rail line has several stops near the west bank Esplanade, and the Portland Streetcar has stops near the RiverPlace Boardwalk and South Waterfront promenade. On the east side of the river, streetcar and light rail stops are some distance away from the water's edge.

Climate Change and Sea Level Rise Concerns

Sea level rise will impact Portland even though it is far inland from the ocean because the Willamette River has daily tidal flows that extend to the city and beyond.[3] Sea level rise along the Oregon Coast is projected to be slightly less than average global sea level rise because of regional land uplift, and some of this rise will translate up the river leading to greater flood risk. Portland's waterfront promenades are currently reasonably protected from flooding because most of them sit atop high seawalls and riprap embankments, although the floating parts of the east bank Esplanade are sometimes closed during high water events. According to the *Tom McCall Waterfront Park Masterplan*, ordinary high water reaches to 2 feet below the top of the west bank seawall on which the Esplanade sits, a 100-year flood would overtop it by over 8 feet, and a 500-year flood would overtop it by 13 feet.[4] In 1996, a major flood almost topped the west bank seawall and came close to flooding the downtown.[5] The frequency and severity of overtopping floods is likely to increase in the future because of sea level rise compounded by the more intense rainfall events projected for the region because of climate change.[6] When flooding is anticipated, the city deploys an extra flood barrier by affixing panels to the guardrail lining the west bank Esplanade. It is conceivable that at some time in the future the seawall edge will have to be raised and this might mean design changes to the Esplanade.

Given Portland's stick-to-it history in relation to creating a public waterfront, there are good reasons to expect that they will meet any future challenges that come with climate change with creativity. Meanwhile, the city has adopted a watch-and-see approach, as articulated in its recently prepared *Climate Change Preparation Strategy*,[7] is considering the possibility of redesigning parts of Tom McCall Park to accept flood waters, and has plans to continue expanding its waterfront promenade system. Ideas include more floating pontoons extending north from Tom McCall Waterfront Park, beyond the Steel Bridge, and possibly expanding part of the west bank Esplanade with a lower level walk cut into the seawall.[8]

Portland's riverfront promenade loop is a wonderful community achievement in a very challenging physical environment marked by periodic floods and freeway infrastructure. It stands as a testament to a city having a dream and making that dream come true over extended years despite many obstacles, and to the courage the city has had to correct its mistakes, namely the Harbor Drive Freeway. It also speaks to the greater whole that can come from a piece by piece knitting together of vastly different parts of an urban fabric, and teaches that a grand riverfront promenade loop does not need to have a single comprehensive design or be built all at once.

Central Waterfront Promenades, Bilbao, Spain

Promenades line both sides of the Nervión River where it passes through central Bilbao, northwest of the old medieval center. Those on the southern left bank were built over the last two decades in conjunction with redevelopment projects that brought the famed Guggenheim Museum Bilbao; some of those on the right bank are recent and others date from earlier times. Multiple bridges connect the promenades, some easier to cross by foot or bicycle than others, creating multiple possible promenade loops and an overall connected promenade system that is almost three and a half miles long. Though connected, the promenades on each side of the river create their own linear experience because they have different spatial characteristics and design detailing.

Bilbao's promenade loop came into being with the city's de-industrialization. Bilbao is the largest city in the autonomous Basque region of northeastern Spain, and has been a major manufacturing and port city since the latter half of the nineteenth century.[9] The city is located in a narrow river valley that wends through mountainous countryside. The central city lies about 9 miles inland of the Bay of Biscay, where the Bilbao estuary meets the Atlantic Ocean. Urbanization stretches along the Nervión River to the sea, encompassing a number of smaller cities, and until the 1980s the river's left bank was almost entirely lined with shipyards and heavy industry.[10] Industrial decline began in the 1970s and many riverfront industrial sites became derelict, including those in Bilbao's central area.

Beginning in the mid-1980s, local and regional governing bodies began devising and implementing strategies to arrest Bilbao's decline, which had been exacerbated by the major flood of 1983 that devastated the historic city and other waterfront areas. Planning efforts resulted in the creation of a *Master Plan for Bilbao* (1989) and a *Strategic Plan for the Revitalization of Metropolitan Bilbao* (1991).[11] These plans envisioned making Bilbao a world-class metropolitan center by transforming the city's physical environment and improving its image. A key strategy was the creation of large emblematic projects along the riverfront.[12] In 1992, a non-profit development corporation called Bilbao Ria 2000 was set up to carry out redevelopment schemes, with shareholders including the City of Bilbao, the Basque government, the provincial government, the Port Authority, and two railroad companies.[13] Ria 2000

operates similarly to a private development firm but uses public resources of land and money to bear the speculative redevelopment risk.[14]

Redevelopment efforts focused first on an area called Abandoibarra, a derelict 86-acre site on the left bank of the central area that was formerly occupied by the Euskalduna shipyards. In addition to clearing the land and constructing new buildings and landscapes, the project involved removing a rail line, overcoming a more than 30-foot grade change, constructing a new tramline, and building three bridges over the river, two of them for pedestrians only.[15] The area is today home to the Guggenheim Museum, the Euskalduna Palace Congress and Music Center, a major shopping mall, a maritime museum, various university facilities, an iconic tower office building, and luxury housing. The waterfront is lined with wide and lushly planted parks and a highly designed pedestrian promenade runs all along the water's edge.

The success of Abandoibarra spurred private redevelopment of a 10½-acre waterfront site just to the east of it, which came to be known as the Isozaki Gateway project. Here there are luxury residential buildings with some upscale ground floor commercial uses.[16] The water's edge is lined with a narrow park strip through which runs a simply designed waterfront promenade.

No major redevelopment projects happened across the river on the right bank, but some existing walkways along the water's edge were upgraded with new paving and tree plantings.

Promenade Design Characteristics

The many individual promenade segments that make up Bilbao's promenade loop have markedly different characters. The left bank promenades are exuberant in their design and have recreational, cultural, and commercial attractions directly on them. They reflect a conscious attempt to turn a long stretch of the waterfront into a major destination. The right bank promenades are more modest in their design and more locally oriented.

Within Abandoibarra, the waterfront promenade runs for two-thirds of a mile between the Euskalduna Music Center and La Salve Bridge, which lies just past the Guggenheim. Here the promenade has two separate walkways, one at a higher level than the other. The un-treed lower walkway, which lies at the water's edge atop a high seawall, is 22 feet wide and lined on its inland side with long benches offering 50 feet of seating at a stretch. Along the water's edge is a sleek steel rail. The upper walkway, some 5½ feet higher, is 26.5 feet wide, lined on both sides with rows of trees, and edged with parks containing playgrounds, basketball courts, and broad lawns. The trees are closely spaced, at 22 to 25 feet on center, in a pattern of palms and sweet-smelling linden trees. Tall light fixtures with an

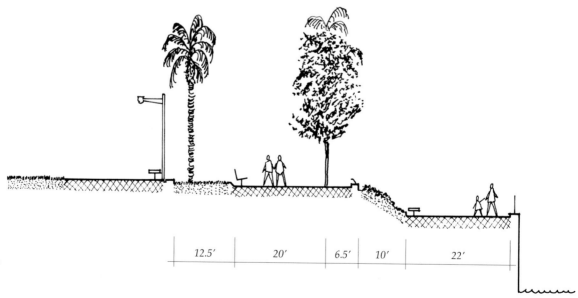

Section: Abandoibarra
Promenade
Scale: 1" = 20'

12.5'   20'   6.5'   10'   22'

industrial aesthetic are interspersed within the line of trees. Back to back benches line the waterside of this walk, and more widely spaced single benches line the inland edge.

The upper and lower walkways are mostly separated by a sloping, planted bank, but every so often the upper walk juts out to the edge of the lower walk in a prow-like shape that holds a massive, sculptural light fixture, over 50 feet tall, made of rusted steel and opaque glass. These fixtures create an impressive visual rhythm along the promenade and are its most memorable element.

Toward the western end of Abandoibarra, the upper and lower walks widen, the upper walk slopes down and becomes nearer the height of the lower walk, and the lower walk becomes a wooden deck. Near the Guggenheim, at the eastern end of Abandoibarra, the walks merge to cross a narrow bridge.

Within the Isozaki Gateway area, the waterfront promenade runs for about three-quarters of a mile between the La Salve Bridge and the Arsenal Bridge, across which lies the old city center. Here the water's edge is lined by a traditional looking nautically designed rail with integrated light fixtures, painted white, which ties this whole length of promenade together even though other design elements vary. Along the first stretch are two separate walks that are close in elevation but separated by a sitting height wall. A tramline runs alongside the promenade within a grassy strip and in some places a row of linden trees at the edge of the grass gives shade to pairs of benches lining the upper walk. After the tramline turns away from the waterfront just before the Ayuntamiento Bridge, the promenade shifts to a single level and there are one or two rows of linden trees depending on the width of the walk.

Bicyclists and pedestrians mix all along the left bank promenades. There are also dedicated bike lanes paralleling the promenades within the adjacent park spaces and along the street adjacent to the tramline.

The right bank promenade has four different segments, each with a different layout and design. The one constant element is the same traditional-looking white painted railing with integrated light fixtures that is found on the Isozaki Gateway section of the left bank promenade.

Heading northwest along the right bank from the Arsenal Bridge, the water's edge is at first lined with a broad plaza through which walkers and bikers can freely move. At its far end the plaza has covered stalls used for public markets. West of the Ayuntamiento Bridge, after a large traffic circle that is the only place along the promenade loop where it is necessary to cross a street, the promenade becomes a linear space paralleling the river. The first half-mile stretch runs alongside a two-lane roadway, the Paseo Campo Volantin. Though the cross section varies somewhat, in general there is a walk atop a seawall along the river's edge, then a wide grassy slope, and then an upper level walk. Both the upper and lower

Section: Isozaki Gateway Promenade
Scale: 1" = 20'

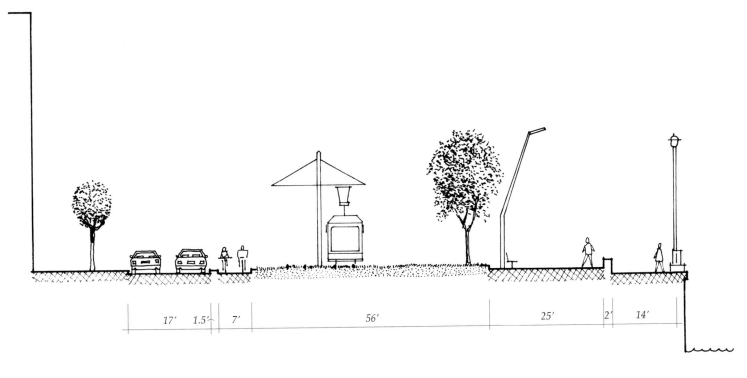

| 17' | 1.5' | 7' | 56' | 25' | 2' | 14' |

The upper and lower promenades along Abandoibarra are close together at the development's western edge

Abandoibarra promenade with its upper and lower levels

PART 1 An Assembly of Waterfront Promenades

The promenade running through the Isozaki Gateway area where the tram line runs adjacent to it

walks are about 15 feet wide. Tall London Plane trees shade the upper walk but the lower walk is open to the sun. Benches along the lower walk, set at 30-foot spacing, look out to the river. Similarly spaced benches along the upper walk look toward the street. A low wall topped with a fancifully designed wrought iron rail, painted green and with integrated double-globed light fixtures, separates the promenade from a two-way bike path, which runs along the edge of the street. The roadway itself is 27 feet wide, and has one traffic lane in each direction and a parking lane on the far side. Residential buildings, four to eight stories high, start 30 feet back from the curb behind planted terraces.

From the La Salve Bridge to somewhat before the Deusto Bridge, a distance of about two-fifths of a mile, a 12-foot-wide walkway runs along the water's edge, bounded by a narrow planting strip with closely spaced (20-foot on center) broad-leafed deciduous trees, bike lanes, and the same two-lane traffic roadway. Here the Deusto University and other education facilities are the major fronting land use. Benches line the promenade at regular spacing. A row of modestly designed light fixtures of recent vintage separate the bike and auto lanes.

After this, for a stretch of about one fifth of a mile that passes under the Deusto Bridge, the promenade becomes purely utilitarian and more than a little bleak: a 6-foot-wide walk with no trees, the bike lanes, and the roadway. Beyond this, after the roadway curves away, the promenade continues for almost another quarter of a mile along the edge of a park. The walk widens to 15 feet and a grassy tree-lined strip separates the walk from the bike lanes. The other side of the park is bounded by a neighborhood of low-income housing, other residential properties, and industrial-commercial buildings, many of which seem to be undergoing change.

After the promenade ends, it takes some doing to work one's way up to the new Euskalduna bridge on a long hairpin-shaped ramp. Once there, it is easy to conclude that the effort is worth it because of the bridge's unique design: fully one-half of it is devoted to pedestrians and bicyclists who can move under a sheltering canopy.

All in all, from Euskalduna Bridge to Arsenal Bridge, seven bridges connect the two sides of the river, all of which can be crossed on foot. All except the Deusto Bridge, a drawbridge, were built

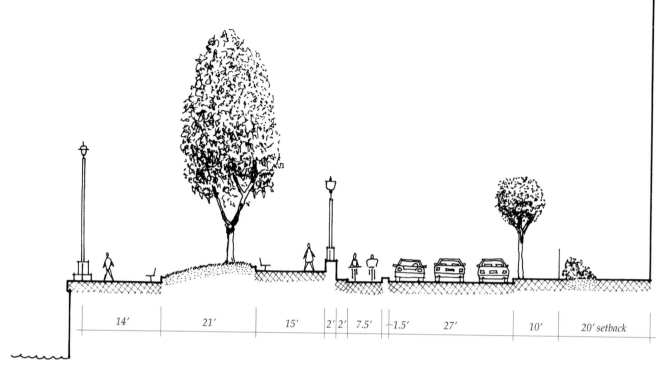

| 14' | 21' | 15' | 2' | 2' | 7.5' | 1.5' | 27' | 10' | 20' setback |

**Section: Paseo Campo Volantin
Promenade**
Scale: 1" = 20'

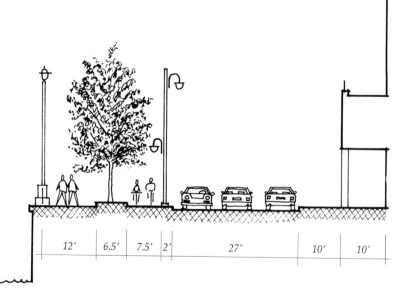

| 12' | 6.5' | 7.5' | 2' | 27' | 10' | 10' |

Section: Deusto Promenade
Scale: 1" = 20'

People walking along the right bank Paseo Campo Volantin promenade

after the 1998 consolidation of the port near the ocean, which allowed low-level bridges to be built along the river.[17] Five of the bridges carry vehicle traffic as well as bicycle paths and pedestrian walks, and two are for pedestrians only. Stairways and ramps connect all the bridges to the promenades. The Zubi Zuri pedestrian bridge, designed by Santiago Calatrava, is a soaring cable-stayed arch structure with a glass block walkway.

Promenade Use and Connectivity

All the promenade segments see activity but none get particularly crowded. At times more people can be seen moving along the simply designed right bank promenade near the university than just across the river on the fancier left bank promenade near the Guggenheim. On a warm and sunny early evening in late June, before the traditional Spanish late evening dinnertime, 696 people moved along the right bank in an hour and 498 moved along the left bank. Along both banks, most of the people were strolling leisurely with only a few jogging (7%). Fifteen percent of the people on the right bank were biking versus 6 percent of those on the left bank. On the left bank, most of the walkers (59%) chose to use the shaded upper walkway while most of bikers and joggers (68%) chose the un-shaded lower level.

The promenades along both sides of the river are easily accessible along their length. On the right bank, a fine grain of streets leads to the waterfront and there is much nearby housing. The two-lane

The narrow Deusto promenade

roadway abutting the waterfront is not heavily trafficked and is easy to cross at intersections. The left bank block structure is somewhat larger, especially in Abandoibarra, but it is still relatively permeable. The new waterfront park connects directly with an older park that is easily traversed from nearby central area streets. The new tramline, with four stops near the waterfront, can bring people from a distance.

Climate Change and Sea Level Rise Concerns

Although Bilbao is some distance inland of the Bay of Biscay, it will be impacted by future sea level rise because the Nervión River has large tidal flows and storm surge can reach upriver to Bilbao and beyond. At Bilbao, the daily tidal range can be as much as 4.67 meters (15.3 feet)[18] and storm surge can raise the water by as much as .3 meters (1 foot).[19] Bilbao's river bulkheads currently handle the daily water level shifts with ease but will be pressed to handle them if the base water level elevates with sea level rise. The European Environment Agency projects that relative local sea level rise along Spain's northern coast will be similar to or slightly less than average global sea level rise,[20] which according to recent projections of the Intergovernmental Panel on Climate Change could be a much as .98 meters (3.2 feet) by 2100.[21] If sea level rise translates up the river, which it is likely to do unless a barrier is created at the estuary mouth, Bilbao will be more at risk of flooding than it already is.

The Nervión River is flood prone because the steep topography surrounding it channels rainfall downhill quickly. Heavy rainfall events have been known to cause massive floods, such as in 1983. The European Union Centre for Climate Adaptation warns that with climate change Western Europe may experience more severe storms[22] and more frequent and more intense river flooding.[23] The Basque region has adopted a climate change adaptation plan but a clear strategy for adaptation of the Nervión River has not been articulated. Efforts are focusing on improving storm water management. Given all that Bilbao has done in the last decades to bring up the quality of its riverfront and make it publicly accessible, it seems likely that it will develop creative adaptation plans as necessary.

Bilbao's waterfront revitalization has been both criticized and lauded. It is criticized for contributing to the city's gentrification and increasing the cost of housing and retail space in nearby areas.[24, 25] In addition, while the project was successful at bringing more tourists to the city, apparently it has not generated as much international investment as was anticipated.[26] On the other hand, the Guggenheim Bilbao has put the city on the international map, and many residents are proud of this.

Bilbao has made a major effort to establish a publicly oriented waterfront over a long area. While the new left bank efforts in their exuberance contrast with the more sedate right bank efforts, they all seem to be achieving the aim of inviting people to promenade along the water's edge.

The Abandoibarra promenade as it skirts around the Guggenheim Bilbao Museum

San Antonio River Walk, San Antonio, Texas, USA

Scale: 1:400,000

Once a shallow and meandering spring-fed river prone to seasonal flooding along which a Spanish presidio and mission were established in the late 1600s, the San Antonio River today is a highly engineered and micro-managed urban water body within a 15-mile linear park that snakes through the sprawling city of San Antonio. Along its banks is a river walk that is the city's main focal point, notwithstanding the historic prominence of the Alamo.

The river in its natural state brought challenges to early settlers. It alternately ran dry during droughts and flooded during storms, becoming unsightly during the former and causing great damage and loss of life during the latter. As the city grew around the river its meandering nature required multiple crossings, accomplished first via planks on floating barrels and later via iron bridges, both of which were often destroyed in the floods.[27] Other cities might have straightened and channelized the river or put it into an underground pipe, but San Antonio, inspired by turn of the twentieth-century City Beautiful ideas, chose to keep its river, although in altered form, to landscape its banks, and to make its edges accessible by building river walks. The flooding problem was finally solved in 1987 with the construction of a tunnel, 24 feet in diameter and 140 deep, beneath the central city, into which river water could be diverted during floods.[28]

San Antonio's River Walk has been built in stages. The vision to turn the banks of a u-shaped meander of the river passing through the downtown into a garden-lined River Walk recessed below street level, fronted by small shops, and styled on the water gardens of Mexico City, was the brainchild of San Antonio architect Robert H. H. Hugman, who sketched the proposal in 1929. Though much debated, the idea caught people's imagination and something akin to it was implemented in the 1940s with the help of federal Works Progress Administration (WPA) funds.[29] Gardens and walks were built all along the meander, and also along a short stretch of river north of it. Little was built fronting onto the walk until the 1960s, when hotels, restaurants, and shops were built along it as part of the city's hosting of the 1968 Hemisfair. At the same time, a walkway-lined canal was built to connect the River Walk with a new convention center and the fairgrounds, east of the downtown. The River Walk was a celebrated feature of the fair, and it has been an internationally known attraction ever since.

Between 2008 and 2013, the River Walk was extended northward with a 3½-mile segment called the Museum Reach, conceived as a spine for cultural venues and urban housing, and southward with an 8-mile segment called the Mission Reach, which involved a massive aquatic and riparian habitat restoration. These new segments, costing $384.1 million were funded by multiple sources, including the City of San Antonio, the local county, the San Antonio River Authority, the U.S. Army Corps of Engineers, and the privately run San Antonio River Foundation.[30]

Promenade Design Characteristics and Use

The River Walk is today a continuous 15-mile-long recessed linear park corridor that snakes through the city. Within the downtown core, the river and the walks along it are a full story below street level, varying from roughly 14 to 20 feet down. In all, the River Walk passes under 37 street crossings and several highway crossings.

Different sections of the River Walk have different characters and different design details. The intensely developed downtown loop of the River Walk has a canyon-like quality. The river "right-of-way" is about 70 feet wide and the walks are about 14 feet below street level. Basements of buildings, whose main entries are at street level, have been converted to eateries and shops facing the River Walk. Above are more restaurants that can be accessed from street level or from the River Walk via elevators and stairs. For the most part, there are walks along both sides of the river. They are typically about 8 feet wide and may be right at the water's edge, set back from the water a short distance behind landscaping or a line of tables and chairs, or cantilevered over the water. Trees and landscaping are in abundance and in many places the inner edges of the walks are lined by low stonewalls. The river itself is very shallow, only about 3 feet deep. During the day its murky greenish brown color is enlivened by the play of dappled light through the trees and reflections of the many multi-colored umbrellas that shelter tables along the river's edge. At night, the river is alive with the reflected sparkle of many lights.

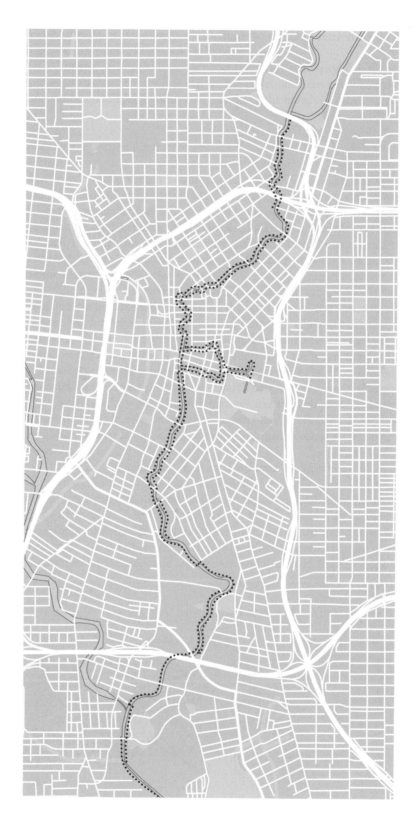

Scale: 1:40,000

The walks of the downtown loop are very crowded in the evenings, and somewhat less crowded, but still quite full, during the lunch hour. On a Saturday evening in mid-March, 3,450 people per hour were counted moving along both walks combined past a fixed point on the central part of the River Walk. Around noon the following Sunday, 1,984 people per hour were counted moving past

PART 1 An Assembly of Waterfront Promenades

Cafes at river level and up above at street level

the same location. These numbers are toward the highest seen on any of the promenades studied. The moving crowds were in addition to the crowds seated at outdoor restaurant tables. All in all, the downtown River Walk loop is not a place for casual promenading. Although most people are there with others, there is much single file walking. The walking can be in fits and starts as pedestrians back up. Crowded? "You couldn't stir this with a stick," said one passerby. A constant parade of river barges, carrying up to 40 people each, adds more movement and activity to the scene. Many of the people on the River Walk are tourists. According to a recent study, 11.5 million people visit the downtown River Walk each year, and most of them, some 81 percent, come from beyond the local county.[31]

The eastern end of the downtown loop is pierced by a straight segment of river that was built for the 1968 Hemisfair to connect the fairgrounds with the River Walk. Here the river canyon widens to about 120 feet, edges are lined with stone-faced retaining walls, and the walks undulate through heavy landscaping and small parks with benches. At its t-shaped end, one leg of the water extends to the city's convention center and the other leg extends into a shopping mall. Convention-goers and mall-goers walk along this segment to get to the more commercialized section. There are far fewer people here and they stroll leisurely.

Just north of the downtown loop is a mile-long segment that was built as part of the original 1940s WPA project. Here commerce gives way to stone-faced retaining walls and a park-like ambience. The walks are relatively narrow, 6 to 8 feet wide, and there are many tall trees and planting beds. There is both shade and sun, and many benches. Far fewer people use this part of the walk than the central part, and those that do seem a mix of locals and visitors. Many people were observed jogging, walking dogs, or eating while sitting on benches. Up above at street level is a rather bleak landscape of low-scale industrial buildings, large surface parking lots, and multi-story parking garages, although there are some notable buildings, such as the Tobin Center for the Performing Arts, which fronts on the River Walk and has landscaped steps leading down to it. In more than a few places, surface parking lots come to the top edge of the retaining walls, so that looking up one can see the front ends of parked cars through the trees. In 2002, some of the surface parking lots along it were turned into landscaped parks that cascade down to the water and mosaic tile art pieces were installed under bridges. Some adjacent property owners have opened portals onto the River Walk, with stairs leading up to street level buildings.

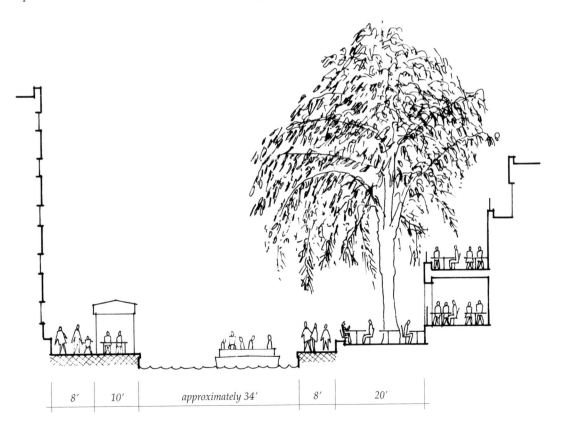

Section: San Antonio River Walk in the downtown area
Scale: 1" = 20'

| 8' | 10' | approximately 34' | 8' | 20' |

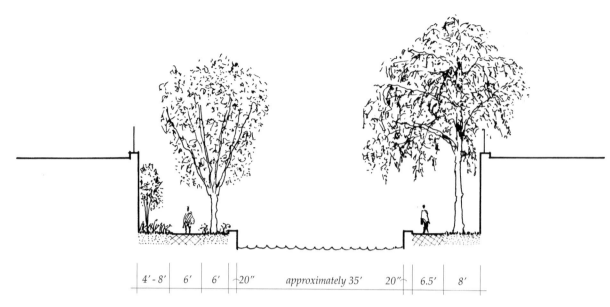

4'-8' | 6' | 6' | 20" | approximately 35' | 20" | 6.5' | 8'

Continuing north is the new Museum Reach section, which takes the place of what had been a muddy and overgrown riverbed. Toward its start is a 9-foot-tall dam that has a lock for raising and lowering the river barge taxis that also ply this stretch of water. In many places landscaped slopes lead from street level down to the walks, and the water's edge has been designed to emulate a more natural environment with pools, riffles, rocks, and water plants. Two major building complexes anchor this stretch of the river: the San Antonio Museum of Art toward the southern end and the Pearl Brewery mixed used district at the northern end. They are both adaptive reuses of former industrial buildings that include new structures oriented toward the river. South of the Pearl Brewery a new neighborhood of mid-rise condominiums oriented toward the river is under construction. Here, at the river's edge, is a pop-up café housed in shipping containers, surrounded by picnic tables and sporting a bocce ball court, which is a popular place for young and not so young people to have a beer. Colorful

The downtown section of the River Walk is always crowded with people

The promenade connecting between the main River Walk and the Convention Center has a bucolic feeling

Art under the freeway

art installations are in place under overhead bridges, including a school of brightly painted fiberglass sunfishes suspended high in the air below Interstate 35.

The number of people walking along the Museum Reach is considerably less than in the downtown. On a Sunday late afternoon in mid-March, 316 people per hour were observed moving along the walks on both sides combined. Overwhelmingly people were strolling, some 86 percent, but there

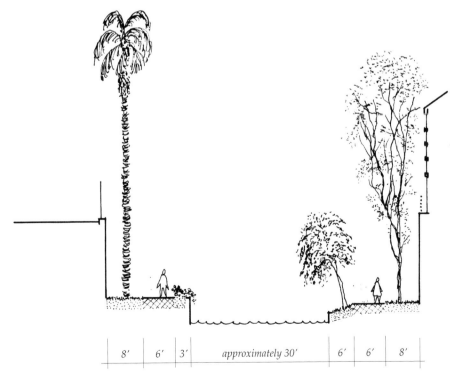

Section: San Antonio River Walk toward the start of the Museum Reach
Scale: 1" = 20'

| 8' | 6' | 3' | approximately 30' | 6' | 6' | 8' |

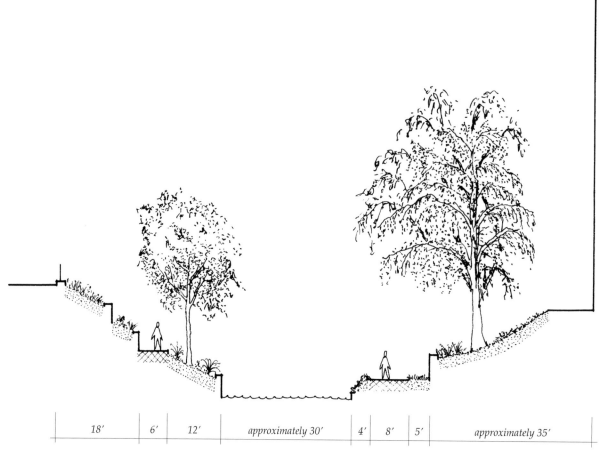

| 18' | 6' | 12' | approximately 30' | 4' | 8' | 5' | approximately 35' |

Section: San Antonio River Walk Museum Reach, far northern end
Scale: 1" = 20'

were also a handful of runners, fast walkers, and bikers. Many tourists choose to ride in the barges that ply the length of the Museum Reach rather than to walk on the promenades.

Immediately south of the downtown loop is a one-mile section called the Eagleland Segment, which runs through the historic King William neighborhood. Here the large rear yards of sizable homes back onto the river, with some protected by high walls and planting and others open to the view with only low fences. Grassy slopes extend from the backyards to low retaining walls along the river, and narrow pedestrian paths meander along the river's edge through randomly planted trees and shrubbery.

The 8-mile Mission Reach starts south of South Alamo Street. Here, the river widens and broad areas along it are planted with native grasses and shrubs. The formerly channelized riverbed has been reconfigured to have something of its original meandering form, and riffles and pools have been created. A combined walking/biking trail parallels the river, crossing from one side to the other at various places. There is little shade along the trail because there are few trees. The shade provided by the many highway and roadway bridges that pass overhead provides the few walkers and bikers who use the paths with a welcome respite from the sun.

In large measure, the River Walk is the center of San Antonio and yet it stands in stark contrast to the rest of the city. It is a lushly vegetated linear park running through an arid urban landscape. Most of the trees in the urban core are along the River Walk. Their canopies rise about street level, creating a sinuous green line through the city. From the many bridges, one can look into the tree canopy and get inviting glimpses of the water below. Almost all the commercial energy of the city is oriented toward the River Walk. Most of the city's best hotels face onto it and most of the city's best restaurants are located along it. Conversely, many streets in the central downtown core are lined with parking garages. The city's primary downtown commercial street, Houston Street, which is situated a block away from River Walk, is considerably less lively than would be expected of a big city's main street. This waterfront promenade is clearly the lifeblood of its city.

The Museum Reach

The Museum Reach where
it passes by the San Antonio
Museum of Art and a newly
developing residential
neighborhood

The Mission Reach

Cheonggyecheon Stream Walk, Seoul, South Korea

Scale: 1:400,000

The recently restored Cheonggyecheon stream in central Seoul is lined on both sides with continuous pedestrian promenades. Long covered by a street and elevated freeway, the stream now courses for three and a half miles through a recessed linear park. The walkways and sitting areas along it offer a calm and bucolic respite from the surrounding high-density, bustling cityscape.

Cheonggyecheon stream was at the heart of ancient Seoul and through a quickly executed government effort it is now again a central part of the modern city. Seoul is an enormous city of over ten million people that sits toward the western side of the Korean peninsula and spreads around the Han River, which flows west into the Yellow Sea. More than 500 years before the city's period of rapid growth that took place between the 1960s to the 1990s, the city had its start as a walled city surrounding the Cheonggyecheon stream, a small, intermittent tributary of the Han River. The stream would occasionally flood, and so it was early on enclosed with stone retaining walls. By the early 1900s, the stream had become a sewer conduit and was fouled with industrial waste. Not unlike other cities that dealt poorly with their watercourses, in the 1950s the stream was decked over with an eight-lane road. To add insult to injury, a four-lane elevated freeway was built above the road in the mid-1970s, part of a larger highway system.[32] In 1997, the freeway was found to be in poor condition and only passenger vehicles were allowed to use it.[33] At the same time, a groundswell of environmental concern was growing that called for restoring the buried stream. This became a central issue in the 2002 mayoral campaign and the candidate who backed restoration, Myung-Bak Lee, won the election. The new mayor, who later became President of South Korea, made restoring the stream his top priority. He quickly established the Cheonggyecheon Restoration Headquarters and appointed a Citizen's Advisory Committee, and restoration work soon began.[34]

The freeway and surface roadway were demolished in 2004 and, remarkably, 27 months later the restoration was complete, at a cost of about US $380 million.[35] The metropolitan government funded the whole project, in part with money that had been earmarked for rebuilding the highway. The restored stream corridor starts in the downtown then runs eastward through a series of densely built neighborhoods, eventually merging with a naturally flowing stream that feeds into the Han River.

Scale: 1:40,000

Some people feared that the restoration would cause traffic chaos because the freeway and the street under it carried some 168,000 vehicles per day.[36] To overcome these concerns, the city implemented a number of transportation improvements, including expanding public transit hours, increasing bus services, and cracking down on illegal parking. Access to the many buildings facing the restored stream corridor was maintained by retaining the outermost lanes of the former wide roadway as one-way streets. Twenty-two bridges were constructed over the stream, including one restoration of an ancient bridge and one reinterpretation of another ancient bridge. The other bridges all have different designs; seven are for pedestrians only.

Restoring the stream involved a number of challenges. A central concern was ensuring a constant flow of water in the naturally intermittent stream. To solve this problem, 120,000 cubic meters of water per day is pumped into the stream from the Han River and subway system groundwater.[37] The water emerges from a waterfall fountain that spills from the edge of a downtown plaza and downstream merges with other tributary streams before entering the Han River. A second challenge was containing occasional floods. This was resolved by creating a stream canyon cross section deep enough to contain a 200-year flood. The stream bottom is some 18 feet below street level in the downtown section, as much as 28 feet below street level in its middle section, and about 13 feet below at its eastern end. A third challenge involved maintaining water quality during storm events, a problem because the city has a combined sewer and storm water system. To address this, a special double-box storm water and sewer channel was built along the banks of the stream, with floodgates installed under bridges.[38]

Promenade Design Characteristics

The stream corridor follows a straightforward overall design. Stream banks are tiered, starting with a planter just below the rim, then masonry-faced straight or sloped walls, then walkways of varying width and material, and then banks at the water's edge. The walkways range from 2 to 8 feet above the normal shallow water level. Steps lead down to the water at various locations along the path, and in some places stepping stones allow crossing the stream. Stream banks are planted with native trees, shrubs and grasses. Most sections of the walkway on the northern side of the stream are more formally designed than those on the southern side. They typically are wider, have a paved surface, and bring people to the water's edge, while those on the south side may have a soft surface, are often at a higher elevation, and are usually more enclosed with planting. Nighttime lighting comes from downlights mounted on the tiered retaining walls and accent lighting fixtures located at event spaces and under

Section: Cheonggyecheon stream near the downtown at Gwanggyo bridge
Scale: 1" = 20'

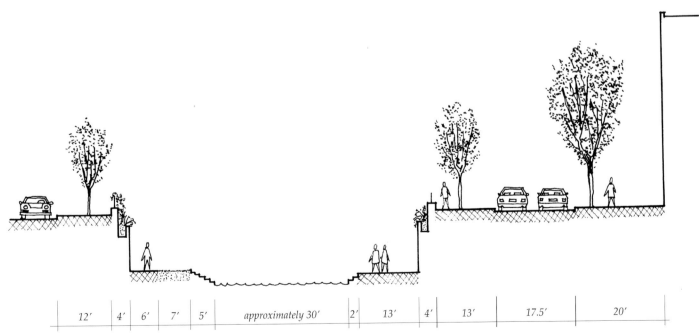

| 12' | 4' | 6' | 7' | 5' | approximately 30' | 2' | 13' | 4' | 13' | 17.5' | 20' |

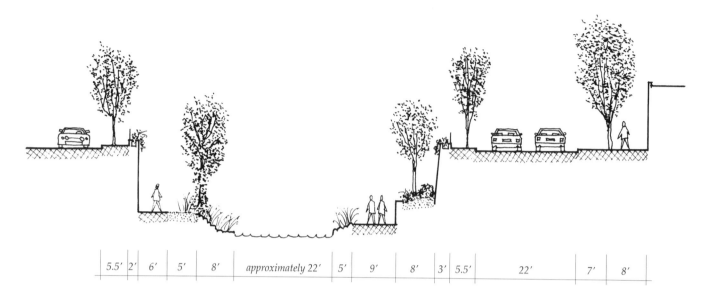

| 5.5' | 2' | 6' | 5' | 8' | approximately 22' | 5' | 9' | 8' | 3' | 5.5' | 22' | 7' | 8' |

Section: Cheonggyecheon
stream east of the downtown
near Supyogyo bridge
Scale: 1" = 20'

Cheonggyecheon stream near
the downtown during lunch hour

the bridges. Public art is integrated along the stream corridor, including a wall of ceramic tiles depicting the 8-day procession of an eighteenth-century king, and a wall covered with ceramic tiles created by local citizens.

Notwithstanding the common design elements, the character of the stream corridor changes along its length, with more hardscape at its beginning and more natural landscaping toward its end. The downtown section is sometimes used for festival events during which lanterns are strung over the river and colorful statues are placed within it. Land uses along the corridor also change. It is fronted by high-rise office and commercial buildings in the central business area, by two- to three-story buildings containing small retail and industrial establishments along its middle stretches, then by a stretch

The more informal central
section of the stream corridor

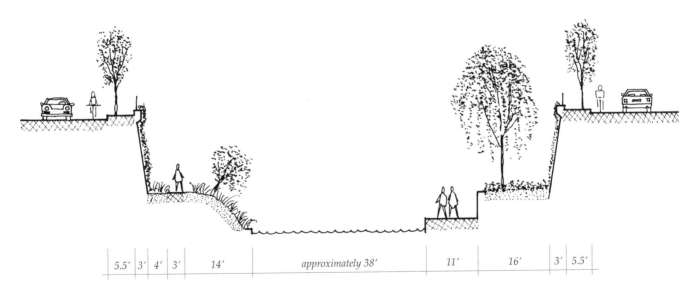

| 5.5' | 3' | 4' | 3' | 14' | approximately 38' | 11' | 16' | 3' | 5.5' |

Section: Cheonggyecheon
stream toward its eastern end
near Dasangyo bridge
Scale: 1" = 20'

Narrow one-way streets with tree-lined sidewalks run along the stream corridor at street level

of tall residential buildings, and finally, at its eastern end, by lower-scale residential and commercial buildings.

Promenade Use and Connectivity

The stream corridor promenades are relatively easy to get to, with many nearby subway stops and bus routes and a fine grain of surrounding streets. Many streets lead directly to the stream corridor: 40 from the north and 29 from the south. The narrow one-way access roads that line the corridor at street level are easy to cross and have tree-lined sidewalks. The trees were planted as part of the stream restoration project. Stairways and ramps, at least one per block, lead from the roadways into the stream corridor. In the downtown area there is also at least one elevator.

Surveys conducted in 2005, shortly after the restored stream corridor was opened to the public, found that almost 90 percent of people coming to the stream came via public transportation, most having traveled for at least 30 minutes and about a third for more than an hour.[39] Most people visited on Saturdays, and most came during daylight hours. People coming to the stream were of all ages and they came primarily to rest or to walk. Areas toward the beginning and ending of the stream corridor were the most popular.

In 2015, the walks closest to the downtown area saw the most weekday usage. On a warm weekday in late May, over 1,100 people per hour were observed moving along the stream walk just before noon, roughly evenly distributed on each side. The numbers almost doubled shortly after noon, during the lunch hour, to 2,208 people per hour. Most people were strolling (75%) and the rest were walking fast. Most people were with others rather than alone and many of the groups seemed to be made up of office co-workers.

Cheonggyecheon stream corridor toward its far eastern end where reminders of the freeway remain as sculptural elements

The walkways along the restored Cheonggyecheon stream have become a major focus of pedestrian activity in the city. Studies have found an increase in pedestrian activity near the promenade, and a shift in pedestrian activity away from parallel streets to the stream corridor.[40] The promenades serve to gather people together, and observations suggest they provide a milieu in which people of different generations mix.

As successful as the stream restoration project seems to be, it has been criticized on several grounds. First and foremost are concerns about displacement and gentrification. A great deal of displacement did occur when the stream corridor was restored because about 3,000 street vendors who previously operated under parts of the elevated freeway were forced to move elsewhere.[41] People were fearful that more displacement of small-scale businesses would occur, and some of this seems to have happened, with industrial uses replaced by commercial and office uses. Since the stream was restored, land prices and rents in the downtown area have risen, with the greatest increases being for properties nearest the stream.[42] Admittedly, changes to the city's urban fabric are being spurred not only by the stream restoration but also by the planning activity that has followed it, including the 2004 *Downtown Development Plan*, the 2007 *Urban Renaissance Masterplan*, and a series of international design competitions, including one for the Dongdaemun Design Plaza and Park, which was won by Zaha Hadid Architects. Second, users have expressed concern about the lack of public toilets along the stream corridor and the lack of enough access for disabled people.[43] There are fewer ramps connecting to street level than there are stairs, and those ramps that exist are widely spaced. Finally, people have expressed environmental concerns because the stream relies on pumped water. However, the stream corridor has had environmental benefits because it attracts birds, fish, and insects into the central city. In addition, following the stream restoration the central city has seen decreased surface temperatures and increased wind flows.[44]

The stream corridor attracts wildlife into the central city

Notes

1   Portland Parks and Recreation, "Governor Tom McCall Waterfront Park Master Plan," May 2003, 13–17.
2   "Portland Neighborhoods: Riverplace," accessed August 10, 2015, www.portlandbridges.com/portland-neighborhoods/00-Riverplace.html.
3   Multnomah County and City of Portland, "Climate Change Preparation Strategy: Preparing for Local Impacts in Portland and Multnomah County," 2014, 10.
4   Portland Parks and Recreation, "Governor Tom McCall Waterfront Park Master Plan," 35.
5   John Killen, "Flood of 1996: Nearly Two Decades Ago, Huge Flood Struck Portland, Oregon City," *OregonLive.com*, February 10, 2015, accessed June 17, 2016, www.oregonlive.com/history/2015/02/flood_of_1996_two_decades_ago.html.
6   Climate Leadership Institute, "Preparing for Climate Change in the Upper Willamette River Basin of Western Oregon: Co-Beneficial Planning for Communities and Ecosystems," Executive Summary (March 2009), accessed June 17, 2016, http://climlead.uoregon.edu/programs/scenariosplanning.html.
7   Multnomah County and City of Portland, "Climate Change Preparation Strategy: Preparing for Local Impacts in Portland and Multnomah County."
8   Portland Parks and Recreation, "Governor Tom McCall Waterfront Park Master Plan," 73–76.
9   Jorg Ploger, "Bilbao City Report" (Center for Analysis of Social Exclusion, 2007), 6.
10 Ibid., 7.
11 Arantxa Rodriguez and Elena Martinez, "Restructuring Cities: Miracles and Mirages in Urban Revitalization in Bilbao," in *The Globalized City: Economic Restructuring and Social Polarization in European Cities*, ed. Frank Moulaert, Arantxa Rodriquez, and Erik Swyngedouw (Oxford; New York: Oxford University Press, 2003), 181–207.
12 Lorenzo Vicario and P. Manuel Martinez Monje, "Another 'Guggenheim Effect'?: Central City Projects and Gentrification in Bilbao," in *Gentrification in a Global Context: The New Urban Colonialism*, ed. Rowland Atkinson and Gary Bridge (London; New York: Routledge, 2004), 158.
13 Ploger, "Bilbao City Report," 17–18.
14 Jean-Paul Carriere and Christophe Demaziere, "Urban Planning and Flagship Development Projects: Lessons from Expo 98, Lisbon," *Planning Practice and Research* 17, no. 1 (2002): 71, doi:10.1080/02697450220125096.

15 Arantxa Rodriguez and Elena Martinez, "Restructuring Cities: Miracles and Mirages in Urban Revitalization in Bilbao," 192–195.

16 Lorenzo Vicario and P. Manuel Martinez Monje, "Another 'Guggenheim Effect'? The Generation of a Potentially Gentrifiable Neighbourhood in Bilbao," *Urban Studies* 40, no. 12 (November 1, 2003): 2387, doi:10.1080/0042098032000136129.

17 Alfonso Vegara, "New Millennium Bilbao," in *Waterfronts in Post-Industrial Cities* (London; New York: Spon Press, 2001), 91.

18 "Tide Times and Tide Chart for Bilbao," accessed October 13, 2015, http://www.tide-forecast.com/locations/Bilbao-Spain/tides/latest.

19 Marta Marcos et al., "Effect of Sea Level Extremes on the Western Basque Coast during the 21st Century," *Climate Research* 51 (2012): 237–248.

20 "Global and European Sea-Level Rise (CLIM 012) – Assessment Published Sep 2014" (European Environment Agency, 2014), accessed July 22, 2015, www.eea.europa.eu/data-and-maps/indicators/sea-level-rise-2/assessment.

21 J. A. Church et al., "2013: Sea Level Change," in *Climate Change 2013: The Physical Science Basis. Contribution of Working Group I to the Fifth Assessment Report of the Intergovernmental Panel on Climate Change* [Stocker, T.F., D. Qin, G.-K. Plattner, M. Tignor, S.K. Allen, J. Boschung, A. Nauels, Y. Xia, V. Bex, and P.M. Midgley (eds)]. (Cambridge, United Kingdom and New York, NY, USA: Cambridge University Press, 2013), 1182.

22 "Storms – Spain – Climate Adaptation," accessed October 18, 2015, www.climateadaptation.eu/spain/storms/.

23 "River Floods – Spain – Climate Adaptation," accessed October 18, 2015, www.climateadaptation.eu/spain/river-floods/.

24 Arantxa Rodriguez and Elena Martinez, "Restructuring Cities: Miracles and Mirages in Urban Revitalization in Bilbao," 198.

25 Vicario and Monje, "Another 'Guggenheim Effect'?"

26 Arantxa Rodriguez and Elena Martinez, "Restructuring Cities: Miracles and Mirages in Urban Revitalization in Bilbao," 201.

27 Lewis F. Fisher, *American Venice: The Epic Story of San Antonio's River* (San Antonio, TX: Maverick Books, 2015), 6–21.

28 Ibid., 170.

29 Ibid., 90–127.

30 Ibid., 178.

31 Steve Nivin, "Impact of the San Antonio River Walk," April 2014, accessed October 10, 2015, www.sanantoniotourism.com/downloads/research/River%20Walk%20Impact%20Study%20Final%20-%20April%202014.pdf.

32 Peter G. Rowe, ed., *A City and Its Stream: The Cheonggyecheon Restoration Project* (Boston, MA: Graduate School of Design, Harvard University, 2010), 17–24.

33 Ibid., 32.

34 Ibid., 32–43.

35 Ibid., 43, 86.

36 Jin-Hyuk Chung, Kee Yeon Hwang, and Yun Kyung Bae, "The Loss of Road Capacity and Self-Compliance: Lessons from the Cheonggyecheon Stream Restoration," *Transport Policy* 21 (May 2012): 166, doi:10.1016/j.tranpol.2012.01.009.

37 Bianca Mariarinaldi, "Landscapes of Metropolitan Hedonism The Cheonggyecheon Linear Park in Seoul," *Journal of Landscape Architecture* 2, no. 2 (September 1, 2007): 63, doi:10.1080/18626033.2007.9723389.

38 Peter G. Rowe, *A City and Its Stream: The Cheonggyecheon Restoration Project*, 82, 109.

39 Ibid., 127–131.

40 Heeji Lim et al., "Urban Regeneration and Gentrification: Land Use Impacts of the Cheonggye Stream Restoration Project on the Seoul's Central Business District," *Habitat International*, 39 (July 2013): 199, doi:10.1016/j.habitatint.2012.12.004.

41 Peter G. Rowe, *A City and Its Stream: The Cheonggyecheon Restoration Project*, 102.

42 Lim et al., "Urban Regeneration and Gentrification," 199.

43 Peter G. Rowe, *A City and Its Stream: The Cheonggyecheon Restoration Project*, 132.

44 Y.-H. Kim et al., "Does the Restoration of an Inner-City Stream in Seoul Affect Local Thermal Environment?" *Theoretical and Applied Climatology* 92, no. 3–4 (July 17, 2007): 239–248, doi:10.1007/s00704-007-0319-z.

Chapter 5

Park Promenades Along Former Industrial Waterfronts

It is one thing to stroll along a waterfront promenade lined with commercial enticements and a very different thing to stroll along a waterfront promenade in a peaceful green park. The one continues the hustle and bustle of the city, the other gives respite from it.

Many urban waterfronts have long been lined with shipping and industrial uses, or with freeways, but this is changing. When the shipping and industrial uses have gone into decline, some cities have chosen to rebuild the water's edge with linear parks, perhaps even removing a freeway to do so. Although the reclaimed waterfront parks are often relatively narrow and no more than a stone's throw away from the crush of the city, the combination of the greenery in them and the water views from them creates a calm and tranquil environment. Typically they are lined with waterfront promenades because their lineal nature invites them.

This new generation of waterfront parks and the promenades within them are not all alike, far from it. One difference is that some are formally designed and others informally designed. In some, vestiges of the former industrial landscape remain, are celebrated, and are incorporated as new kinds of park spaces; in others, the former industrial landscape has been largely erased. Some include ecological features at the water's edge, some concentrate on providing access to water activities, and some do both.

Five of the six promenades that follow, three in New York City, one in Lisbon and one in San Francisco, are within large and ambitious park projects. The other one, in Charleston, is within a considerably smaller park and has a particular elegance.

Waterfront Park Promenades, Charleston, South Carolina, USA

The overarching impression one gets of Charleston Waterfront Park is a sense of calmness. This was the vision held for it by long-time mayor Joe Riley, under whose tenure it was built, and the vision was beautifully realized. The 12-acre linear park was built in 1990, replacing industrial uses. It lies along the southeast edge of the Charleston peninsula just east of downtown, facing the Cooper River, and its design is structured around two parallel promenades. One runs at the water's edge, following the gentle curve of the shoreline and offering views over restored salt marshes toward Charleston Harbor. The other runs under two rows of tall and closely spaced oak trees. The two walkways offer the choice, during the day, of walking in either sun or shade. Between the promenades are large grassy lawns that attract many activities: flying kites, picnicking, or just lying around. A wooden pier jutting into the water at the northern end of the park is very much a third promenade.

Scale: 1:400,000

The promenades and the whole park are noteworthy for fine materials and careful detailing. Though modest in length—the park is less than half a mile long and the pier is just 370 feet long—the promenades invite lengthy strolling back and forth, first on one path and then on another.

Contributing to the peaceful ambience of the park is the residential nature of most of the development that faces it. Four-story multi-family buildings along the northern section of the park directly abut it or are held back behind a narrow cobblestone paved roadway that gives access to ground floor

Scale: 1:40,000

The waterfront promenade
curves along the wetland

Pineapple Fountain

parking structures. Two-story houses front the southern section of the park, beyond a narrow asphalt roadway that offers public parking on both sides.

Though peaceful, the park is not without foci of activity. Two fountains welcome children to play in their water: the Splash Fountain at the park's northern entry, and the smaller Pineapple Fountain situated in a small plaza toward the middle of the park.

Promenade Design Characteristics

The design details of each promenade are distinctly different. The waterfront promenade is 20 feet wide and surfaced with decomposed granite. A low granite wall backed by a line of closely spaced palmetto trees defines its inner edge, in front of which is an almost continuous line of traditionally designed wooden benches. A beautifully designed metal railing sitting atop a granite curb, which tops a 6-foot-high sea wall, defines the outer edge of the promenade. A line of regularly spaced light fixtures rise from the railing, visually emphasizing the sweep of the shoreline and the curve of the promenade.

The tree-shaded promenade is 12 feet wide and surfaced with rustic brick pavers laid in a her-ringbone pattern. The oak trees lining the path arch over it, creating a continuous overhead canopy of branches and leaves. The close spacing of the trees helps create this effect: they are spaced 20 feet apart across the path and 27 feet apart along it. Paired benches set between the trees line both sides of the promenade. On the water-facing side, half of the benches face the walk and half face the water in back-to-back arrangement. A row of light fixtures also lines this edge of the path. Inland of the promenade two more rows of oak trees arch over a succession of seating areas.

At its southern end, the park narrows and the two promenades merge into a single informally designed path that steps down closer to water level and curves along the edge of the salt marshes. The path leads to a wide, rustic-feeling wood-planked floating fishing pier that lets people get down to the water.

The pier promenade is both straightforward and whimsical in its design. It is 32 feet wide and surfaced with wood planks. For a good part of its length, half of its width is covered with long gable-roofed pergolas. Old-fashioned porch swings hang from beams in these structures and people vie to sit on them; not only is it fun to swing, doing so creates a welcoming breeze on a warm day. Many other benches, particularly toward the end of the pier, invite sitting in the sun. A bridge at the end of the main pier gives access to a narrower perpendicular pier almost 300 feet long that is lined with more benches and leads at one end to a small floating dock where people can get close to the water.

Section: Charleston Waterfront
Park
Scale: 1" = 20'

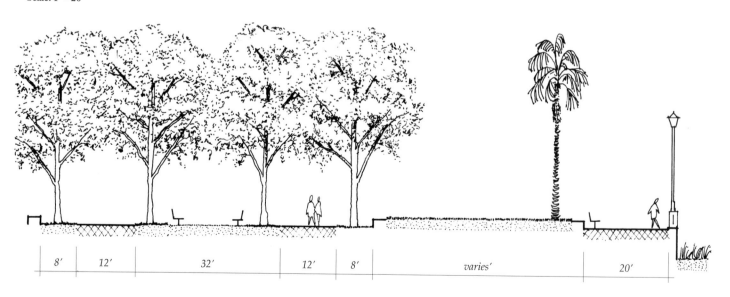

The waterfront promenade

The tree-shaded promenade

The pier promenade with its pergolas

Promenade Use and Connectivity

The promenades draw people in steady but not high numbers. Within the park, at any given moment people are usually roughly evenly distributed between the sunny waterfront path and the shaded tree-lined path. Posted signs say no biking or skating is allowed in the park and this is respected. On a weekend morning in early summer on a day that was sunny and warm, 184 people per hour were counted on both promenades combined. Most people (about 90%) were walking with others rather than alone. Most were strolling (about 80%) while the others were jogging or walking fast. The latter overwhelmingly preferred the waterfront path while those walking leisurely somewhat favored the shaded path. The pier sees more than twice as much promenading as the other two promenades combined, 480 people per hour, perhaps because being out over the water is so enticing. Here, almost everyone strolls leisurely.

People in the park and using the promenades seem a mix of locals and tourists, often clearly mostly the later. The city's cruise ship dock is just to the north and both crew and passengers use the park when ships are at dock. During the brief moments they can be ashore, crew often come to the park in droves in order to use the free Wi-Fi that is available.

The spatial structure of the nearby urban fabric makes the park highly accessible. Seven streets lead to the park and all except one are narrow and cobblestoned, making them great to walk on for pedestrians but less inviting to vehicles. The exception is the northernmost street that leads to the main park entry, which is the extension of a main downtown cross street. Wider and serving more cars, most moving slowly and looking for parking, it is lined with restaurants, cafés, and hotels. The park is well equipped with public restrooms, which also adds to its accessibility. A public art gallery overlooking the park has public restrooms in it that are open even when the gallery isn't, as do two public parking garages that are unobtrusively tucked into the neighborhood fabric a block away from the park.

Climate Change and Sea Level Rise Concerns

Charleston is one of the cities in the United States most vulnerable to the impacts of climate change and sea level rise. The historic floods of October 2015, which inundated large parts of the city, give

a grim picture of the challenges that the city faces. Charleston sits on a series of marshy islands and peninsulas that lie at the confluence of the Ashley and Cooper Rivers, which merge into Charleston Harbor and then connect with the Atlantic Ocean. Much of the city is less than 4 feet above the current high tide line and substantial areas have long experienced regular flooding during high tide events and major storms. Since 1975, the city has sought to deal with the flooding by building drainage projects aimed at slowly draining flooded streets by pumping the water into tunnels 140 feet underground, where it can be stored and later pumped back into the harbor.[1]

As impressive as this drainage system may be, it will not protect the city from the greater and more frequent flooding that will come with climate change and sea level rise. Scientists are uncertain whether Charleston will become wetter or drier with climate change, but in recent years storms have been both more intense and more frequent and this pattern may well continue. Problems will be exacerbated by the greater than global average sea level rise anticipated for the Charleston area. In the past 100 years, the local sea level has risen over one foot,[2] and calculations for relative local sea level corresponding to the 2012 National Climate Assessment's intermediate high global sea level rise scenario[3] project that sea levels could rise an additional 3.9 feet by 2100.[4] In spite of these realities, the city is doing little to prepare or adapt. In 2011, the city adopted a new comprehensive plan, the *Century V Plan*, which says nothing about climate change or sea level rise.[5]

Steps at the edge of the park

For the time being, Charleston's Waterfront Park is better protected against current and future flooding than many other waterfront areas because it is raised about 3 feet higher than adjacent city streets. The elevation change is subtly achieved at its entrances via terraced steps and ramps.

In many ways, Charleston's Waterfront Park and its promenades are unassuming. There is a feeling of them just belonging there rather than calling attention to themselves through spectacle. Other cities could do worse.

Hudson River Promenades

The Hudson River side of Manhattan Island is completely lined with linear parks, some more developed than others. Long stretches of these parks incorporate elements of a transitioning industrial landscape. Waterfront promenades run along the more developed park spaces and a bikeway connects through all of them. From south to north, the parks begin at Battery Park City, which has multiple waterfront parks, then comes the Hudson River Park, Riverside Park South, Riverside Park, Fort Washington Park, Fort Tyron Park and Inwood Hill Park. The walks and cycle paths in the latter three parks are simple trails wending through overgrowth. Those in Riverside Park, which lies between 72nd and 155th streets, are straightforward 15- to 20-foot-wide asphalt paths atop a seawall that was built as part of Robert Moses' West Side Improvement project, which expanded the park into the Hudson River to create room for the Hudson River Parkway and a number of sports fields. In places the paths run directly adjacent to the high traffic parkway. Those in Riverside Park South, which lies between 59th and 72nd streets, were created in the 2000s as part of the Trump Tower development. Here the paths in some places are narrow asphalt paths set under the elevated Joe DiMaggio Highway and elsewhere are wooden boardwalks and paved paths curving through constructed wetlands.

The promenades in Hudson River Park and at Battery Park City are more formally designed and are the focus here.

Battery Park City Esplanade, New York City, New York, USA

Scale: 1:400,000

The Battery Park City Esplanade was lower Manhattan's first waterfront promenade and has long been a calm oasis because it is well removed from major traffic streets. It was created in the 1970s as part of the 92-acre master-planned Battery Park City development that was built on reclaimed land at the southwestern end of Manhattan Island, replacing a number of dilapidated piers that had long been used for handling produce destined for the large produce market that existed in the area.[6] The massive amount of fill required to build Battery Park City came from excavations for the World

Scale: 1:40,000

Trade Center and other large projects. The development, which is overseen by the Battery Park City Authority, a New York State Public Benefit Corporation, consists of a mix of high-rise and mid-rise office and residential buildings set within an irregular grid of large blocks. A series of parks, large and small, line the entire water's edge of Battery Park City, a distance of about a mile. The esplanade is a continuous combined walking and biking path, always placed right at the water's edge, that connects them all.

Promenade Design Characteristics

The esplanade is for the most part all of a piece and simple in its design. In most areas it is 20 feet wide and surfaced with hexagonal asphalt pavers (the same pavers as can be found on Fifth Avenue along Central Park). The water's edge is lined with a curved metal railing sitting atop a low granite wall from which rise traditionally designed light fixtures spaced 40 to 50 feet apart. Clusters of traditionally designed wooden benches are placed near the railing, letting people sitting on them look directly over the water. Along one section, perhaps the most gracious, the main promenade is joined by a narrower parallel walkway, one or two steps higher up, that is lined on both sides with rows of closely spaced trees and regularly placed benches. Along another section, near a ferry terminal, a row of closely spaced trees in staggered pattern straddle a line of waterside benches. One short segment has a completely different and more informal design than the rest. Here, the railing, light fixtures, and benches are made of rustic wood construction, and clusters of trees and heavy boulders edge the promenade.

There are many things to look at while walking along or sitting on the esplanade. Views can be had across the Hudson River toward New Jersey's high-density waterfront developments and at the southern end of the promenade the Statue of Liberty comes into view. Ferries, both crossing the Hudson River and serving stops along the Manhattan shore are constantly zipping along and a changing kaleidoscope of boat traffic up and down the river continually attracts one's eye. In the evening, many people come to watch the sunset.

Most of the buildings fronting the parks are residential, contributing to the peaceful ambiance, except at a central yacht harbor basin where there is cluster of office buildings, a shopping mall,

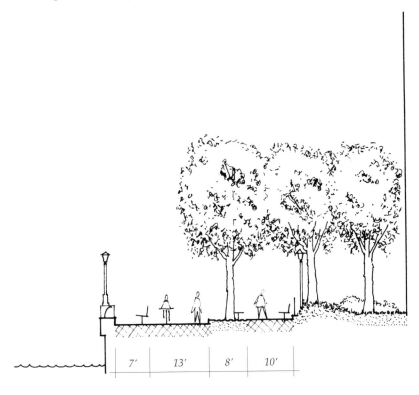

Section: Battery Park City Esplanade, area with parallel walkway
Scale: 1" = 20'

7'   13'   8'   10'

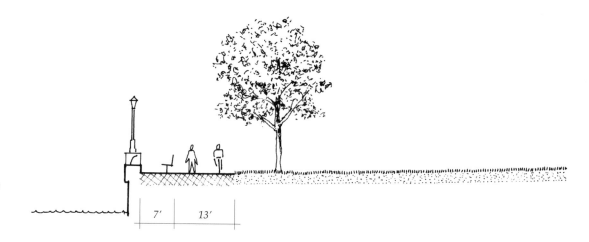

7'   13'

Walking, running, sitting, and
fishing are all favorite activities
along the esplanade

The informally designed part of
the esplanade

and a handful of cafés. The frontage buildings are mostly tall, which lends something of an urban quality to the scene. Their presence is somewhat shielded from immediate view by trees, except again at the yacht harbor, where the esplanade widens into a broad paved plaza and there is no adjacent park.

Promenade Use

The esplanade draws people year round, including on cool and overcast days. Perhaps slightly more people come on weekends than during the week, but the flows of people walking remain fairly constant. For example, in early November, 408 people per hour were counted moving along it on a weekend afternoon versus 348 on a weekday afternoon. During these times, roughly an equal number of men and women were using the promenades, and most people were walking in groups, particularly

Rows of trees and benches line the part of the esplanade with a second parallel walkway

on the weekday. Most people were strolling, though on the weekend there were also a number of runners and fast-walkers. Only a few people were on bikes, perhaps because the shared walkway makes biking slow going, but also because bikers have the option of riding on the parallel Hudson River Greenway, a dedicated bike route that runs just east of Battery Park City.

Climate Change and Sea Level Rise Concerns

Battery Park City is better protected from future sea level rise than other parts of Lower Manhattan. The bulkhead lining is about 3 feet higher than the bulkheads lining other areas, and its buildings are raised another 2 to 3 feet higher, beyond sloped park areas.[7] It suffered much less inundation during Hurricane Sandy[8] and there was no building damage although water did overtop the bulkhead and inundate the parks.[9]

Sea level rise in New York City is projected to be in the range of 11 to 21 inches by the 2050s, and as much as 6 feet by 2100.[10] With sea level rise, Lower Manhattan's flood zone will increase, including at Battery Park City.[11] In 2013, the city issued a plan to protect itself against sea level rise, which included the idea of building a deployable flood barrier around Lower Manhattan, conceptualized as a low wall, lined with benches and landscaping, onto which higher flood protection panels could be attached when necessary. The plan doesn't envision extending the deployable flood barrier around Battery Park City.[12] In 2014, a U.S. Department of Housing and Urban Development (HUD) competition resulted in the idea of building a protective system of waterfront berms around Lower Manhattan, a project dubbed the Big U, and a first phase of this project has been funded.[13] The berm design has not been fully developed, but initial sketches for it did not focus on Battery Park City.

Hudson River Park Promenade, New York City, New York, USA

The 550-acre Hudson River Park is work in progress that is being carved bit by bit out of a storied and partially still functioning industrial landscape of shipping piers. The park runs from Battery Park City north to 59th Street, a distance of some 4 miles, occupying a narrow foreshore and a number of former shipping piers of various sizes. Old, old timers remember this area as one of pier after pier of luxury ocean liners and cargo ships, places where the Cunard Queens, the French Normandie, the SS United States and SS America, and the Holland America Line ships used to dock. This too is where countless immigrants arrived and from where they were transported to Ellis Island. In the late 1950s, transatlantic passenger sea travel stopped with the advent of transatlantic commercial jets and the piers became used for cargo shipping. This lasted into the 1980s, when this use shifted elsewhere and the piers became used for parking and various city-owned utility uses.[14]

Not so old timers also remember the elevated West Side Highway that used to run from Canal Street to 59th Street just inland of the piers. The highway was built in the 1930s, shut down

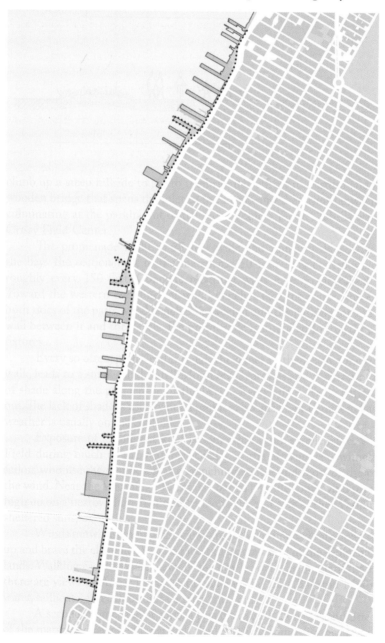

in the 1970s after it fell into disrepair, dismantled in the late 1980s, and replaced in the early 2000s with West Street, a surface thoroughfare with signalized intersections. It is officially called the Joe DiMaggio Highway, but is often still referred to as the West Side Highway.[15] The vision for creating Hudson River Park coincided with the roadway reconstruction. Not only would it open up the waterfront for public uses, it would also create accessible open space for nearby neighborhoods that were without adequate public parks.

Hudson River Park was established in 1998 and is being created through a unique public–private partnership overseen by the Hudson River Park Trust. It is being built in stages as land and funding becomes available. City, state, and federal governments and private philanthropists have funded capital improvements of the park, while funding for day-to-day operations and maintenance comes from rents and income generated by park facilities.[16]

The areas of park foreshore that have so far been developed are those adjacent to Tribeca and Greenwich Village between Battery City and Pier 52, those adjacent to Chelsea between Piers 59 and 66, and those adjacent to Piers 84, 95, 96, and 97 further north. Waterfront pedestrian promenades are major design features of the developed foreshore areas. Promenades also run along the edges of some of the pier structures that have been turned into public parks, recreation areas, and cultural venues.

Promenade Design Characteristics and Connectivity

The Hudson River Park offers an amazing waterfront experience that surmounts the reality of being bounded along its whole length by the six- to eight-lane West Side Highway, which carries considerable traffic. The local streets of many neighborhoods lead into the far side of the highway and there are signalized crosswalks at some intersections, hence giving regular access to the park, but crossing the wide street can feel formidable. The posted speed of the highway was recently reduced to 25 miles per hour but traffic often moves much faster.

Running between the highway and the park is a cycle track that is part of the Hudson River Greenway, which runs the whole length of the island. The cycle track is 20 feet wide where it parallels the constructed southern part of the park and is buffered from the highway by a 10-foot-wide planted strip and lined on both sides with trees. This greenery helps to integrate it into the park. Along Chelsea and the unconstructed sections of the park the cycle track is often narrower and tree planting can be sparse and irregular.

The developed foreshore and piers south of Pier 52 provide a foretaste of what the whole park and its promenade may well eventually be like. Here the park occupies a thin sliver of land along the water and flows out onto six large piers that have been developed with open spaces and recreational amenities including beach volleyball courts, a miniature golf course, playgrounds, and a community boathouse. The foreshore part of the park varies in width and is about 90 feet wide at its widest point.

Section: Hudson River Park Promenade
Scale: 1" = 20'

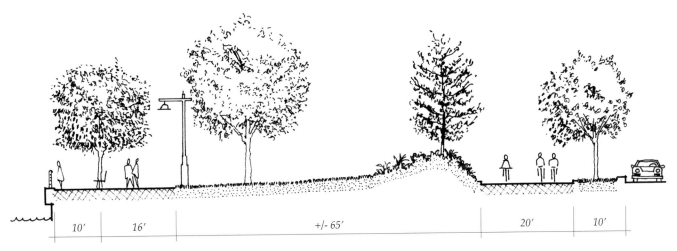

10'   16'   +/- 65'   20'   10'

Hudson River Park Promenade
as it runs past Pier 46

The Hudson River Greenway runs along the West Side Highway,
separated from the park by planting and the roadway by a line of trees

The promenade on Christopher Street Pier (Pier 45)

A 20- to 26-foot-wide pedestrian promenade runs at the water's edge with the rest of the space devoted to landscaped spaces or facilities such as basketball courts, a skate park, and dog parks. The landscaped spaces are planted with trees and grasses, and typically have berms at the outside edge to visually and somewhat aurally shield the promenade from West Side Highway traffic. Most of the promenade is paved with granite pavers and lined with stainless steel railings designed to have something of a nautical feel. Opposite where streets lead in on the other side of the highway, the promenade is surfaced with wooden planks laid on the diagonal—a way of emphasizing the cross-axis. In places along the promenade there are lines of trees near the water with benches placed under them. Tall light fixtures line the inside edge of the path, with additional down lights integrated into the rail stanchions.

The three piers that have been developed with parks have promenades around their edges, greatly extending the total promenade length available and offering a variety of experiences. For instance, the promenade on the south side of the elegantly designed Christopher Street Pier is surfaced with wooden planks that give the feel of a beach boardwalk, an ambience that is further emphasized by other nautical looking elements, whereas the promenade on the pier's north side is surfaced with aggregate pavers.

Promenade Use

People strolling and jogging along the promenade on a cool November day

The Hudson River Park is a major open space for Manhattan's southwestern neighborhoods and is heavily used by residents and tourists alike. The promenade invites people to it throughout the year. It, and the pier parks, can get quite crowded during the warm summer months. In colder weather, the promenade is particularly used for exercise.

On an early November weekend late morning, 900 people per hour were counted moving along it. Most people were young (54%) or middle-aged (38%), with only a few elderly (5%) and children (3%). Most people were either running or fast-walking (57%), many were strolling (41%), and a few were biking. Over 60 percent of people were on their own rather than with others, a much higher proportion than typically observed on the promenades studied. At the same time, 414 people per hour moved along the cycle track next to the West Side Highway, most were biking (77%), some were running (22%) and the rest were on skateboards. By way of comparison, the combined number of people on both the promenade and the bike path during this non-peak time of year (1,314 people per hour) was quite a bit higher than the number of people using Vancouver's highest used promenades during peak time in the summer.

Climate Change and Sea Level Rise Concerns

All of Hudson River Park sits on landfill and old bulkheads bound the shoreline. Most piers are supported by wooden pilings. As the park has been constructed, the bulkhead has not been upgraded and neither the foreshore nor the piers have been designed to address sea level rise or be resilient to storm surge flooding. During Hurricane Sandy, storm surge overtopped the seawall and piers, inundating the park and flowing several blocks inland.[17] The park sustained over $20 million worth of damage, which included heaving pavements and playgrounds.[18] The city is exploring strategies to modify the park to better protect adjacent areas from flooding but no plans have yet been completed.[19]

Meanwhile, the 2015 report of the New York City Panel on Climate Change predicts that sea levels around New York City could rise as much as 6 feet by 2100.[20] Maps prepared by Climate Central's Surging Seas project indicate that with this much water rise all of Hudson River Park would be inundated.[21] Creating Hudson River Park has been and continues to be an enormous undertaking that represents enlightened caring for the waterfront, but future sea level rise and the impacts of events such as Hurricane Sandy bespeak the amount of work still to be done.

Brooklyn Bridge Park Promenades, New York City, New York, USA

Scale: 1:400,000

The multiple waterfront promenades in Brooklyn Bridge Park sit within a recently created 85-acre linear park that stretches for 1.3 miles along Brooklyn's northwestern shoreline, from just north of the Manhattan Bridge south to Atlantic Avenue. The park occupies a narrow foreshore and five piers, and an elevated freeway runs along most of it. The main promenade is a curvilinear path wending along the foreshore. It gives views of and access to the water while moving people through successive park environments having different qualities, both bucolic and industrial. It is a remarkably pleasant promenade with many attributes.

Brooklyn Bridge Park is a work in progress being carved out of a gritty, derelict industrial area and being shaped by extensive community participation. Its site, an area of flat land sitting at the base of a high bluff upon which sits the upscale Brooklyn Heights neighborhood, was long occupied by major cargo shipping activities and goods warehouses. In the 1950s, the elevated double-decked Brooklyn-Queens Expressway was built along the face of the bluff. To appease residents of Brooklyn Heights, the freeway structure was topped with a pedestrian promenade (see Chapter 10), but the 60-foot-high structure isolated the foreshore. In the 1960s, shipping began to go elsewhere.[22] By 1989, the piers and warehouse structures were largely vacant and local citizens, groups joined together under the rubric of the Brooklyn Bridge Park Coalition to advocate for turning the area into a park. The idea was widely embraced, and planning for the park went on for many years while logistical issues were sorted out and funding sources were identified.

In 2002, the Brooklyn Bridge Park Development Corporation was created to oversee the park, and in 2005, the firm of Michael Van Valkenburgh Associates prepared a masterplan for it.[23] It was understood that the park would need to be self-sustaining and generate its own revenue for operating expenses, and so the plan called for carving off some of the foreshore for development sites, including one historic warehouse building, with revenue from these projects going to the park.[24] Park construction began in 2009 and has proceeded in stages. By 2017, most of the foreshore and four of the piers have been developed, with construction funding coming from various city and state grants. Buildings have been erected on several of the development sites, including condominiums and a hotel.

Scale: 1:40,000

Promenade Design Characteristics

The main promenade weaves along the foreshore south of the Brooklyn Bridge. Other promenades go around the four piers that have developed with public parks and recreation spaces. A fifth pier has yet to be developed. Many wonderful views are to be had from the promenades: the Manhattan skyline across the East River, the Brooklyn and Manhattan Bridges, the constant boat traffic on the East River, and, not least, the Statue of Liberty in the distance. There are many closer water views to be had as well, including a forest of wooden pylons that once supported a pier, and wetlands along the water's edge.

The main promenade has an informal character. It is surfaced with decomposed granite and lit with irregularly spaced industrial-looking light fixtures strapped to tall wood poles. At its northern end it is about 33 feet wide, which includes a 10-foot-wide walk, a 15-foot-wide bicycle path, and an 8-foot-wide zone for benches. A line of granite pavers demarcates the bike path, but pedestrians regularly ignore it and use the whole width of the promenade. Elegant wood benches are arrayed along the waterside of the path in long lengths, up to 110 feet, and configured in arcs aligned with the curving path. Further south, the pedestrian path is separated from the bicycle path by planting beds that are lined with large granite boulders and landscaped with tall grasses. Toward its mostly unfinished southern end, the promenade runs for a distance atop a narrow platform squeezed between the shore and a designated development parcel. The platform is lined with a long string of waterside picnic tables and has been dubbed the Picnic Peninsula.

The main promenade is in places located some distance back of the water's edge and in some places directly next to it. The meeting of land and water beyond the promenade takes many different forms. Most of the shore is protected with sloping riprap revetments, but some areas, especially near the piers, are protected with bulkheads. Multiple ways are provided to get near or into the water: a small beach, some concrete platforms, a curving ramp from which kayaks can be launched, an iron beam laid on its side that serves as a waterside seat.

The promenade has a variety of inland edge conditions. A narrow middle section of the park runs immediately adjacent to the elevated expressway and so minimizing the impact of its traffic was a design major objective for this area. Here, the promenade is edged with a tall and steep berm that is planted with grass and trees. The berm blocks the sight of traffic and maybe the worst of its noise. North and south of this area, development parcels front the promenade, some of

**Section: Brooklyn Bridge Park
Promenade
Scale: 1" = 20'**

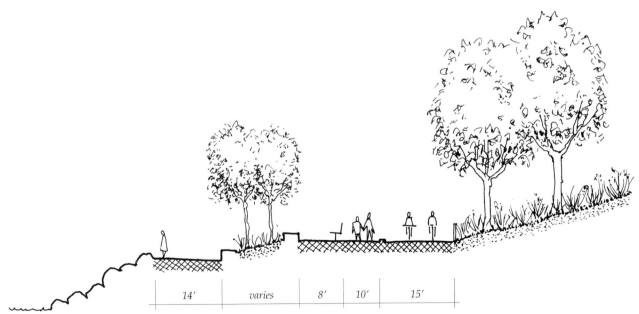

14' varies 8' 10' 15'

The Brooklyn Bridge Park Promenade
at its northern end where it runs
behind the berm on Pier One and is
lined with long benches

The promenade where it divides
into multiple paths

which have been built and some of which are vacant lots. Some of the as yet un-built parcels will have commercial uses in them that will face the park. For now, commercial uses are confined to areas near the base of the Brooklyn Bridge, where there is an outdoor café and an ice cream shop.

The piers and the promenades on them have different characters. Pier One, which is the pier closest to the Brooklyn Bridge and sits parallel to the foreshore rather than jutting out into the water, is mostly covered by a large berm that is heavily planted with trees, but its outer edge is lined with a promenade. The paved walk is relatively wide, surfaced with pavers, and lined with a simple metal railing. In places along it are long lines of benches like the ones on the main promenade, and one stretch has a group of colorful metal table and chairs. The walks around Pier Two, which is developed with basketball courts, playgrounds, and a large lawn facing the water, are utilitarian concrete paths lined with benches made of massive timber beams.

The waterfront promenade on Pier One

Promenade Use and Connectivity

The main promenade is the most used and it draws large crowds. On a sunny but cool afternoon in November 2014, 1,212 people were observed moving along it in an hour. Overwhelmingly they were strolling, almost 90 percent, with relatively few jogging or walking fast, and fewer still on bicycles. Most (85%) were in groups of two or more people. People of all ages were present, but mostly young and middle-aged adults. There were remarkably few young children at this particular time and many more women (60%) than men. People were engaged with each other and with their surroundings, and very few were listening to music on headphones or using phones.

The promenade is somewhat difficult to get but this doesn't stop visitors from coming. People coming from Lower Manhattan can take a ferry across the East River and get off at a ferry terminal in Brooklyn Bridge Park, on Pier One. They can also cross the Brooklyn Bridge on its promenade (see Chapter 11) and then make their way down to the park, but doing so requires walking some distance along city streets because the bridge approach ends a long distance inland of the shore. People coming

The promenade meanders along the foreshore through naturalized landscaping

A steep berm buffers the central part of the promenade from the adjacent expressway

from downtown Brooklyn can walk to it via steeply sloping Old Fulton Street, or a handful of other streets. People coming from Brooklyn Heights are supposed to able to walk to it via a pedestrian bridge built to connect Brooklyn Bridge Park with the Brooklyn Heights Promenade, but this bridge was closed shortly after it was built because of structural problems. Other than the ferry, getting to the promenade by public transit is difficult because subway stops lie some distance away and there are few nearby bus stops.

Already popular, it is hard to escape the conclusion that the Brooklyn Bridge Park promenade will in the future become an even more popular destination for New Yorkers and visitors alike, in spite of its somewhat isolated location.

Climate Change and Sea Level Rise Concerns

One of the many differently designed stretches of resilient shoreline

Brooklyn Bridge Park was designed to be resilient to flooding and withstand future sea level rise. Its shoreline is strengthened with riprap, marshes and wave-absorbing revetments, and its plant materials are salt tolerant.[25] As the foreshore has been built, topography has been created to raise it above future flood plains associated with sea level rise, and the several piers that have been planted with greenery have also had topography raised on top of them.[26] Sections of the promenade were placed within the undulating topography rather than at the water's edge atop a bulkhead for the very purpose of protecting it from flooding, and to create a more resilient and interactive water's edge than a hard bulkhead allows. Although Brooklyn Bridge Park experienced considerable storm surge from Hurricane Sandy, which raised New York inner harbor waters more than 4 feet higher than previously recorded high water marks,[27] it fared very well, sustaining much less damage than most of New York City's other waterfront areas.[28]

Passeio das Tágides and Passeio do Tejo, Lisbon, Portugal

Scale: 1:400,000

Lisbon, which lies at the mouth of the Rio Tejo (Tagus River) estuary just above where it connects with the Atlantic Ocean, is currently in the process of creating a much-written-about waterfront promenade along its central waterfront (see Chapter 12). The city already has two lesser-known waterfront promenades, built several decades ago, which run through parks a good distance north of the city center. They are examples of waterfront promenades built as major features of a peripheral revitalization project anchored by a temporary event, in this case an international world fair. They are rather sleepy but also compelling.

The promenades are very different in their designs as are the parks they run through. The heavily treed Passeio das Tágides runs along the formally structured and commercialized Parque das Nações (Park of Nations), a former exposition area. The open Passeio do Tejo runs along the more natural Parque Tejo e Trancão (Tagus Park), which is part of a large nature reserve created following the exposition.

The Passeio das Tágides was built as part of Expo 98, the world's fair that Lisbon used as a catalyst for redeveloping a derelict and heavily polluted industrial dock and petrochemical area in the northeastern part of the city, around which many impoverished immigrants lived in large social housing estates.[29] The fair followed from ideas contained in the 1992 *Strategic Plan for Lisbon*, whose driving vision was to regenerate the city, and make it the Atlantic capital of Europe.[30] The fair was touted as a way to rediscover the river, create a new distinctive urban center, and make Lisbon a global city.[31] Included within the fairgrounds were an aquarium, a sporting arena, a 600-berth marina, an iconic waterfront sail-shaped building called the Vasco de Gama tower, and a 3¼-mile-long waterfront

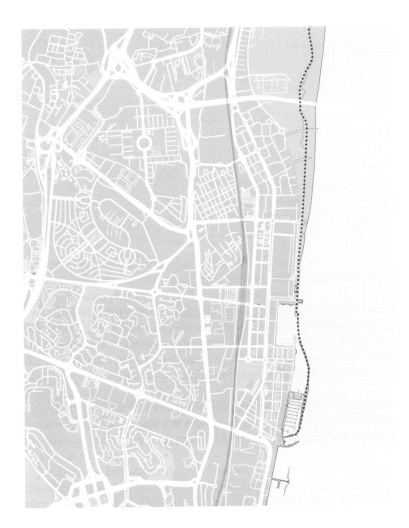

Scale: 1:40,000

gondola ride. The Passeio do Tejo was completed several years later with the construction of Tagus Park on redevelopment lands not included within the fairgrounds. Together, the two waterfront promenades opened up to the public an over 5-kilometer length of waterfront that had previously been inaccessible.[32]

The waterfront parks and the fairground were but a small part of a much larger redevelopment project. The entire project covered almost one and a half square miles (350 hectares or 865 acres) of which the fairgrounds occupied slightly less than 15 percent (50 hectares or 124 acres) and the Tagus Park occupied 24 percent (84 hectares or 208 acres).[33] The rest of the land was developed into mixed-use areas that included an "international" business district (for national and multinational corporate headquarters), an immense shopping center, university facilities, and housing for 25,000 residents. Major new infrastructure projects included the nearby Gare do Oriente train station, a metro line servicing the area and linking it to both the airport and downtown, an elevated highway system, the 13-kilometer-long Vasco de Gama bridge that crosses the Tagus estuary, and an extensive natural wastewater treatment system within Tagus Park. Little expropriation was required for the redevelopment project because most of the land was publicly owned, but 278 poor families squatting on the land were displaced.[34]

The redevelopment project was begun by the public sector and completed by the private sector. A quasi-public company, Parque Expo 98, whose main shareholders were the state and the city of Lisbon, was set up to implement the redevelopment and to coordinate the infrastructure projects.[35] Funding came from the state, bank loans, fair receipts, and profits from the Oceanarium, Arena, and other businesses in which Parque Expo 98 held a stake.[36] To ensure occupancy and build-out after the fair, the fair buildings were sold to private developers prior to the fair opening and so were many serviced land parcels throughout the redevelopment area. Today, within the former fairgrounds the aquarium and gondola ride remain, the Vasco de Gama tower has been repurposed as a hotel, another building has been turned into a casino, and numerous small buildings near the water now house restaurants and eateries. Much of the housing that has been built is up-market.[37]

Promenade Design Characteristics

The two promenades are very different in their designs and notably in the amount of shade on them, an issue in Lisbon's warm and sunny climate. Both the Passeio das Tágides and the Passeio do Tejo look east toward the river and the sun moves across them as the day progresses.

Throughout much of the day, the 17-foot-wide Passeio do Tejo promenade is in full sun as there are no trees immediately on it. Clusters of trees set back from the park's edge, some of which have

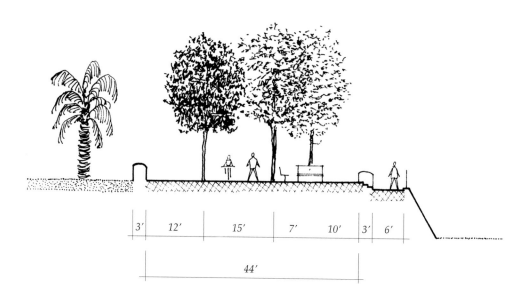

Section: Passeio das Tágides
Scale: 1" = 20'

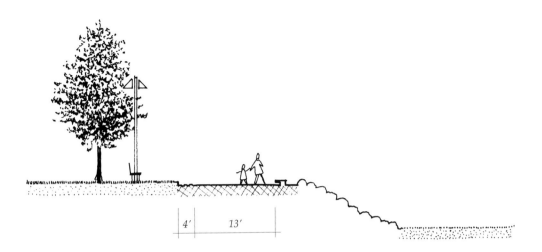

Section: Passeio do Tejo
Scale: 1" = 20'

benches under them, cast shade on the promenade in the late afternoon. The walk itself is surfaced in beige colored concrete brick pavers and lined along its inner edge with a row of grey cobblestones.

The Passeio das Tágides offers both sun and shade. The whole promenade is about 53 feet wide and is divided into distinct channels. A narrow 6-foot-wide path runs at the water's edge next to a sloping revetment, which is topped with a simple metal guardrail. The inner side of the walk is lined with a sitting height wall topped with a curved granite cap that acts as a curb to the main walking path, which is about 18 inches higher up. In the morning, the water's edge path is in full sun and later in the day it is in partial sun.

The main walking path runs under three rows of pine trees and is always shady. The trees give an overall impression of regularity but in reality have different spacing that gets successively closer moving inland: 35 feet, 27 feet, 21 feet. It is possible to walk anywhere under the trees, but randomly

Passeio das Tágides

The lower promenade of Passeio das Tágides where it widens under the trellis structure

located groups of colorfully painted poured concrete benches occur within the two tree rows closest to the water and so people tend to walk between the second and third rows. A poorly marked designated bike path runs here, but few bikers use it and it is mostly ignored.

The path at the water's edge is surfaced with white cobbles and the upper promenade is surfaced with concrete aggregate pavers, striped at intervals with strips of grey cobbles. The surface undulates everywhere, lending an informal character.

In one place the upper promenade narrows and the lower walk widens to accommodate benches and a vine-and-flower-laden trellis structure. Toward its southern end, where the Passeio das Tágides extends into a marina basin and has water on both sides, lower promenades line each side. A handful of restaurants and eateries line the Passeio das Tágides, set within gardens, and seem not to draw overly lively crowds.

Both promenades offer opportunities to get close to the water because they flow at their ends onto wooden piers extending over the water. The Passeio do Tejo along its way gives access to two 160-foot-long piers and approaching the Vasco de Gama Bridge itself becomes a pier. The pier is 13 feet wide, surfaced with horizontal wood planks, and lined with benches and light fixtures, inviting both gathering and evening use. The pier's custom metal railings seem vaguely inspired in their design by the aesthetic of the massive cable-stayed Vasco de Gama Bridge, which dominates the view. North of the bridge, the promenade continues as a walk along the shoreline. At its southern end, the Passeio das Tágides leads onto an 18-foot-wide pier lined with simply designed white painted tubular metal railings. The pier is surfaced with wood planks set in square pallets arranged in alternating horizontal and vertical directions. Many boards are warped and some pallet sections move when walked on so walking here can be challenging for the faint at heart.

Passeio do Tejo in the late afternoon

Promenade Use and Connectivity

Both the Passeio das Tágides and the Passeio do Tejo are only moderately well used. For instance, on a warm and sunny weekday early afternoon in mid-June about 270 people per hour were observed moving along the Passeio das Tágides and they were all walking. There were no bikers or runners. Later that same day, in the early evening before the traditional late dinner hour, the numbers increased to 422 people per hour of which almost 25 percent were jogging and another 9 percent were on bikes. At the same early afternoon time only a handful of people were on the Passeio do Tejo, while during the early evening time there were many more people, including a number of joggers and bikers and what seemed to be many family groups.

These promenades seem to be minor rather than major tourist attractions and appear to be mostly used by local business people and immediate residents, perhaps because of their relative inaccessibility. Neither promenade is easily accessible via subway, nor do the city's trams run this far out from the city center. The closest metro stop, located near the Oriente train station, is about a third of a mile from the Passeio das Tágides. Getting to the promenade from the stop requires walking through a commercial mall and through a somewhat barren area in front of the Casino. The only other nearby metro stop is almost half a mile from the Vasco de Gama tower at the southern end of the Passeio do Tejo. Getting to the promenade from it requires passing along a major arterial street. While the promenades are easy to get to from the adjacent neighborhoods that were built as part of the redevelopment project, they are not easy to get to from the many lower-income housing estates further out because the railroad line that runs along the periphery of the redevelopment area creates a barrier.

The pier at the end of the Passeio das Tágides

The pier at the end of the Passeio do Tejo

People strolling along the Passeio das Tágides in the shade of the trees

Indeed, the redevelopment project is criticized for having paid little attention to the local context. The lower-income people on the outskirts of the redevelopment area may now be able to more easily get into the central city because of the transportation improvements, but they are cut-off from the new waterfront development and its amenities by the surface railroad tracks. In addition, few of the jobs associated with Expo 98 or the development that followed went to the low-income residents.[38]

Climate Change and Sea Level Rise Concerns

It is unclear how sea level rise will impact the Passeio das Tágides and the Passeio do Tejo. Both promenades sit about 10 feet above the sand of the estuary shore. The water in the Tagus estuary rises and falls throughout the day with sizable tidal flows.[39] At times the water comes close to the top of the revetments lining the promenades, and at other times it is quite a distance out, exposing expanses of sand. At extreme high tide events the revetments may be overtopped, but this is unusual.

Studies of the potential climate change impacts on the Tagus estuary have little to say about what will happen along this part of the coastline, focusing instead on areas to the south at the mouth of the estuary. The European Environment Agency projects that relative local sea level rise along Portugal's Atlantic coast will be similar to the global average. The Intergovernmental Panel on Climate Change predicts that by 2100 the average global sea level might rise by as much as .98 meters (3.2 feet). With that level of water rise, both the Passeio das Tágides and the Passeio do Tejo promenades would likely be regularly inundated at high tides.

Pier along the Passeio do Tejo during low tide condition

Golden Gate Promenade at Crissy Field, San Francisco, California, USA

The Golden Gate Promenade at Crissy Field, which runs along San Francisco's northern waterfront just east of the Golden Gate Bridge, is a perfect example of the baseball movie *Field of Dreams* adage "if you build it they will come." Until the mid-1970s, Crissy Field was a military airfield, part of the Presidio Army Base, and there was no public waterfront access. Today, it boasts the city's most popular waterfront promenade, heavily used by walkers and bikers throughout the year.

Crissy Field is a 130-acre relatively flat open space that stretches along the waterfront for about one and a third miles. It sits on what was originally marshland that was filled for the 1915 Panama-Pacific Exposition. After the fair, Crissy Field was incorporated into the Presidio Army Base and became an Air Coast Defense Station. A runway was built on it, which remained in operation into the early 1970s. In 1994, the Presidio Army Base was decommissioned and turned over to the National Park Service to become America's first urban national park. Crissy Field has been incorporated into the 125-square-mile Golden Gate National Recreation Area, which stretches along the coast north and south of the Golden Gate Bridge, and is managed by it in association with the Presidio Trust. The trust partially restored the wetland, improved the existing dunes and planted them with native vegetation, built an extensive raised lawn where the airfield had been, improved beaches along the bay, built several picnic areas protected with berms, constructed two parking lots, and created the Golden Gate Promenade.

Promenade Design Characteristics

The promenade runs the whole length of Crissy Field. Its long central part is sandwiched between the dunes and the raised lawn, and passes beside the re-constructed marsh. At its western end, it runs between grass-covered berms and first a beach and then a breakwater, culminating at a small café and gift shop, "The Warming Hut." From here, walkers, runners, and cyclists can continue on, if they wish, along a paved road to Fort Point at the base of the Golden Gate Bridge, or they can

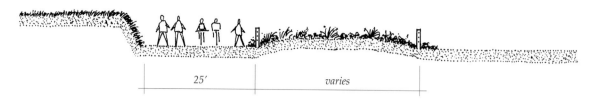

25'   varies

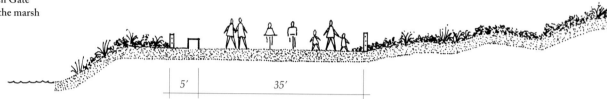

5'   35'

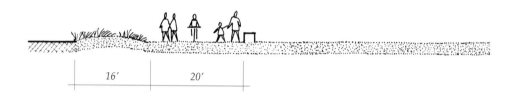

16'   20'

climb up a steep hillside to get to the bridge itself. At its eastern end, the promenade passes over a wooden bridge that spans the inlet to the marsh and then runs between the beach and a parking lot, culminating at the parking lot of the Saint Francis Yacht Club. Toward its end is another café, the Crissy Field Center.

The promenade is 20 to 35 feet wide and unpaved. It gently curves, following the arc of the bay. The section next to the marsh has 50-foot-long concrete block benches along it, spaced roughly every 150 feet. Concrete retaining walls edging the raised lawn also serve as benches. Toward the western end, lines of wood benches face the water. The eastern section has seating on both sides of the path, wood benches between it and the parking lot and a low concrete sitting-height wall between it and the beach. The promenade is intended for daytime use only, and so has no light fixtures.

Every so often, paths lead through the dunes to the beach. One such path, an accessible board-walk, leads to a small stand of tall Monterey Cypresses and a cluster of benches. This is the only area of shade along the promenade or the beach. Everywhere else is always in full sun, when the sun is out. The lack of shade is usually not a problem because San Francisco has a temperate climate and the weather is usually on the cool side.

Exposure of a different kind is somewhat more problematic. Winds can be strong at Crissy Field during much of the year, particularly in the afternoons—witness the large number of board sailors who use the east beach as a launching zone—and most of the promenade is fully exposed to the wind. Near the Warming Hut, grassy berms provide some wind protection, as do eucalyptus trees high up on a nearby bluff. Picnic tables along the east side of the Warming Hut are in a favored wind-sheltered sunspot.

Winds notwithstanding, the views from the promenade are quite spectacular, and people bundle up and brave the elements. Walking west there are views of the Golden Gate Bridge and Marin head-lands. Walking east there are views of the city beyond the dome of the Palace of Fine Arts. All along there are views of Angel Island, Alcatraz, and the East Bay and Marin hills, to say nothing of the water, sailboats, and cargo ships coming and going.

A second promenade of sorts, a paved sidewalk along Mason Street, which runs on the far side of the marsh and lawns, also parallels the bay but at some distance from it. It is striped with two-way

The Warming Hut

The Golden Gate Promenade
where it runs next to the marsh

The Golden Gate Promenade
where it runs between dunes and
the raised lawn

Golden Gate Promenade approaching the Golden Gate Bridge

bike lanes and a walking path, and travels along a series of old airplane hangars and maintenance buildings, which have been retrofitted to house a variety of mostly youth-oriented sports activities, including climbing walls, trampolines, and a swimming pool. Not far behind Mason Street runs Doyle Drive, the U.S. 101 approach to the Golden Gate Bridge. Elevated in some sections, recently tunneled in others, and usually full of traffic, it is a constant presence. Work is underway to top the tunneled areas with a landscaped corridor that will connect the main parade ground of the Presidio with the waterfront.

Promenade Use and Connectivity

The Golden Gate Promenade attracts walkers, runners, and bikers, and so movement on it flows at different paces. There is no marked bicycle path, but everything seems to work just fine, with people by and large staying to the right whichever direction they're moving in. Most bikers don't go very fast, slowed by the unpaved surface and the need to negotiate around people on foot.

On a sunny but windy Saturday early afternoon in late March, 945 people per hour were observed moving along the promenade. Most people were strolling, but almost 25 percent were running, and another 25 percent biking. Fewer people visit the promenade on weekdays. On a weekday afternoon in early February, slightly fewer than 300 people moved along it in an hour. Again, they were mostly strolling. Most people come to the promenade with others, and they seem a mix of local residents and out-of-towners. There are often notable numbers of people speaking foreign languages and many bikers are on rented bikes. Often, most of the people on the promenade at any given time are young adults, reflecting the demographics of San Francisco.

Climate Change and Sea Level Rise Concerns

Crissy Field and the Golden Gate Promenade are going to be seriously impacted by sea level rise. A 2012 report prepared by the National Research Council projects that by 2100 the local sea level will be .42 to 1.67 meters (1.4 to 5.5 feet) higher than it is today.[40] If sea level rise approaches the upper end of this range, all of Crissy Field except the raised lawn area would flood during a 100-year storm event, from a combination of storm surge, large waves, and high tides. A sign with

Views of the Golden Gate Bridge and the Marin headlands can be had from the shaded sitting area

a graphic showing this future reality is prominently displayed along the promenade on the railing of the bridge spanning the marsh inlet. Near to the sign is a pole adorned with colored balls that indicate how high the water level would reach under various sea level rise scenarios. From where the sign is located there is a good view of the Golden Gate Bridge, and the sign alarmingly notes that should the entire Antarctic ice sheet melt the water level in San Francisco Bay would be as high as the bridge's deck.

San Francisco is barely starting to grapple with how to address the impacts of sea level rise on its 37 miles of shoreline and no plans have yet been developed to reinforce the water's edge of Crissy Field to protect against the future flooding. In 2016, the city issued the *San Francisco Sea Level Action Plan*, which presents a vision for mitigating sea level rise and coastal flooding.[41] The city expects to have a citywide sea level rise adaptation plan completed by 2018.

Notes

1   "The Front Lines of Climate Change: Charleston's Struggle," accessed October 6, 2015, www.climatecentral.org/news/the-front-lines-of-climate-change-charlestons-struggle-16934.
2   Ibid.
3   National Oceanic and Atmospheric Administration, "Global Sea Level Rise Scenarios for the United States National Climate Assessment," NOAA Technical Report, (December 6, 2012), accessed June 2, 2016, http://scenarios.globalchange.gov/sites/default/files/NOAA_SLR_r3_0.pdf.
4   Climate Central, "Sea Level Rise and Coastal Flood Risk: Summary for Charleston County, SC. Surging Seas Risk Finder File Created June 13, 2014," June 13, 2014, accessed June 10, 2016, http://ssrf.climatecentral.org.s3websiteuseast1. amazonaws.com/Buffer2/states/SC/downloads/pdf_reports/County/SC_Charleston_Countyreport. pdf.
5   City of Charleston, South Carolina, "City of Charleston Century V 2010 Comprehensive Plan Update," February 22, 2011, accessed October 9, 2015, www.charleston-sc.gov/index.aspx?nid=285.

6   The City of New York, "A Stronger, More Resilient New York" (Office of the Mayor, 2013), 373, www.nyc.
    gov/html/sirr/html/report/report.shtml.
7   The City of New York, "A Stronger, More Resilient New York," 373.
8   Ibid., 372.
9   Editor, "Two Years Ago 'Hurricane Sandy: Battery Park Unscathed,'" *BatteryPark.TV*, accessed July 31,
    2015, www.batterypark.tv/first-precinct/hurricane-sandy-battery-park-unscathed-compared-to-rest-of-
    new-york.html.
10 "New York City Panel on Climate Change 2015 Report Executive Summary," *Annals of the New York
    Academy of Sciences* 1336, no. 1 (January 1, 2015): 11, doi:10.1111/nyas.12591.
11 The City of New York, "A Stronger, More Resilient New York," 379.
12 Ibid., 384.
13 "Rebuild by Design Finalists," n.d., accessed June 9, 2016, www.rebuildbydesign.org/winners-and-finalists/.
14 "The History of Chelsea Piers - New York City - NYC," accessed October 8, 2015, www.chelseapiers.com/
    company/history.cfm.
15 Hilary Ballon and Kenneth T. Jackson, eds., *Robert Moses and the Modern City: The Transformation of New
    York*, 1st ed (New York: W. W. Norton & Co, 2007), 204–205.
16 "Hudson River Park Trust," *Hudson River Park*, accessed October 7, 2015, www.hudsonriverpark.org/
    about-us/hrpt.
17 The City of New York, "A Stronger, More Resilient New York," 373.
18 Hudson River Park Trust, "Hudson River Park Mission Statement and 2012 Performance Measurement
    Report," 2012, 2–3, www.hudsonriverpark.org/assets/content/general/Mission_Statement_and_
    Performance_Measurement_Report_Aug2013.pdf.
19 The City of New York, "A Stronger, More Resilient New York," 393.
20 "New York City Panel on Climate Change 2015 Report Executive Summary," *Annals of the New York
    Academy of Sciences* 1336, no. 1 (January 1, 2015): 11, accessed July 20, 2015, doi:10.1111/nyas.12591.
21 "New York | Surging Seas: Sea Level Rise Analysis by Climate Central," accessed June 17, 2016, http://
    sealevel.climatecentral.org/ssrf/new-york.
22 New York State Urban Development Corporation, DBA The Empire State Development Corporation,
    and Brooklyn Bridge Park Development Corporation, "Brooklyn Bridge Park Civic and Land Use
    Improvement Project Modified General Project Plan," December 18, 2006, 3–4, accessed October 9, 2015,
    http://brooklynbridgepark.s3.amazonaws.com/s/518/2006%20General%20Project%20Plan.pdf.
23 Bruner Foundation, Inc., "Partnering Strategies for the Urban Edge: 2011 Rudy Bruner Award for Urban
    Excellence," 2011, 44–46, accessed October 9, 2015, www.brunerfoundation.org/rba/pdfs/2011/CH2.pdf.
24 "About BBP (Project Development) - Brooklyn Bridge Park," accessed June 26, 2016, www.
    brooklynbridgepark.org/pages/project-development.
25 The City of New York, "A Stronger, More Resilient New York," 17, 195.
26 The City of New York, "Coastal Climate Resilience Urban Waterfront Adaptive Strategies," June 2013, 70,
    www.nyc.gov/html/dcp/pdf/sustainable_communities/urban_waterfront_print.pdf.
27 The City of New York, "A Stronger, More Resilient New York," 372–373.
28 Ibid., 17, 249.
29 Jean-Paul Carrière and Christophe Demazière, "Urban Planning and Flagship Development
    Projects: Lessons from Expo 98, Lisbon," *Planning Practice and Research* 17, no. 1 (2002): 73,
    doi:10.1080/02697450220125096.
30 Jeremy Alden and Artur da Rosa Pires, "Lisbon: Strategic Planning for a Capital City," *Cities* 13, no. 1
    (February 1996): 32, doi:10.1016/0264-2751(95)00111-5.
31 Carrière and Demazière, "Urban Planning and Flagship Development Projects: Lessons from Expo 98,
    Lisbon."
32 Teresa Craveiro and Manuel da Costa Lobo, "Integrating the City" (42nd International Planning Congress
    ISoCaRP, n.d.), 3, accessed August 5, 2015, http://www.isocarp.net/Data/case_studies/889.pdf.
33 Carrière and Demazière, "Urban Planning and Flagship Development Projects," 73.
34 João Cabral and Berta Rato, "Urban Development for Competitiveness and Cohesion: The Expo 98 Urban
    Project in Lisbon," in *The Globalized City: Economic Restructuring and Social Polarization in European Cities*,
    ed. Frank Moulaert, Arantxa Rodriquez, and Erik Swyngedouw (Oxford; New York: Oxford University
    Press, 2003), 221.
35 Ibid., 215.
36 Carrière and Demazière, "Urban Planning and Flagship Development Projects," 77.
37 Ibid., 76.
38 João Cabral and Berta Rato, "Urban Development for Competitiveness and Cohesion," 220–221.

39 João Miguel Dias, Juliana Marques Valentim, and Magda Catarina Sousa, "A Numerical Study of Local Variations in Tidal Regime of Tagus Estuary, Portugal," *PLoS ONE* 8, no. 12 (December 2, 2013), accessed August 3, 2015, doi:10.1371/journal.pone.0080450.

40 Committee on Sea Level Rise in California, Oregon, and Washington; Board on Earth Sciences and Resources; Ocean Studies Board; Division on Earth and Life Studies; National Research Council, *Sea-Level Rise for the Coasts of California, Oregon, and Washington: Past, Present, and Future* (Washington, D.C.: The National Academies Press, 2012), 107–108.

41 City and County of San Francisco, "San Francisco Sea Level Rise Action Plan," March 2016, accessed June 9, 2016, http://sf-planning.org/sea-level-rise-action-plan%20.

Chapter 6

Promenades in the Shadow of Freeways

Many cities have freeways along their waterfronts that cut people off from the water's edge, and some cities are trying to correct this problem. San Francisco took down its elevated waterfront freeway after it was damaged in the 1989 Loma Prieta earthquake, thus undoing what everyone had come to understand was a terrible mistake of the 1960s freeway building era, and built a transit boulevard and pedestrian promenade in its place (see Chapter 12). New York City took down the elevated West Side Highway that ran along the Hudson River in Lower Manhattan, building a surface arterial in its place and creating a waterfront park containing pedestrian and bicycle promenades (see Chapter 5).

Some cities wanting to connect with their waterfronts, but seeing no way of doing away with an elevated waterfront freeway, have chosen to build pedestrian promenades and bicycle paths next to or under the freeway structure. New York City is taking this approach along the East River side of Lower Manhattan and Hong Kong is doing so along its Kwun Tong waterfront in East Kowloon. Other cities with elevated waterfront freeways may wish to look to these examples for inspiration about design approaches.

East River Waterfront Esplanade, New York City, New York, USA

Scale: 1:400,000

New Yorkers have long been cut off from most of Manhattan's East River waterfront because the wide FDR Drive highway runs along it, in some places elevated and elsewhere at grade. Heading north from the southern tip of the island, the roadway emerges from the tunnel that circles the Battery, rises into an elevated structure that continues for almost 2 miles, then becomes at- or slightly below grade until it reaches the Triborough Bridge, where it merges into Harlem River Drive. Along its 9½-mile length, FDR Drive runs close to the water's edge except at a few locations, creating a major barrier between the water and adjacent neighborhoods.

Since 2005, the city has been planning and building a new public open space, the East River Waterfront Esplanade, under the elevated section of FDR Drive. The first phase opened in 2011 and completion is expected in 2019.[1] The elevated highway structure and its traffic create a gritty, tough urban context: noise, shadow, and a multitude of old columns, beams and drainage pipes, many rusty. But water attracts people and here are to be had views of the very busy East River, with its ferry and commercial shipping traffic, and across to Brooklyn. The project is a heroic effort to create a community park and waterfront promenade in a very challenging urban context. Following the extensive flooding of this area in 2012 from the storm surge associated with Hurricane Sandy, the context is understood to be even more difficult.

Revitalizing the East River waterfront with public open space was a major part of Mayor Bloomberg's 2002 *Vision for Lower Manhattan*,[2] and the East River Waterfront Esplanade emerged as a key project. Construction of the 2-mile-long Esplanade, which upon completion will run from Broad Street in the Battery north to the East River Park, and include the renovation of three piers, became a project of the New York City Economic Development Corporation, a non-profit corporation that provides economic development services for the city.[3] The esplanade's design was developed through a yearlong planning process conducted by the City Planning Department that involved stakeholders from six adjacent neighborhoods, including areas as disparate as the Wall Street financial district, the South Street Seaport festival marketplace, and Chinatown. Along with the goal of

Scale: 1:40,000

East River Waterfront Esplanade northeast of Pier 11

creating a "spectacular waterfront esplanade," other objectives developed during the planning stage were: reconnecting nearby neighborhoods with the waterfront, completing the Manhattan Greenway cycle track that runs around Manhattan Island, maximizing year-round waterfront use, creating a bio-diverse aquatic habitat, and shaping built form to recall the area's maritime history.[4]

Promenade Design Characteristics

The esplanade is being fitted into three different existing conditions. Between the East River Park and the Brooklyn Bridge, it is wholly under the highway structure, sandwiched between South Street, which runs alongside the highway, and bulkheads at the water's edge. Between the Brooklyn Bridge and the busy ferry terminal at Pier 11, it runs under the elevated highway but also extends toward the water atop various parallel platforms and pier structures that jut beyond the bulkhead. From Pier 11 to the Battery, it is squeezed between the waterfront bulkhead and the edge of the rising highway structure. The overall design plan calls for a pedestrian promenade along the water's edge, a two-way bicycle path along South Street, and glass-enclosed pavilions under the highway structure for community, cultural, and commercial activities.[5]

The segments of the Esplanade that have so far been completed—namely from the Battery to Pier 15, which lies somewhat south of the Brooklyn Bridge—give some sense of what the whole will eventually feel like. In the meantime, temporary walking and biking paths have been inserted in the other areas.

The esplanade begins north of the Battery Maritime Building along an initial at-grade stretch of FDR Drive. Here, the promenade is a narrow sidewalk atop the bulkhead that lines the water's edge. It is paved with classic New York City hexagonal pavers, laid in multicolor patterns, and has a few highly designed benches along it. Paralleling the sidewalk is a two-way bicycle track, which is raised slightly higher than the adjacent roadway, separated from it by a rolled curb. North of Pier 6, which has a helicopter terminal, the sidewalk widens and is separated from the bikeway by planters lined with benches.

Beyond Pier 11, FDR Drive becomes fully elevated and the cycle track veers inland to run along the side of South Street, separated from it by bollards. The sidewalk merges into a wide pedestrian space that is partly under the highway and partly on various platforms overhanging the bulkhead. Just north of the ferry pier, the platforms are metal grates spanning over a constructed living shoreline, elsewhere the platforms are solid. In all, the pedestrian space is about 110 feet wide, approximately half under the highway. A succession of planters, which have wooden benches integrated into them, define a walking path near the water. The water's edge is protected with a sleek metal rail and lined, in several places, with benches. Along one stretch, eight barstools attach to the railing and here the wood

**Section: East River Waterfront
Esplanade, northeast of Pier 11
Scale: 1" = 20'**

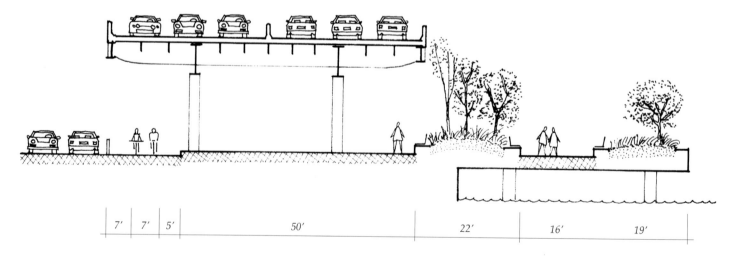

PART 1 An Assembly of Waterfront Promenades

People strolling along the East River Waterfront Esplanade on a cold November day

The East River Waterfront Esplanade north of the Brooklyn Bridge, where the promenade is completely under the freeway

Relaxing on the upper deck of the Pier 15 park

top cap widens into a narrow but very usable bar top, upon which people can set their food and drink. Under the freeway structure is a glass-enclosed pavilion that houses a bar. When the bar is open, tables and chairs associated with it spill onto the walkway.

This segment of the promenade ends at Pier 15, which has been rebuilt into a two-story structure that is both a park and a cultural and recreation venue. Above are lawns, movable Adirondack chairs, and spectacular views across the river. There are also views of the historic ships berthed alongside the pier. Below are two pavilions used for art events and water related activities. From the esplanade, people can climb to the upper deck and walk on promenades lining the 500-foot length of the pier.

Between Pier 15 and the Brooklyn Bridge, the esplanade is at first almost completely under the freeway as it passes a series of piers used for industrial purposes, and then widens to be both under the freeway and atop a long parallel platform overhanging the bulkhead, which has been developed as a linear park.

From the Brooklyn Bridge to East River Park, a stretch that passes under the Manhattan Bridge, the elevated highway structure runs almost right at the water's edge and the esplanade is almost completely underneath it. This segment has not yet been built to its final form. In some areas, temporary walking and bicycle paths are marked out next to the freeway columns. Elsewhere, a walking path near the water's edge is paved with multi-colored hexagonal pavers and simply designed exercise areas have been constructed under the freeway. Views toward the water are blocked for a long stretch where the esplanade runs past Pier 36, which houses recreational facilities in repurposed bulkhead buildings. Plans are to turn this pier into a landscaped park in the future.

At its northern end, the esplanade merges into the walkway that lines the water's edge of East River Park, which sits on a stretch of reclaimed land lying between FDR Drive and the shoreline.

In a design move intended to unify the whole length of the esplanade and give it a sense of identity, the outermost beam supporting the highway has been painted purple and studded with a string of lights that can be seen from across the river, in Brooklyn. The conceptual design calls for more lighting within panels attached to the underside of the highway structure.[6] It is envisioned that the panels will be made of sound attenuating materials that will help mitigate traffic noise.

Promenade Use and Connectivity

The only part of the Esplanade that as yet sees much use is the part south of Pier 15. Both tourists and locals frequent the elevated park on Pier 15, and many people walk or bike along the waterfront

Bar stool seating along the esplanade, with the Pier 15 park beyond

Bench at the water's edge tucked in behind a planter

between it and the Battery, some going to the ferry pier or the helicopter pier. During the middle of the day, workers from nearby establishments come to the esplanade to sit on the benches or bar stools facing the water and eat their lunch. In the evening, many people come to the bar under the highway for drinks. The less developed parts of the esplanade are for the most part frequented only during the day and mainly by local residents who come to fish off the bulkhead or work out using the exercise facilities. Intrepid bicyclists also use them, sometimes as part of a ride around the whole island.

Getting to the esplanade is relatively easy south of the Brooklyn Bridge because many streets lead into South Street. It is more difficult north of the bridge because the adjacent block structure is larger, and so fewer streets lead to the water. South Street itself is relatively easy to cross because it is not too wide. Getting to the part of the esplanade south of the Brooklyn Bridge via public transit is fairly easily accomplished because there are multiple subway stops five to six blocks inland and also many nearby bus stops. Getting to the northern part is more difficult because there are fewer nearby transit stops.

The conceptual design plan for the esplanade includes proposals for linking it with adjacent neighborhoods through the construction of small linear parks or greenways, such as tree-lined sidewalks and medians, reaching into the neighborhoods. Some of these have been built and others are still on the drawing board.

Climate Change and Sea Level Rise Concerns

An unreconstructed part of the esplanade where it runs wholly under the highway

The effort going into building the East River Waterfront Esplanade is proceeding in the face of a serious threat from sea level rise. The sea level at Lower Manhattan is expected to rise by 11 to 21 inches by 2050, and as much as 6 feet by 2100.[7] Areas inland of the esplanade fared badly during Hurricane Sandy because they are particularly low-lying, and many blocks of Wall Street and the Lower East Side were inundated.[8] Since Sandy, a proposal has been made to construct a deployable flood barrier beneath the elevated highway that can be lowered during flood events. This movable panel idea is part of a larger sea level rise adaptation plan called The Big U, which proposes building a berm around the southern tip of Manhattan Island and another berm along the Lower East Side, north of the East River Park.[9] The latter berm, dubbed the Bridging Berm because it not only creates a berm along the waterfront but also bridges over FDR Drive, was funded in 2014 with a $335 million federal grant from the Department of Housing and Urban Development (HUD).[10] In 2015, the city pledged $100 million toward building a flood protection system around Lower Manhattan up to the Lower East Side that will include floodwalls and berms, and hopes to receive up to $500 million more from HUD to build more ambitiously along the lines of the BIG U plan.[11]

The East River Waterfront Esplanade began as an ambitious project to connect neighborhoods with the waterfront despite the existing highway, and to complete a waterfront promenade around Manhattan. The project may become more ambitious as it is redesigned to deal with sea level rise and climate change issues. In the process, a unique public open space is coming into being. Architectural critic Paul Goldberger has summed up the East River Waterfront Esplanade nicely when he refers to it as being "sleek, gritty, and urban at the same time."[12]

Kwun Tong Promenade, East Kowloon, Hong Kong, China

Scale: 1:400,000

As Daniel Burnham famously once said: "Make no little plans..." So it is in Hong Kong. The recently completed waterfront Kwun Tong Promenade is but one piece of an ambitious plan to build a second Central Business District for Hong Kong in an outlying industrial area of East Kowloon. It is envisioned that the so-called CBD2 will eventually contain twice as much office space as the city's central area. Given this context, the promenade, which lies adjacent to an elevated six-lane freeway and was the first open space project of the plan to be implemented, is surprisingly modest in its design.

People have been known to refer to Kwun Tong as the dark side of Hong Kong because of its gritty industrial nature. Kowloon wraps around the northern and eastern sides of Victoria Harbour and Kowloon Bay, opposite Hong Kong Island, and Kwun Tong is its easternmost part. In the 1920s, the city's Kai Tak airport was built on a large spit of reclaimed land extending into the bay parallel to the Kwun Tong shoreline. By the 1960s, Kwun Tong was densely filled with factories and residential tenement blocks. The area began to transition in the 1990s, when many factories left to relocate in Mainland China. In 1998, the airport was moved to a new location north of the city, draining more businesses and employment from the area.[13] The government intended to undertake a massive development project on the former airport lands, making plans to create 299 hectares (1.2 square miles) of new land around the spit, but citizen protests forced the government to abandon the landfill idea.[14] The protests were emboldened by an ordinance passed in 1997 to protect central Victoria Harbour from further land reclamation, though the ordinance didn't protect this part of the harbor.[15]

The government continued to pursue other redevelopment strategies. In 2001, all industrial land in Kwun Tong and nearby Kowloon Bay was rezoned for business.[16] In 2007, a plan was adopted for the Kai Tak spit, which called for creating "a distinguished, vibrant, attractive people-oriented community."[17] Several years later, a 488-hectare (1.9 square mile) redevelopment area was created, which encompassed the Kai Tak spit, lands directly north of the spit, and the Kung Tong and Kowloon Bay business areas. In all, the area was home to 30,000 firms supporting over 260,000 jobs.[18] The

Scale: 1:40,000

PART 1 An Assembly of Waterfront Promenades

conceptual redevelopment masterplan envisions not only creating a new Central Business District but also adding 90,000 new residents.[19] It is anticipated that the Kai Tak spit will be built out by 2022, and that by then the other areas will also be well along in their redevelopment.[20] Major elements of the plan include a new monorail system, new greening projects, and new waterfront amenities for both residents and tourists.

Efforts are underway to rebrand the area with a more positive image than it has had. Key catalyst projects constructed so far include the Kwun Tung promenade, built on land formerly occupied by the publicly owned Kwun Tong Public Cargo Working Area, where small ships were loaded,[21] and a large and lavish cruise ship terminal at the end of the Victoria Harbour side of the former airport spit. These two projects have very different pedigrees and orientations. The cruise ship terminal was designed by Norman Foster's firm and will be able to berth the very largest cruise ships. The promenade was designed by Hong Kong's Architectural Services Department and is meant to primarily serve the needs of local residents, although some features are aimed at attracting tourists.

Promenade Design Characteristics

The Kwun Tong Promenade has a straightforward elegance that belies its gritty context. It is some-what over half a mile long (950 meters) and was built in stages, with a short first section opening in 2010 and the rest in 2015. It occupies a 10.2-acre linear strip of land about 188 feet wide, the inner half of which lies under the elevated freeway structure. The promenade has two different walkways, both 20 feet wide, which are separated by lawns. One walk is at the water's edge and the other partially under the freeway. The lawns between the walkways are in some areas planted with trees, and their inner edges are lined with a series of fitness stations, some oriented toward the elderly, some toward children, and some toward everyone else. The fitness stations are sheltered by metal trellis structures, planted with flowering vines, which give them some shade.

Other much larger metal structures give shade to parts of several broad plazas that interrupt the lawns and connect the walkways with each other. One of these is a linear structure with a shaded upper level deck that people can climb up to and walk along. Other linear structures shade viewing stands situated along the lawns, where people can sit on stepped seats and gaze across the lawn toward the water.

The two walkways have different characters and design detailing. The walkway near the water is a wood-plank boardwalk. Along some sections, an outer 6½ feet of boardwalk steps down toward the water about a foot or so, and the continuous step along its edge can act as a seat. The guardrail protecting the water's edge is made of wood and glass. Backless wooden benches line the outer edge of the walkway, set at regular spacing. The walkway near the freeway is surfaced with pavers and also

Section: Kwun Tong Promenade
Scale: 1" = 20'

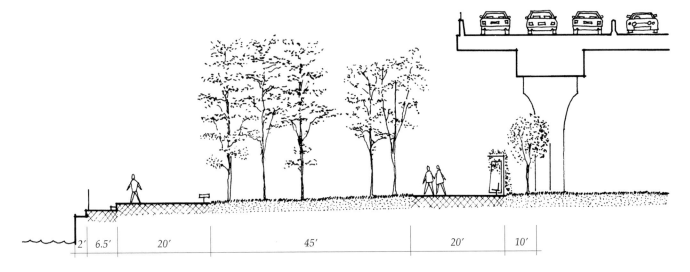

The promenade at the water's edge is designed as a boardwalk

lined with regularly spaced benches, these ones set within vine-covered metal shelters that back up to the freeway structure. A line of trees backed by a fence runs behind the shelters, shielding the area under the freeway from view. Access under the freeway is via widely spaced plazas, which are studded with art pieces meant to recall the area's industrial past. One of these plazas contains public restrooms. Some areas under the freeway have been developed with amenities, including a sensory garden and a play area for children.

At the southern end of the promenade stands a landmark metal sculpture meant to look like piles of compressed recycled paper. At night, this piece flashes with multi-colored lights, and uplights embedded all along the boardwalk also flash changing colors. The lights illuminate sprays of mist emanating from pipes under the boardwalk, creating something of a spectacle display.

The elevated freeway both detracts from the pleasantness of the promenade and contributes to it. The noise of traffic moving on the freeway is a constant presence and the traffic fumes make for poor air quality, but at the same time, the elevated structure casts welcome shade on the inner walkway during morning hours. The waterfront walkway is in full sun throughout the day, so when it's hot, as it often is, it can be more comfortable to walk next to the freeway than next to the water.

Looking over the lawn and the waterfront promenade toward the new cruise ship terminal on Kai Tak spit

Future development may result in changes to the locally oriented character of the promenade. The Kai Tak Fantasy International Ideas Competition, held in 2014, sought proposals for the southern tip of the Kai Tak spit and the water basin between it and the Kwun Tong Promenade. Many of the proposals submitted envisioned elaborate redesigns of these areas.[22] Given the speed with which redevelopment is projected to occur in Kwun Tong, things may feel very different here in the not too distant future.

Promenade Use and Connectivity

The promenade does not yet see much regular use. On a hot and humid Saturday morning in late May, very few people were on the promenade with the exception of a large group of elderly Chinese visitors on a bus tour who were dropped off there for about an hour. However, according to a Public Works Subcommittee report of 2012, some 30,000 people per month visited the first stage of the promenade when it was first opened.[23]

Getting to the promenade can be a challenge. The two metro stations that service it are about half an hour by metro away from Hong Kong Island's central district and the trip requires two train transfers. Both stations are a distance from the waterfront, and walking to it takes determination because streets leading there are heavily trafficked and bordered by high buildings that create a canyon effect and trap exhaust fumes. Sidewalks are minimal and often lined with fences to keep pedestrians out of the traffic lanes. Two traffic circles located a block away from the promenade are particularly difficult to navigate on foot because fences along them force pedestrians to walk half a block beyond the circles to get to crosswalks. The redevelopment masterplan calls for creating better pedestrian connectivity and so perhaps the journey to the waterfront will be easier in the future.[24]

The street that parallels the promenade for most of its length, Hoi Sun Road, has been traffic calmed and is easy to cross. It has one lane of traffic in each direction and parking on both sides. Many of the buildings along it are newly constructed high-rises with gleaming glass facades—they are probably a portent of buildings to come throughout the redevelopment area. Given the very dense adjacent

Sculptural artwork under the freeway

The inner promenade along the freeway is lined with trellis-shaded benches

Landmark sculpture

Jogging along the waterside promenade on a hot May morning

Street connecting the main metro station and the waterfront

development, arriving at the promenade feels like a great relief, even like a breath of fresh air, despite the elevated freeway and its pollutants.

Climate Change and Sea Level Rise Concerns

The Kwun Tong Promenade may be at risk from future sea level rise. The land on which it and much of Kwun Tong sits was reclaimed prior to Hong Kong's 1990 public works directive that requires projects sensitive to sea level rise be designed with the assumption that sea levels will rise 10 millimeters per year, or 39 inches in 100 years.[25, 26] The seawall on which the promenade sits was rebuilt when the promenade was constructed but it doesn't appear to have been raised above the height of the surrounding neighborhood, and the glass panels of the edge railing do not seem designed to withstand flooding. If these observations are correct, then more work may have to be done in the future to address sea level rise.

Local experts project that by 2100 the relative sea level rise in Victoria Harbour may be as much as 1.07 meters (42 inches).[27] However, the International Panel on Climate Change projects that global sea level could rise by as much as .98 meters (3.2 feet) by 2100, and other climate change assessment bodies project that it could rise even higher.[28] For Hong Kong, the effects of sea level rise will be exacerbated by the storm surge impacts of tropical cyclones, which regularly hit the region and have in the past caused extensive flooding of Hong Kong's low-lying coastal areas, especially when associated with high tide events.[29] With climate change, these typhoons are expected to increase in both frequency and severity.[30] The Kai Tak spit will help protect the Kwun Tong Promenade from the worst of the extra wave action that accompanies typhoons, but the area will be vulnerable to storm surge flooding.

Notes

1 "East River Waterfront Esplanade," *NYCEDC*, accessed September 11, 2015, www.nycedc.com/project/east-river-waterfront-esplanade.

2 Office of Mayor Bloomberg, "A Vision for Lower Manhattan," October 11, 2002, accessed June 25, 2016, www.renewnyc.com/content/avisionforlowermanhattan.pdf.

3 "History," *NYCEDC*, accessed September 11, 2015, www.nycedc.com/about-nycedc/history.

4 The City of New York, "Transforming the East River Waterfront," accessed September 11, 2015, www.nyc.gov/html/dcp/pdf/erw/east_river_waterfront_book.pdf.

5 Ibid., 40.

6 Ibid., 45.

7 "New York City Panel on Climate Change 2015 Report Executive Summary," *Annals of the New York Academy of Sciences* 1336, no. 1 (January 1, 2015): 11, doi:10.1111/nyas.12591.

8 The City of New York, "A Stronger, More Resilient New York" (Office of the Mayor, 2013), 373, accessed July 28, 2015, www.nyc.gov/html/sirr/html/report/report.shtml.

9 "BIG U," *Rebuild by Design*, accessed July 15, 2015, www.rebuildbydesign.org/project/big-team-final-proposal/.

10 "New York's New $335 Million Storm-Surge Barrier Will Transform the Lower East Side – Next City," accessed July 15, 2015, https://nextcity.org/daily/entry/new-yorks-new-335-million-storm-surge-barrier-will-transform-the-lower-east.

11 "$100M Project Will Protect Lower Manhattan from Major Storms – NY Daily News," accessed September 11, 2015, www.nydailynews.com/new-york/100m-project-protect-manhattan-major-storms-article-1.2338430.

12 "On the East River Waterfront Esplanade – The New Yorker," accessed July 15, 2015, www.newyorker.com/news/news-desk/on-the-east-river-waterfront-esplanade.

13 Doug Meigs, "New Central Rises in Kowloon East|HongKong Focus|chinadaily.com.cn," November 10, 2011, accessed August 17, 2015, www.chinadaily.com.cn/hkedition/2011-11/10/content_14068150.htm.

14 Mee Kam Ng, "Power and Rationality: The Politics of Harbour Reclamation in Hong Kong," *Environment and Planning C: Government and Policy* 29 (2011): 688.

15 Ibid., 677.

Exercise stations along the
promenade have colorful,
whimsical designs

16   "Energizing Kowloon East - Background," accessed August 18, 2015, www.ekeo.gov.hk/en/about_ekeo/
     background.html.

17   "Kai Tak Development – Overview of Kai Tak Development," accessed August 17, 2015, www.ktd.gov.hk/
     eng/overview.html.

18   "Energizing Kowloon East - Vision and Mission – Vision," accessed August 17, 2015, www.ekeo.gov.hk/
     en/vision/vision/index.html.

19   "Kai Tak Development – Overview of Kai Tak Development."

20   "Energizing Kowloon East – FAQs," accessed August 18, 2015, www.ekeo.gov.hk/en/faqs/index.html.

21   "Item for Public Works Subcommittee of Finance Committee, 439RO-Kwun Tong Promenade
     (stage 2)," June 13, 2012, accessed August 17, 2015, www.legco.gov.hk/yr11-12/english/fc/pwsc/papers/
     p12-30e.pdf.

22   "Energizing Kowloon East – Kai Tak Fantasy," accessed August 17, 2015, www.ekeo.gov.hk/en/activities/
     KT_Fantasy_winning_entry.html.

23   Ibid., 3.

24   Energizing Kowloon East Office, "Kowloon East Conceptual Masterplan 4.0," January 2015, accessed
     October 11, 2015, www.ekeo.gov.hk/en/conceptual_master_plan/index.html.

25   Environmental Resources Management - Hong Kong, Limited, "A Study of Climate Change in Hong
     Kong – Feasibility Study" (Environmental Protection Department, The Government of the Hong Kong
     Special Administrative Region, December 2010), 55.

26   Kwok Pui Tin, "An Assessment of Potential Future Sea-Level Rise and Its Impacts on Coastal
     Development in Hong Kong, M. Sc." (University of Hong Kong, August 2013), 59, http://hub.hku.hk/
     bitstream/10722/192995/1/FullText.pdf?accept=1.

27   "Projections of Hong Kong Climate for the 21st Century - Mean Sea Level Projection," accessed October
     6, 2015, www.hko.gov.hk/climate_change/proj_hk_msl_e.htm.

28   J. A. Church et al., "2013: Sea Level Change," in *Climate Change 2013: The Physical Science Basis.
     Contribution of Working Group I to the Fifth Assessment Report of the Intergovernmental Panel on Climate
     Change* [Stocker, T.F., D. Qin, G.-K. Plattner, M. Tignor, S.K. Allen, J. Boschung, A. Nauels, Y. Xia, V. Bex,

and P.M. Midgley (eds)]. (Cambridge, United Kingdom and New York, NY, USA: Cambridge University Press, 2013), 1182.

29 T. C. Lee and C. F. Wong, "Historical Storm Surges and Storm Surge Forecasting in Hong Kong; Hong Kong Observatory Reprint 734" (JCOMM Scientific and Technical Symposium on Storm Surges (SSS), Seoul, Republic of Korea, 2 – 10/6 2007), 2 – 3, www.iwaponline.com/wpt/006/0081/0060081.pdf.

30 B.Y. Lee, W.T. Wong, and W.C. Woo, "Sea-Level Rise and Storm Surge – Impacts of Climate Change on Hong Kong," April 12, 2010, 4, www.weather.gov.hk/publica/reprint/r915.pdf.

Chapter 7

Spectacle Promenades

The Marina Bay Waterfront Promenade in Singapore, and the Tsim Sha Tsui and Central District Promenades in Hong Kong are as much about creating spectacle to draw people to them at night as they are about providing a place for people to stroll during the day when the glaring sun and normal high heat and humidity in these cities can make being outside very uncomfortable. These promenades are designed to be especially attractive to tourists and great places to see spectacular nightly light shows over the water. Each of the promenades has other spectacle draws as well: a casino, an immense Ferris wheel, an Avenue of Stars. There are also nearby hotels, shopping centers, and other commercial and cultural attractions. A driving idea behind these promenades, as well as other spectacle promenades in other cities, is to be "world-class" and contribute to making their city a top travel destination. To be sure, the promenades are more than just spectacle venues. They are meant to attract people to the waterfront during the day, as well as for the evening shows, and thus are designed for strolling as well as gathering. It is useful to take note of the physical design characteristics of these high-end tourist-oriented promenades and the planning contexts in which they were created.

Marina Bay Waterfront Promenade, Singapore

Scale: 1:400,000

Singapore has embarked on an ambitious plan to greatly expand its central business district and at the same time rebrand its image as a vibrant and exciting world-class city, attractive to international professionals and executives as well as tourists.[1] Large-scale land reclamation and the creation of a new fresh water reservoir and flood control barrier are central to the plan, as is a large casino resort with iconic buildings and a large new park with iconic landscaping. A 3½-kilometer (2.2-mile) waterfront promenade is a highly advertised feature of the new development.[2]

The Marina Bay project is emblematic of Singapore's modernization and development strategy which has evolved over the last 50 years. Singapore is a small (718 square kilometers or 277 square miles) island city-state of almost 5.5 million people that is located at the tip of the Malaysian peninsula. Long under British rule, it became an independent nation in 1965 and since then has increased its land area by almost 25 percent through land reclamation.[3] The state owns almost 80 percent of the country's land, and since the country's birth has been pursuing a massive urban renewal program directed by its Urban Redevelopment Authority.[4] Singapore's central area faces onto Singapore Strait, the southwestern arm of the South China Sea which separates it from Indonesia. Historically the waterfront here, at the mouth of the Singapore River, was the main gateway where people and goods entered the city.[5] In the 1970s and 1980s, after port activity was moved elsewhere, the government embarked on the Marina Bay project, reclaiming 360 hectares (1.4 square miles) of land beyond the end of the river and east along the coast, enclosing within these new lands a 240-hectare (.92-square mile) water body.[6] In 2008, the water body was turned into a fresh water reservoir with the building of the Marina Barrage at the new mouth to the sea, a structure designed to both keep seawater out and discharge excess storm water from the Singapore River and other rivers.[7]

The first development of these new lands was on the northern side of the new bay in what is known as Marina Centre. Here, hotels and shopping centers were built in superblocks that turned their backs to the new water body. The water's edge was seen as problematic because of the daily 3-meter tidal flow and also because the Singapore River flooded regularly.[8] After the barrage was built,

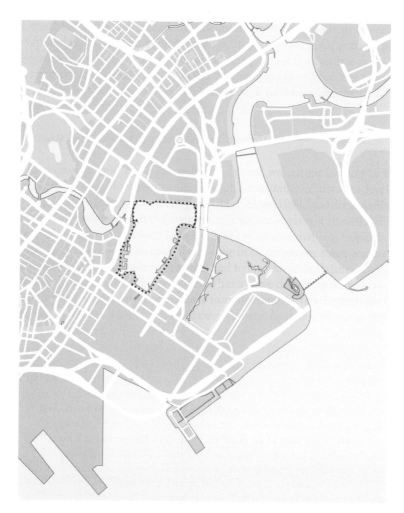

Scale: 1:40,000

Marina Bay at night

PART 1 An Assembly of Waterfront Promenades

water in Marina Bay could be held at a constant level and development began to face it rather than shun it. In the mid-2000s, the water's edge of Marina Centre was addressed with the construction of a large viewing gallery facing a floating dock topped with a stadium playing field.

Development of the reclaimed land east and south of the reservoir began after it was designated an entertainment area. The first construction consisted of a large public park and botanical garden, the Gardens by the Bay, built on the western part of these lands. In 2005, after an unprecedented year of public consultation, the government decided to reverse its long-standing anti-casino policy and allow them into the country. The rationale was to keep Singapore competitive as a major Asian destination by rebranding it as a fun city. Marina Bay South was designated as a site for an "Integrated Resort" casino, and the contract to build it was given to a consortium that included the Las Vegas Sands and the architect Moshe Safdie.[9] The project that was built is a massive complex which, along with the casino, includes a giant barrel-vaulted shopping mall, an expo and convention center, a theater, and three hotel towers, containing more than 2,500 rooms, that are connected at the top by a "sky park," which from below looks vaguely ship-like. The casino opened in 2010 along with new public open spaces at the water's edge containing pedestrian and bicycle paths. These paths connect with older paths along the other side of the reservoir so that now promenades and bicycle paths line the entire water's edge of the reservoir.

Promenade Design Characteristics

The older promenade segments on the north and west sides of the reservoir are simply designed. They include a pedestrian bridge that leads to an open viewing plaza, and a walk along a mix of older and newer buildings that culminates at a small plaza holding the city's famed Merlion statue, a fish figure with a lion's head that the city adopted as a tourism logo some years ago and has since become the city's mascot.

The newer promenade segments are more highly designed, in keeping with the spectacle nature of the casino complex. One promenade crosses a pedestrian bridge that spans the reservoir at a narrowing that leads to the barrage. The bridge, known as the Helix Bridge because its spiraling design was inspired by the double helix structure of DNA, has several viewing pods along it that jut out over the water. At night, the bridge's overhead structural elements and ground surface are lit with multi-colored lights.

Section: Marina Bay Waterfront Promenade, near the shopping mall and casino
Scale: 1" = 20'

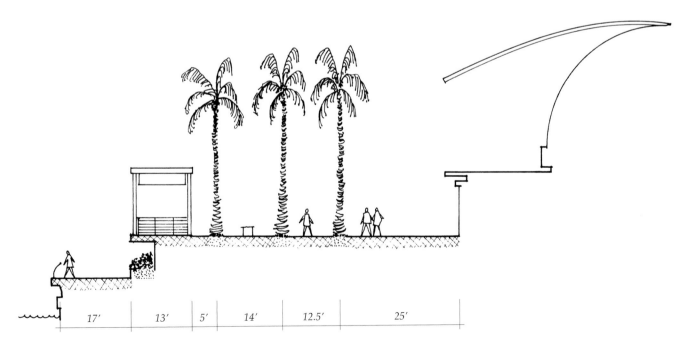

17'   13'   5'   14'   12.5'   25'

The lower level boardwalk curves
sinously along the water's edge

The upper level promenade near
the shopping mall and casino

People enjoy sitting in the shade offered by the belvedere along the upper promenade near the shopping mall, even though there are no benches

The Helix Bridge

Breeze-shelter

Jogging in the shade of the palm trees on the upper promenade

The promenade near the casino, which parallels and is fronted by the long glass covered barrel-vaulted shopping mall building, is elegant in its design. Here, the promenade has two levels. The upper level is a paved walk planted with three rows of closely spaced palm trees that create two allées, one of which offers a shady place to walk or bike and the other a shady place to sit on open-weave wooden box-like benches. Along the way, several belvederes extend from the path toward the water. These structures have wood decking, canvas awnings, and stainless steel railings. Along the shopping mall side, several eating and drinking pavilions open onto the walk.

The lower promenade level, some 7 feet down, is a wide curving boardwalk that sweeps along the water's edge and is bordered by an artfully designed and detailed inward-curving stainless steel rail. Bridges extending from the promenade lead to glass enclosed "crystal pavilions" that house luxury stores, also accessible from the shopping mall via underwater tunnels. During the day, the boardwalk is always in full sun, except its innermost edge, and the only place to sit is on planters that are tucked under the belvederes.

Beyond the shopping mall, the promenade continues on in two levels, past a park and a visitors' center. Run through the palm trees on the upper level is a tubular stainless steel mist-emitting structure. Sensors in it respond to the presence of people and climatic conditions, producing a cooling mist when appropriate.

At the corner of the reservoir, the promenade makes a sharp northwest turn and only the upper level promenade continues on. Here, the walk is lined with several rows of closely spaced feathery trees interspersed with three "breeze-shelters" that have motion-activated fans run by the solar panels in their overhead canopies.

The cooling structures are an attempt to mitigate the harshness of Singapore's climate, which works against public use and enjoyment of outdoor public open space. Singapore is located near the

People watching the night-time water and light spectacle

equator and temperatures throughout the year are typically in the 80s and 90s Fahrenheit, with little cooling at night. But the greater issue is the very high humidity that exacerbates the high temperatures and makes being outside uncomfortable. With good reason, most of the public life in Singapore takes place in air-conditioned shopping malls. It also explains why the several other waterfront promenades in Singapore, including those along nearby Clark's Quay, have been given over to smoking areas and are lined with cigarette depositories.

Promenade Use and Connectivity

Other than the walk in front of the Merlion statue, which attracts many people for photo taking, the most used parts of the promenade are those in front of the casino, shopping mall, and on the double helix bridge. Even here, the numbers of users aren't particularly high and only bikers tend to go for any distance. During the day, most people try to walk and bike where there is shade and so avoid the lower level boardwalk.

Elegantly designed railing and light fixture along the lower level boardwalk

On an early Sunday afternoon in late May, 384 people per hour were observed moving along the upper level of the promenade near the shopping mall. Most people (72%) were strolling, a number were biking (19%), and the remaining few were either running or on skates, skateboards, or scooters. At the same time, many more people were walking along the two levels of walkways inside the air-conditioned shopping mall that parallel the outdoor promenade.

A surge of outdoor activity occurs two or three times nightly when people throng out of the shopping mall, hotel, and casino to witness 13-minute-long light and water spectacles. These shows take place over the water in front of a wood surfaced plaza that transforms into a stepped viewing platform for these events and is located between the upper and lower promenades at a main entry to the shopping mall. The shows are of colored laser lights and video images projected on clouds of mist, whose movements are sequenced to music.

Nighttime spectacle can also be enjoyed within the Gardens by the Bay public park that lies southeast of the casino complex and is easily accessible via another waterfront promenade that forks off beyond the helix bridge and leads along the park to a pedestrian bridge over the Marina Barrage. A defining feature of the garden, which forms a backdrop for this promenade at night, is a grove of metal "super trees," 9 to 16 stories high, whose trunks and canopies are resplendent with multi-colored lights.

Yes, Marina Bay and its promenades are truly about spectacle. That was the intention of the design and it was successfully carried out.

Lack of access may be one reason why the promenade by the casino is so lightly used for strolling. Singapore has an extensive underground metro system and there is a stop at the casino, from which it's an easy walk to the promenade. Except for this, however, it is not easy to get to the promenade because it is not well connected with the city street system. Walkable streets are envisioned for the future, but the city's first big transportation move was to build an expressway around and tunneled under the reclaimed land on which the casino sits.

Starting in 2030, the government plans to develop the "Greater Southern Waterfront," a 1,000-hectare (3.9 square mile) area of land to the southwest of Marina Bay that is currently occupied by shipping terminals, which will be moved elsewhere. The plans call for building a waterfront city that will further the goal of creating a world-class city begun with the Marina Bay development. It is envisioned that a waterfront promenade will run along the entire water's edge of this development, including around a new reservoir that will be created, and extend along the sea-facing edge of the new financial district being built southwest of the casino resort and the new residential neighborhood planned for the land southeast of Gardens by the Bay, a distance of some 30 kilometers (18.6 miles).[10] Once there is more development around Marina Bay, perhaps more people besides tourists will use the promenade near the casino. Perhaps the longer waterfront promenade will attract walking and biking in spite of the difficult climate issues. It will be interesting to see how things develop over time.

Climate Change and Sea Level Rise Concerns

The Marina Barrage protects the promenade around Marina Bay from flooding associated with storm events and it would seem to also afford some protection against future sea level rise, as its top surface is 5½ meters above mean high tide.[11] However, the reclaimed land is at risk from sea level rise. Singapore has in the past constructed reclaimed land 1¼ meters above the highest recorded tide level but has recently changed this policy as it grapples with future sea level rise and the implications of climate change. Sea level rise in Singapore Strait has over the last several decades slightly exceeded global averages, matching trends of the region.[12] With climate change, it is expected that Singapore will experience increased rainfall—annual rainfall currently exceeds 100 inches and daily rainfall of 8 inches is not uncommon—and hence more flooding.[13] Taking these things into account, since 2011 the government has required that reclaimed land be built at 2¼ meters above high tide. Given Singapore's history of massive urban renewal it is more than likely that the government will aggressively deal with protecting the Marina Bay development and in all likelihood the planned coastal promenade will be designed with this in mind.

Tsim Sha Tsui Promenade, Hong Kong, China

Scale: 1:400,000

The Avenue of Stars section of the Tsim Sha Tsui Promenade in West Kowloon, which lies across Victoria Harbour from Hong Kong Island, is probably the most visited public open space in Hong Kong if for no other reason than the views it affords: of Victoria Harbour and the many ferries and ships that constantly ply its waters, of the impressive skyline of Hong Kong Island across the bay, of mountains framing the buildings, and, in the evening, of the multi-media Symphony of Lights spectacle. The rest of the promenade also draws people but in significantly fewer numbers.

Promenade Design Characteristics

The slightly less than 1-mile-long Tsim Sha Tsui Promenade wraps around the southern waterfront of central Kowloon, running from the Star Ferry Terminal east to the entrance to the Cross Harbour Tunnel, and consists of several different sections with markedly different characteristics. The Avenue

Scale: 1:40,000

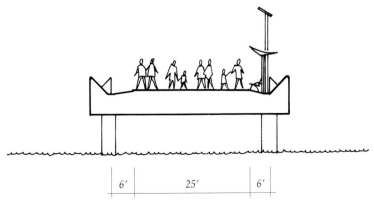

Section: Tsim Sha Tsui
Promenade, Avenue of Stars
Scale: 1" = 20'

Tourists like to compare their handprints with those of stars

of Stars, which comprises roughly the central third of the promenade, is on a segment that juts over the water on a narrow arching pier structure that parallels the shore. West of the Avenue of Stars, the promenade runs through a series of paved open spaces along the sculptural buildings of the Hong Kong Cultural Complex which houses the Space Museum and Museum of Art. To the east, the promenade hugs a narrow strip of land between the shore and a major traffic road. The densely packed skyscrapers of Kowloon's central business district form the promenade's backdrop, most of them office, hotel, and retail buildings.

The Tsim Sha Tsui Promenade was created to draw tourists to this part of the city and the Avenue of Stars segment in particular is highly commercialized. The promenade was constructed in 1982 by the New World Group, a major Hong Kong-based property development corporation. In 2004, the same company paid 40 million Hong Kong dollars (US$5.1 million) to revamp part of the promenade into the Avenue of Stars, designed to pay tribute to movie stars and other notables of the city's film industry. The objective was to cement Hong Kong's position as a world city.[14] Plaques embedded in the paving surface have handprints of over 100 "stars." There are also sculptures depicting the history of the Hong Kong movie industry, a 6-meter-high version of the Hong Kong Film Award statuette, and themed kiosks and carts that sell refreshments and souvenirs. At night, lights in specially designed fixtures lining the promenade and embedded in the paving flash different colors in synchrony with the Symphony of Lights show.

The Symphony of Lights is a nightly 14-minute-long extravaganza participated in by 44 buildings in the central districts of Hong Kong Island and Kowloon. The buildings display decorative light effects on their facades while roving searchlights stream from rooftops. The movement of lights is synchronized with music and a narration celebrating the history and culture of Hong Kong in three different languages: English, Mandarin, and Cantonese.[15] The Avenue of Stars is one of two waterfront places where the music is publicly broadcast. The Hong Kong Leisure and Cultural Services Department oversees the Avenue of Stars, but the New World Group is responsible for managing, maintaining, and operating it.[16]

The promenade section east of the Avenue of Stars, called the East Tsim Sha Tsui Promenade, has a calmer feel. Although it is adjacent to a major road, Salisbury Road, the view and some of the sound of the traffic is buffered by undulating raised mounds planted with ground cover and closely spaced trees.

Promenade Use and Connectivity

The Avenue of Stars is often crowded with people. According to the Leisure and Cultural Services Department, during its first year it attracted approximately one million visitors a month,[17] and people still come in droves. A recent study of tourist behavior in Hong Kong found that many people surveyed considered the Avenue of Stars their favorite city attraction.[18] On a hot and humid breezy

Section: Tsim Sha Tsui Promenade, eastern segment
Scale: 1" = 20'

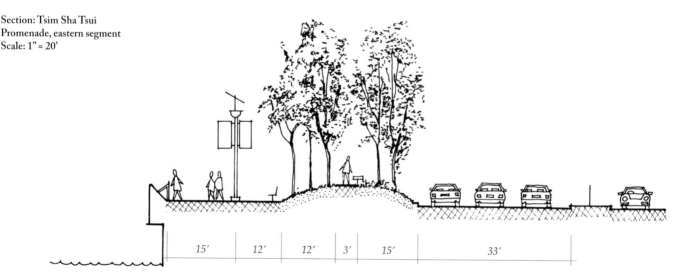

15' 12' 12' 3' 15' 33'

PART 1 An Assembly of Waterfront Promenades

People watching the Symphony of Lights show from the Avenue of Stars

Friday evening in late May 2015, 2,712 people per hour were walking along the Avenue of Stars around the time of the Symphony of Lights show. This number is toward the highest seen on any of the promenades studied. The 36-foot-wide walkway feels quite crowded with this many people. At the same time, many more people were sitting on the benches lining the inside of the walkway and on the railing lining its outside. There is much activity throughout the rest of the day as well. Mostly people stroll and many stop to take pictures of each other in front of the view, interact with the sculptures, and compare their handprints with those of the movie stars.

Fewer people use the more modestly designed eastern part of the promenade although it offers just as good views of the Symphony of Lights show. About a half an hour before the show on the same late May Friday evening, 486 people per hour were observed moving along it, less than 20 percent of the number on the Avenue of Stars. Many people seemed to be locals rather than tourists, and almost a quarter of them were exercising, either running or walking fast.

The large numbers of people who visit the Avenue of Stars do so in spite of it being somewhat difficult to access. To get to it, or to the rest of the promenade, one has to cross Salisbury Road, a six- to eight-lane high traffic artery with expressway characteristics that at its eastern end rises to become the elevated Hung Hom Bypass. Crossing Salisbury Road can be accomplished via several overhead pedestrian walkways that cross the road and land at the East Tsim Sha Tsui Promenade, but that

People walking along the Avenue of Stars in the late afternoon

The more locally oriented eastern part of Tsim Sha Tsui Promenade in the late afternoon

requires walking up and down stairs. Two rapid transit (MTR) stations are near to the promenade but they are located in such a way that pedestrians exiting either one of them must negotiate the big roadway. The many hotels in the area near the Avenue of Stars, and hence the density of tourists staying nearby, helps explain why it is so popular in spite of the access problems. The access difficulties are well acknowledged and plans are underway to improve things.

Change is in the air for the Tsim Sha Tsui promenade. The New World Group perceives the Avenue of Stars as worn and the eastern part of the promenade in need of more attractions and better pedestrian connections. It is proceeding with a major facelift of the Avenue of Stars and has plans to "revitalize" and "re-energize" the East Tsim Sha Tsui promenade by building an elevated observation deck and walkway over half its length and creating connections under the Hung Hom Bypass to connect the eastern end of the promenade with the nearby mega-structure Hung Hom train station complex.[19] Other renovations would include building a new movie themed center, a cultural performance center, eateries, places to drink, and souvenir shops along the promenade.[20] Much is made of the elevated viewing deck as providing both spectacular views of the harbor and a special experience not available elsewhere. It would be accessible directly from the overhead pedestrian bridges that cross the busy Salisbury Road and presumably improve pedestrian access to the waterfront. The objective is to "transform the entire TST Waterfront into one of the best public spaces with one of the world's most striking urban landscapes for the enjoyment of local residents and visitors."[21] The plans were approved by the Town Planning Board in 2015 but may be subject to change because they were met with controversy due to inadequate public consultation, and so the process is being revisited.[22]

Climate Change and Sea Level Rise Concerns

The Tsim Sha Tsui promenade faces challenges from sea level rise. Along with extensive waterfront areas of West Kowloon, it sits on low-lying reclaimed land the edge of which is protected by a hard seawall. The Avenue of Stars and part of the East Tsim Sha Tsui Promenade project past the seawall on pilings and the rest sits atop the seawall. The seawall was not built to address sea level rise because it predates[23] the mandate in place since 1990 that requires projects sensitive to sea level rise to be designed with the assumption that sea levels will rise 10 millimeters per year, or 39 inches in 100 years.[24, 25] Current predictions are that relative sea level rise in Victoria Harbour will be a maximum of 1.07 meters (42 inches) by 2100.[26] Sea level rise will be exacerbated by the storm surge accompanying tropical cyclones, which impact Hong Kong an average of six to seven times a year and have in the past caused extensive flooding of low-lying coastal areas.[27] With climate change such storms are predicted to increase in both frequency and severity.[28] The Tsim Sha Tsui promenade is already closed to the public when cyclones threaten but has not yet experienced massive damage. The redesign plans don't explicitly address the sea level rise issue, although the proposed elevated walkway may be part of a solution.

Central and Western District Promenade, Hong Kong, China

A large land reclamation project is underway along the northern shore of Hong Kong Island's central area, across the harbor from the Avenue of Stars. Among its major features are a tunneled highway, an airport train station, civic and public buildings, parks and open spaces, and a much-advertised waterfront promenade from which people can view the nightly multi-media Symphony of Lights spectacle. The reclamation project has been controversial, and the current emphasis on public amenities is in response to those controversies. The promenade's prosaic name, Central and Western District Promenade, belies its elegance. A middle section of the promenade has been built and the rest is in the pipeline.

This land reclamation project will be the last major landfill of Victoria Harbour, which has seen much fill but is now protected. Hong Kong has been reclaiming land since the mid-1800s in order to create flat land for development because much of its land area is in steep hills, with reclamation accelerating after World War II. Almost the entire central business district on Hong Kong Island is on reclaimed land as is the central area of Kowloon on the other side of Victoria Harbour. By the mid-1990s, sales of reclaimed land had become a major source of government income. Huge areas of Victoria Harbour had been filled and people became alarmed by the city's plan to fill it considerably further. Along with being concerned that the Harbour would become so narrow as to be nothing more than a river, they were expressing displeasure at the mega block developments and multi-lane highways that had been built along the water on previous land reclamations, which had cut neighborhoods off from the water.[29]

In 1997, just as British colonial rule was ending and Hong Kong became a part of China, massive public protests erupted against further land reclamation in Victoria Harbour, which resulted in an ordinance to protect the harbor and stopped about 600 hectares (2.3 square miles) of planned reclamation.[30] The protests expressed a growing view that the city's waterfront should be designed primarily for public access rather than creating wealth for the government and developers.[31]

The Central and Wan Chai reclamations underway along Hong Kong Island's central area, which had begun in the early 1990s, were allowed to proceed in spite of the new ordinance because of the highway and transit infrastructure associated with them that was deemed absolutely necessary, but the total reclamation was reduced to half its original size: from 110.3 hectares (273 acres) to 56 hectares (138 acres).[32] The nature of development on the reclaimed land was also changed. A Legislative Council Complex, the Hong Kong Convention and Exhibition Centre, a massive international finance center and mall complex with high rise buildings atop the new Airport Express station, and six new ferry piers, replacing older ones that had been demolished, had already been built on early phases of the project, but many of the remaining planned commercial developments were stopped. Citizens criticized the government's plan to build more shopping malls and office buildings on the reclaimed land yet to be built and after a several-years-long public consultation process, which has been criticized as not welcoming the input of ordinary citizens and focusing too much on creating a world-class waterfront, the city issued a revised plan.[33] The land being reclaimed in the final phases will be devoted largely to public open space and some leisure-oriented commercial and cultural uses in relatively low-scale buildings.[34]

Promenade Design Characteristics

The Central and Western District Promenade will eventually extend the whole 2-mile length of the reclaimed waterfront, from the ferry piers eastward to beyond the Convention Centre. There has been discussion of extending it further and linking it with a 3¼-mile-long waterfront promenade to the west, Sheung Wan, built in 2009, but this would be difficult to accomplish because of an intervening public cargo working area.[35] While the Sheung Wan promenade is modestly designed and advertised primarily as a fitness trail, the Central and Western District Promenade is much more elaborate. The city's urban design study calls for it to lie within a green oasis, be divided into multiple landscape thematic character zones, give access to viewing platforms, and be anchored by signature public plazas.[36]

As of mid-2015, a middle section of the promenade had been constructed. It extends along the water's edge of recently built and elegantly designed Tamar Park, which sits at the center of the newly constructed civic area with its iconic buildings. Multiple paths offer water views: a main path along the water's edge and higher level curving paths in the park that lead to eight glass-fronted viewing platforms that cantilever over the lower walk. There is a bucolic nature to the park paths and the viewing platforms, some of which are wooden decks and others of which have lawns with a wooden deck edge. The walk at the water's edge is simple in its design: a 20-foot-wide path surfaced with pink and grey concrete pavers, edged by an inwardly curving wood-capped metal railing that extends from the top of a high curb that functions as a wave wall. Custom-designed benches are grouped in 11-foot-wide spaces under all the viewing platform overhangs except under one where there is a small bakery kiosk and a handful of tables and chairs.

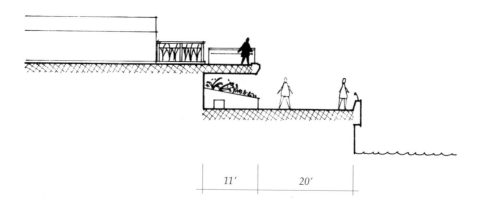

Section: Central and Western
District Promenade
Scale: 1" = 20'

11'   20'

Tamar Park, with the upper level promenade visible in a distance

The lower level promenade has a more utilitarian design than the upper level promenade and Tamar Park

Nighttime lighting is designed for low-level illumination so as not to interfere with viewing the Symphony of Lights show. The lower walk is lit via soft uplights, downlights, and wall sconces integral to the seating areas. The upper level viewing platforms are lit with uplights mounted in the wooden decks and downlights mounted in bollards that edge the lawn areas.

Glass panels line the viewing platforms that extend from the upper level promenade

The lower level waterfront walk will eventually extend in both directions from Tamar Park. As of now it extends west to the ferry docks, passing along the way through an as yet undeveloped area that is fenced off on both sides. Near the ferry docks it passes a gigantic Ferris wheel, the 60-meter-tall (197-foot) Hong Kong Observation Wheel, which people can ride day and night to get spectacular views. The wheel provides an ever-moving visual focal point, especially at night when it is brilliantly lit. To the east, the walk will continue toward and around the massive glass fronted and curved-roof Convention Centre, which is another focal point and also brilliantly lit at night.

Promenade Use and Connectivity

The Central and Western District promenade is not yet highly used. It attracts only a handful of people during the day, mostly office workers, and even fewer people in the evening, even though it offers good viewing of the Symphony of Lights show. It is not yet a destination for tourists, likely because it is difficult to get to and not yet advertised on either tourist maps or MRT station maps. A wide surface highway running inland of the reclaimed land creates a barrier. Except at Tamar Park, much of the land between the waterfront and the highway is not yet developed and is difficult to traverse. A rapid transit (MTR) station gives reasonably good access to Tamar Park, but the several metro stations nearer the ferry piers are quite a way inland and require navigating a long and confusing system of overhead walkways to get to the water.

Residents may not be using the promenade because it is so new and not yet finished, or they may be staying away because there was little public input into its design and it doesn't feel locally oriented.

People sitting along the upper and lower level promenades

The Hong Kong Observation Wheel creates a landmark in the distance

The upper level promenade as it meanders through Tamar Park

Other reasons the promenade is little used may have to do with the many restrictions advertised on way-finding signs: no bicycling, no dogs, and no smoking. Or perhaps people are not gravitating to it because of the lack of almost any shade along it and the desolate surrounds of the walk between the ferry piers and Tamar Park. Probably the promenade will become more used when it is finished and when the planned community facilities along it have been constructed.

Climate Change and Sea Level Rise Concerns

The reclaimed land along Hong Kong's central waterfront is likely to be safe from sea level rise for quite some time if current projections of a maximum relative sea level rise in Victoria Harbour of 1.07 meters (42 inches) by 2100 hold true.[37] Since 1990, land reclamation projects, including this one, have been designed with the assumption that sea levels will rise 10 millimeters per year, or 39 inches in 100 years.[38,39] However, Hong Kong lies in an area that sees tropical cyclones and in the past it has often experienced severe coastal flooding from the storm surge associated with storm events. With climate change, such storms are predicted to increase in both frequency and severity,[40] so even though the new seawall along the promenade has a wave deflecting design, in the future it may not be high enough to keep the lower promenade from flooding. Given the high profile of this waterfront area and Hong Kong's tradition of constant development, no doubt whatever moves necessary will be taken to keep it protected.

Notes

1 Kah-Wee Lee, "Regulating Design in Singapore: A Survey of the Government Land Sales (GLS) Programme," *Environment and Planning C: Government and Policy* 28 (2010): 160.

2 "Urban Redevelopment Authority Fact Sheet on Marina Bay," 2010, accessed August 18, 2015, www.mnd.gov.sg/BudgetDebate2012/files/URA%20factsheet%20on%20Marina%20Bay.pdf.

3 Lin Sien Chia, *Singapore's Urban Coastal Area: Strategies for Management* (Malaysia: WorldFish, 1992), 17.

4 Kah-Wee Lee, "Regulating Design in Singapore," 145–146.

5 "Historic Waterfront" (Singapore Urban Redevelopment Authority), accessed September 9, 2015, www.marina-bay.sg/downloads/Historic_Waterfront.pdf.

6 "Marina Bay and Marina South," accessed August 19, 2015, www.ura.gov.sg/uol/master-plan/View-Master-Plan/master-plan-2014/Growth-Area/City-Centre/Marina-Bay-Marina-South.aspx.

7 Wung Hee Moh and Pei Lin Su, "Marina Barrage – A Unique 3-in-1 Project in Singapore," *Structural Engineering International* 19, no. 1 (February 1, 2009): 17, doi:10.2749/101686609787398399.

8 Ibid.

9 Kah-Wee Lee, "Regulating Design in Singapore," 160–161.

10 "Central Area," accessed September 9, 2015, www.ura.gov.sg/uol/master-plan/View-Master-Plan/master-plan-2014/master-plan/Regional-highlights/central-area/central-area.

11 Moh and Su, "Marina Barrage – A Unique 3-in-1 Project in Singapore," 19.

12 P. Tkalich et al., "Sea Level Trend and Variability in the Singapore Strait," *Ocean Science* 9 (2013): 294.

13 Moh and Su, "Marina Barrage – A Unique 3-in-1 Project in Singapore," 17.

14 "Avenue of Stars," accessed August 18, 2015, www.avenueofstars.com.hk/eng/home.asp.

15 "A Symphony of Lights | Hong Kong Tourism Board," accessed August 18, 2015, www.discoverhongkong.com/us/see-do/highlight-attractions/harbour-view/a-symphony-of-lights.jsp.

16 "LCSD Annual Report 2004 – Leisure Services – Initiatives and Improvements," accessed August 18, 2015, www.lcsd.gov.hk/dept/annualrpt/2004/en/leisure-07.php.

17 "LCSD Annual Report 2004 – Leisure Services – Initiatives and Improvements."

18 Bob McKercher et al., "First and Repeat Visitor Behaviour: GPS Tracking and GIS Analysis in Hong Kong," *Tourism Geographies* 14, no. 1 (February 1, 2012): 151, doi:10.1080/14616688.2011.598542.

19 Vivienne Zeng, "Blight on the Harbour? Proposed Plan to Transform Tsim Sha Tsui Waterfront Triggers Complaints," *Hong Kong Free Press*, accessed August 18, 2015, www.hongkongfp.com/2015/08/11/blight-on-the-harbour-proposed-plan-to-transform-tsim-sha-tsui-waterfront-triggers-complaints/.

20 "Plan 'will Create a More Beautiful Harbor' HK - China Daily Asia," *Data:blog.title*, accessed August 18, 2015, www.chinadailyasia.com/hknews/2015-08/13/content_15303353.html.

21 "Broad Development Parameters of the Applied Use/Development in Respect of Application No. A/ K1/250; Section 16: Planning Application for Proposed Eating Place/Shop and Services/Place of Entertainment/Place of Recreation, Sports or Culture at Eastern Portion of Salisbury Garden, the Avenue of Stars and East Tsim Sha Tsui Waterfront Promenade, Tsim Sha Tsui, Kowloon" (Hong Kong Town Planning Board, June 2015), www.info.gov.hk/tpb/tc/plan_application/Attachment/20150710/s16_A_ K1_250_0_gist.pdf.

22 "Avenue of Stars Closed for Rebuilding – The Standard," accessed October 11, 2015, www.thestandard. com.hk/breaking_news_detail.asp?id=67530&icid=3&d_str=20151007

23 Mee Kam Ng, "Power and Rationality: The Politics of Harbour Reclamation in Hong Kong," *Environment and Planning C: Government and Policy* 29 (2011): 681.

24 Environmental Resources Management – Hong Kong, Limited, "A Study of Climate Change in Hong Kong – Feasibility Study" (Environmental Protection Department, The Government of the Hong Kong Special Administrative Region, December 2010), 55.

25 Kwok Pui Tin, "An Assessment of Potential Future Sea-Level Rise and Its Impacts on Coastal Development in Hong Kong, M. Sc." (University of Hong Kong, August 2013), accessed October 5, 2015, 59, http://hub.hku.hk/bitstream/10722/192995/1/FullText.pdf?accept=1.

26 "Projections of Hong Kong Climate for the 21st Century – Mean Sea Level Projection," accessed October 6, 2015, www.hko.gov.hk/climate_change/proj_hk_msl_e.htm.

27 T. C. Lee and C. F. Wong, "Historical Storm Surges and Storm Surge Forecasting in Hong Kong; Hong Kong Observatory Reprint 734" (JCOMM Scientific and Technical Symposium on Storm Surges (SSS), Seoul, Republic of Korea, 2 – 10/6 2007), 2, accessed October 11, 2015, www.iwaponline.com/ wpt/006/0081/0060081.pdf.

28 B.Y. Lee, W.T. Wong, and W.C. Woo, "Sea-Level Rise and Storm Surge – Impacts of Climate Change on Hong Kong," April 12, 2010, 4, accessed July 29, 2015, www.weather.gov.hk/publica/reprint/r915.pdf.

29 Mee Kam Ng, "Power and Rationality: The Politics of Harbour Reclamation in Hong Kong," *Environment and Planning C: Government and Policy* 29 (2011): 681–684.

30 Ibid., 677.

31 Darren Man-wai Cheung and Bo-sin Tang, "Social Order, Leisure, or Tourist Attraction? The Changing Planning Missions for Waterfront Space in Hong Kong," *Habitat International* 47 (June 2015): 235, accessed September 24, 2015, doi:10.1016/j.habitatint.2015.01.006.

32 Mee Kam Ng, "Power and Rationality," 685.

33 Wing-Shing Tang, Joanna Wai Ying Lee, and Mee Kam Ng, "Public Engagement as a Tool of Hegemony: The Case of Designing the New Central Harbourfront in Hong Kong," *Critical Sociology* 38, no. 1 (January 1, 2012): 100–105, accessed September 24, 2015, doi:10.1177/0896920511408363.

34 "Urban Design Study for the New Central Harbourfront, Executive Summary" (Hong Kong Planning Department, July 2011), accessed September 24, 2015, www.pland.gov.hk/pland_en/p_study/comp_s/ UDS/eng_v1/images_eng/pdf_paper/exec_sum_e.pdf.

35 "Waterfront Development in Hong Kong," n.d., accessed July 29, 2015, http://gia.info.gov.hk/ general/201203/29/P201203290357_0357_91974.pdf.

36 "Urban Design Study for the New Central Harbourfront," 39–40.

37 "Projections of Hong Kong Climate for the 21st Century – Mean Sea Level Projection," accessed October 6, 2015, www.hko.gov.hk/climate_change/proj_hk_msl_e.htm.

38 Environmental Resources Management – Hong Kong, Limited, "A Study of Climate Change in Hong Kong – Feasibility Study" (Environmental Protection Department, The Government of the Hong Kong Special Administrative Region, December 2010), 55.

39 Kwok Pui Tin, "An Assessment of Potential Future Sea-Level Rise and Its Impacts on Coastal Development in Hong Kong, M. Sc." (University of Hong Kong, August 2013), 59, accessed October 5, 2015, http://hub.hku.hk/bitstream/10722/192995/1/FullText.pdf?accept=1.

40 B.Y. Lee, W.T. Wong, and W.C. Woo, "Sea-Level Rise and Storm Surge – Impacts of Climate Change on Hong Kong," April 12, 2010, 4, accessed July 29, 2015, www.weather.gov.hk/publica/reprint/r915.pdf.

Chapter 8

Eco-District Promenades

People around the world are beginning to recognize the importance of building cities in sustainable ways. Some cities have taken the lead by developing new ecological districts that incorporate a holistic approach to sustainable design. These districts are typically designed to have renewable energy sources, provide alternative modes of transportation, discourage automobile use, have a mix of uses so that people can meet their daily needs within the neighborhood, and have a variety of housing types attractive to people of different ages and incomes. The public realm is typically designed to be walkable and bikable and also provide ecological services, such as storm water management, habitat, and bio-diversity. When located along water bodies, eco-districts generally reserve the waterfront for public uses, so that the most compelling place in the community is accessible to everyone. The water's edge is often designed with continuous promenades that welcome people to the waterfront and create linear public open spaces that connect the community and become community social spaces.

The three eco-districts that follow have different density, land use mixes, and relationships with their central cities, and also differently designed waterfront promenades. They are located along different types of water bodies—an ocean, a river that experiences major tidal flows, a lake connected to the sea via canals—which present different opportunities, and also different challenges related to climate change and sea level rise. Their waterfront promenades have different characters and draw different numbers and mixes of people to them, but all are inventively designed.

Hammarby Sjöstad Promenades, Stockholm, Sweden

Scale: 1:400,000

Hammarby Sjöstad is a medium density mixed-use ecological neighborhood under construction at the edge of Stockholm's inner city. It covers three-quarters of a square mile (494 acres or 200 hectares) and upon completion, expected in 2018, will have 26,000 residents and 10,000 jobs.[1] Hammarby Sjö (Lake Hammarby) is at the heart of the neighborhood and promenades line its entire edge. The promenades have a combined length of about three and a quarter miles and constitute a major part of the neighborhood's open space. Those on the north side of the lake are not physically connected with those on the south side, because of intervening canals, but a free public ferry service operating during the day links the two shores, effectively creating a connected promenade system. Various promenade segments are different one from another, offering people who live in the neighborhood the choice of enjoying a variety of waterfront experiences.

Hammarby Sjöstad sits on former industrial land south of the city center. Stockholm spreads over 14 islands and its central area sits at the junction of Lake Mälaren, to the east, and Lake Saltsjön, to the west, which is a bay of the Baltic Sea. Hammarby Sjö lies south of Södermalm, the large island south of the city center that for a long time was the edge of the inner city. After World War I, city-owned land south of the lake became a marginal industrial area and it remained so into the late 1980s, when the city decided to redevelop the area into a mixed-use neighborhood.[2] A masterplan was under development when the city decided to make a bid to host the 2004 Olympics and locate the Olympic Village at Hammarby Sjö. This spurred the idea of designing the area as an ecological district to showcase Stockholm's commitment to sustainability. The Olympic bid was unsuccessful, but the ecological focus remained and a new masterplan was completed in

Scale: 1:40,000

2002. The city prepared the land and constructed streets, and then leased sites to developers for development.[3]

Key public realm ecological features of the neighborhood include: a storm water retention and filtration system, district heating from waste incineration and biogas production, a district-wide recycling system, and green corridors, including several land bridges over an adjacent highway that connect with a natural recreation area. The waterfront promenades contribute to the neighborhood's sustainability because they help make it walkable and bikable as well as highly livable.

Promenade Design Characteristics

Storm water management system within the Hammarby Sjöstad neighborhood

The promenade along the northern side of the lake runs atop the wide, slightly arcing Norra Hammarbyhamnen quay, which is backed by a line of seven- to eight-story buildings arranged in courtyard fashion, and in one location a park. Many large tugboats and barges moor along the quay, lending a working dock feeling. The promenade is roughly 60 to 68 feet wide and mostly surfaced with cobblestones. Its width is divided into linear zones by a line of bollards 5 feet in from the water's edge and a low metal fence some 33 feet in from the bollards, which has occasional gaps. A line of light fixtures is integrated with the fence. Pedestrians and slow-moving public buses, which come by only infrequently, share the area between the bollards and the fence. Just inside the fence is a slightly recessed, 10-foot-wide, two-way cycle track, surfaced with concrete stamped in a brick pattern. Beyond this, a 20-foot-wide cobblestone sidewalk fronts the buildings and park.

Except for an occasional bench along the sidewalk and the grass of the park, there is no place to sit along the promenade apart from about 20 chairs and tables lined up along the sidewalk near a refreshment kiosk at the ferry dock. During the day there is no shade on the promenade except that cast by occasional clusters of linden trees.

The southern side of the lake is lined with a succession of differently design promenades. Starting in the west, the promenade at Hammarby Kaj has a workaday feel. Eight- to nine-story residential buildings with ground floor commercial spaces front onto it, along with a few remaining

The promenade along Norra Hammarbyhamnen

The promenade along Hammarby Kaj

industrial buildings. A narrow 11-foot-wide sidewalk fronts the buildings, followed by a 20-foot-wide two-way road, then another 15-foot-wide walk bounded by a metal guardrail. Next to this walk runs a 13-foot-wide lower walk, some 3½ feet down, accessible by ramps. It has three continuous steps along its waterside, where people sometimes sit and may even picnic on a summer evening. Boats tie up at a few places along the lowest step, which is 2½ feet wide, but elsewhere there is no edge protection, and so walking along it can feel hazardous.

East of Hammarby Kaj, the promenade wends around a park, passes a ferry dock, and then runs along the southwest side of the Sickla canal, passing a line of pleasure boats. It is lined with residential buildings, with those near the ferry dock having ground floor restaurants. Here, the promenade is 28 feet wide and surfaced in concrete. Clusters of linden trees are set toward the middle of the promenade within an 8-foot-wide cobblestone strip. Benches facing the water are set under the trees. A simple metal railing lines the bulkhead. Down below, a 12-foot-wide wooden dock, along which people can walk, cantilevers from the bulkhead's side.

A very different kind of promenade runs along the other side of the Sickla canal and around a promontory that protrudes into the lake. Part of this promenade is a gravel path, but most of it is a 12-foot-wide wooden boardwalk, elevated over a constructed wetland. The main boardwalk meanders through reeds and under overhanging trees for almost a mile. A number of boardwalk spurs lead off into the reeds, ending at docks or seating platforms, where people go to sunbathe, eat a meal, or sit with friends. In some places, wood benches are mounted on the boardwalk. Elsewhere, narrow wooden platforms parallel the boardwalk one step down from it, offering more places to sit or lie down. In short, this is a very sylvan atmosphere. At night, the path is lighted with bollard downlights spaced about 24 feet apart which provide a gentle illumination, contributing to the bucolic feeling.

Beyond the boardwalk, the promenade continues around the lake and along the east side of the Danviks canal. It skirts a park and a wooden bathing platform, and then runs around a marina basin and along a canal. This area has many restaurants and can be lively at night, but the promenade itself has few places to sit and offers little shade.

Promenade Use

People from the neighborhood seem to be the main users of the Hammarby Sjöstad promenades, probably because there are many long-standing waterfront promenades around the city's more central islands and people from neighborhoods on those islands go to them. The boardwalk through the

The promenade along the southwest side of the Sickla Canal near the ferry dock

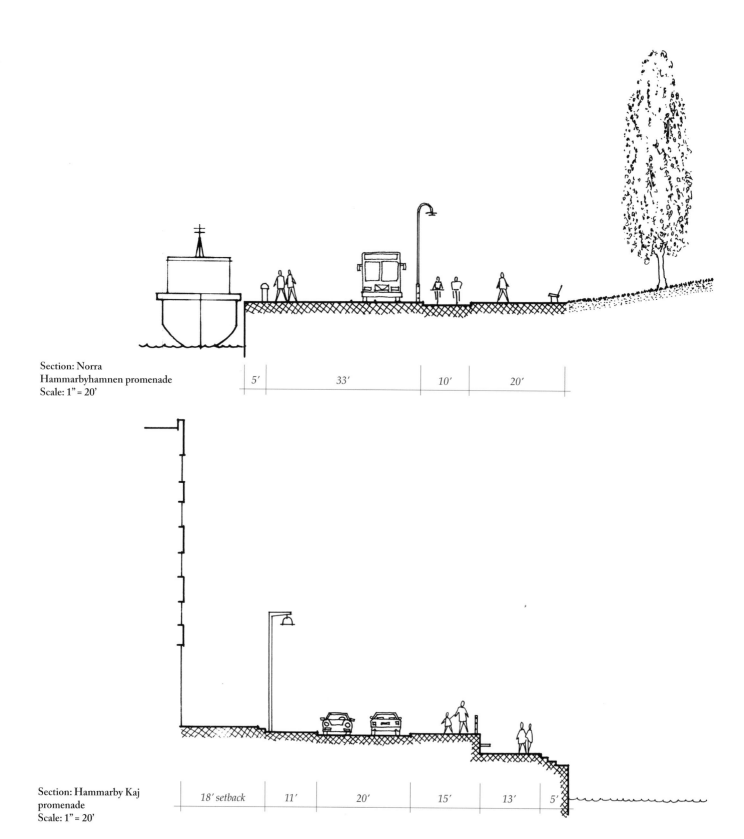

Section: Norra
Hammarbyhamnen promenade
Scale: 1" = 20'

5'   33'   10'   20'

Section: Hammarby Kaj
promenade
Scale: 1" = 20'

18' setback   11'   20'   15'   13'   5'

wetland is the most highly used. Late on a warm summer's evening, as the sun was slowly setting, 354 people per hour moved along it, most on foot (84%), the others biking. Most people were moving leisurely and most were with others, primarily in couples. Less than a quarter of the people observed were alone.

PART 1 An Assembly of Waterfront Promenades

The wetland boardwalk

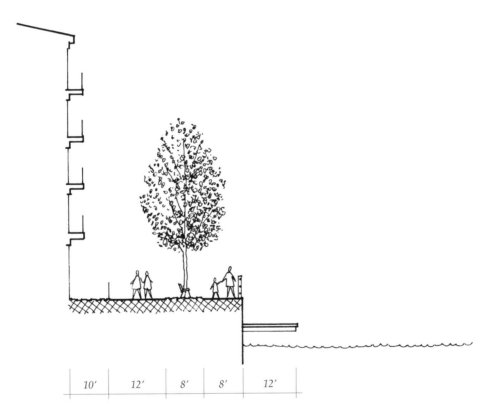

Section: Sickla Canal promenade
Scale: 1" = 20'

Hammarby Sjöstad's waterfront promenades have a comfortable neighborhood feel to them and they are clearly the district's main social gathering place for leisurely activity. The wetland boardwalk is the promenade most in consonance with the ecological focus of the district and also provides a signature identity for the neighborhood. Here, the soft marsh edge provides natural water management and the elevated boardwalk and platforms respect the marsh's functioning and help educate people about natural processes by bringing them into the marsh.

Climate Change and Sea Level Rise Concerns

The wetland boardwalk and community bathing platform

The Hammarby Sjöstad promenades are in an important location relative to Stockholm's complex sea level rise issues. The islands of central Stockholm sit astride four narrow passageways where Lake Mälaren connects with the Baltic Sea. The lake is Stockholm's main source of fresh water, and since 1943, locks and floodgates at these passages have maintained stable water levels in it, keeping salt water intrusion out during high tide events and releasing fresh water into the sea when lake level gets too high during flood events.[4] One of the floodgates is the Hammarby Canal lock at the west end of Hammarby Lake. Currently, the mean water level of Lake Mälaren is 66 centimeters (2.2 feet) above the mean water level of the Baltic Sea.[5] Future sea level rise of the Baltic Sea will be somewhat mitigated by land uplift, which has been occurring at the rate of 4 millimeters a year since the end of the last ice age when the glaciers that used to cover Sweden melted,[6] but it is predicted that by 2100 Lake Mälaren will be only 22 centimeters (8.66 inches) above the Baltic Sea.[7] Climate change will mean increased rainfall, more water flowing into Lake Mälaren, and more risk of flooding around the lake, but with a higher sea level it will be more difficult to discharge lake water into the sea and to keep saltwater intrusion out.[8]

The biggest floodgate between Lake Mälaren and the Baltic is at Slussen, which lies between Södermalm and Gamla Stan, the historic city center island. The city has for some time been planning to rebuild the Slussen lock and the highway and transit infrastructure associated with it. A plan prepared in 2008 envisions a massive renovation including new waterfront public spaces and new development, but controversy has held up its implementation. No plans have been made to rebuild the Hammarby Canal lock, but it's a good guess that something will be done to it in time, perhaps including something that will protect Hammarby Sjö from sea level rise. Meanwhile, the lake's bulkheads seem high enough to protect the neighborhood for some time to come.

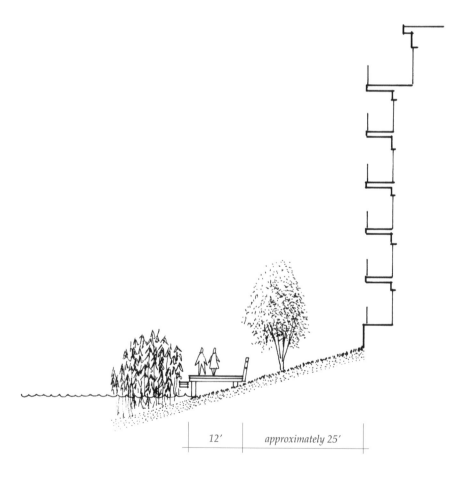

Section: Wetland Boardwalk, along the northeast side of Sickla Canal
Scale: 1" = 20'

12'   approximately 25'

Western Harbour Promenades, Malmö, Sweden

Promenades wrap the seafront of Malmö's Western Harbour ecological district being built on former industrial lands close to the city's downtown. Since their construction about a decade ago, the promenades and the parks through which they run have become among the city's most popular and frequented public open spaces, collectively functioning as something of an urban living room. The promenades are fronted mostly with residential buildings, plus a handful of restaurants and small eateries, and so have a neighborhood ambience. At the same time, they have a distinctly urban feel because of the many people who come to them and the social life that occurs on them. This is particularly true of one promenade segment, called Sundspromenaden (Sound Promenade), which is lined with a long wooden multi-stepped structure that is a favored place for gathering. This gregarious new public space is emblematic of the outgoing and forward-looking image the city is seeking to create for itself.

Malmö lies toward the southern tip of Sweden along the eastern shore of the wide sound that separates the Swedish peninsula from the islands of Denmark. With a population of about 300,000, it is Sweden's third largest city and a major commercial center. Long associated with industry, the city has over the last several decades rebranded itself as a "city of knowledge"[9] and the spearhead of this effort is the new eco-district.

The Western Harbour District, which will eventually cover approximately two-thirds of a square mile (432 acres or 175 hectares), sits on a peninsula of reclaimed land that was created in successive stages from the early 1900s through the mid-1980s, and long occupied by shipbuilding industries and then car manufacturing industries. In the early 1990s, after these industries had left, the city bought the land and began developing the eco-district. The newly founded University of Malmö opened there in 1998, and in 2001 a pedestrian-oriented neighborhood was built along the western edge of the peninsula as part of the European Housing Expo Bo01. Three more neighborhoods have since been built and more are being planned.[10]

The celebrated sustainability features of the district include energy efficient buildings, green roofs, permeable ground surfaces and an open storm water system, energy producing solar panels and

Storm water catchment strategies have been designed into the public realm throughout the Western Harbour District

wind turbines, a district heating and cooling system fueled by natural aquifers, and a community wide recycling system that generates biogas from food waste. A working port surrounded by industrial land abuts the eco-district's eastern edge, so some industrial ambience remains.

Promenade Design Characteristics

The sea-facing northern and western sides of the Western Harbour peninsula are lined with parks that link with an older park along the city's western beachfront. Walking and biking paths in the new parks link with a path in the beach park. Walkers and bikers mix on the new paths and are segregated, though just barely, on the older path. With the exception of the Sundspromenaden, all the paths are simply designed with emphasis being placed on structures that give access to the water.

Moving from east to west starting at the northeast tip of the peninsula, the walk begins with a narrow asphalt path running between a raised riprap revetment and wide, grassy lawns. Toward its middle, this path runs past a wide wooden deck that gives access to three bathing piers. Turning a corner and heading south, the path diverges into two separate paths that go around a landscaped area. One path, surfaced with decomposed granite, runs at the water's edge along a parapet wall that tops a steeply inclined riprap embankment. The other runs at the edge of buildings facing the park, and is surfaced with pavers. The water's edge path gives access to a large elevated viewing platform and to three sets of steps leading down to circular bathing platforms. The paved and unpaved paths come together at a broad plaza, which juts over the sea at an angle.

Next comes the Sundspromenaden, beyond which the path leads south through a wide plaza fronting a small marina, crosses a short wood plank bridge spanning a short canal, and then runs along the side of a longer canal, eventually merging with the almost two-mile-long Ribersborgsstigen path that runs along a series of grassy meadows lying back of dunes fronting the beach. This asphalt-paved path is 25 feet wide and has a white strip painted down its middle and painted icons signifying that

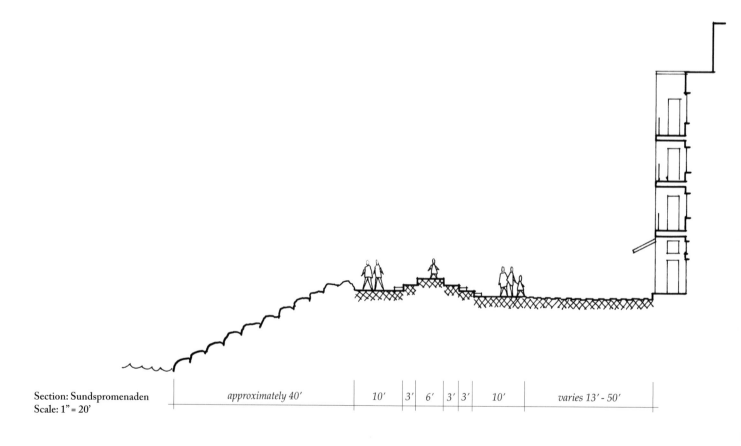

Section: Sundspromenaden
Scale: 1" = 20'

| approximately 40' | 10' | 3' | 6' | 3' | 3' | 10' | varies 13' - 50' |

Sundspromenaden in the early
evening

bikers should keep to the outside and walkers to the inside. Along its length, it gives access to paths
leading across the meadows, dunes, and beach to ten bathing piers, some long and elaborately designed
and others more modest.

The Sundspromenaden segment is about 720 feet long and consists of a multi-level boardwalk
backed by an asphalt path. The dimensions are modest: a 10-foot-wide boardwalk path closest to the
water, a 6-foot-wide raised boardwalk flanked on both sides by continuous 3-foot-wide steps, and a
10-foot-wide asphalt path on the inland side. The promenade sits atop a high riprap embankment and
gives access to the water at one location via broad steps leading down to a bathing platform. There is
no shade along the Sundspromenaden, or any of the other promenades, but this is the far north and
Swedes apparently like to be in the sun whenever they can.

Five-story residential buildings front the Sundspromenaden, some of which have restaurants or
cafés at the ground floor. The buildings are set at an angle to the promenade, creating a series of saw-
toothed plazas at the edge of the promenade's asphalt path, onto which people can and do overflow.
Similar buildings front the park spaces further north. These buildings are designed to provide wind
protection for lower-scale residential buildings inland, because winter winds off the Øresund can
be vicious.

Promenade Use and Connectivity

Bathing platform along the
Sundspromenaden

People use all of the Western Harbour promenades when the weather is the least bit good,
with late afternoons and evenings being particularly popular times to visit them, especially in

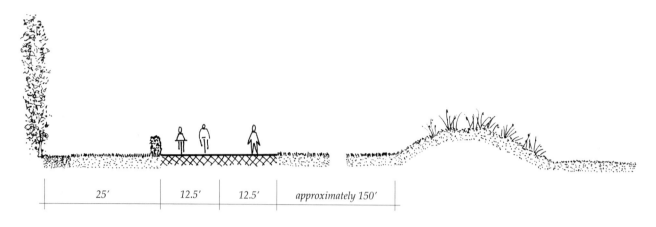

25' 12.5' 12.5' approximately 150'

Section: Ribersborgsstigen path
Scale: 1" = 20'

Ribersborgsstigen path on a
Sunday morning

the summer. The Sundspromenaden is generally the most active area in the evening. On warm summer nights, the step along the raised platform facing the water is often completely full of people watching the long, slow sunset, many enjoying a picnic meal, complete with wine. One hundred and thirty-one people were observed sitting there at 8:15 pm on a Saturday night in July. At the same time, 1,299 people per hour were moving along the promenade. A few used the outer boardwalk at the water's edge, but most pedestrians and all the cyclists used the inner asphalt path, perhaps out of courtesy to not interrupt the views of those sitting. Most people were strolling (80%) and the rest were biking. Most were in couples or groups. Because of the constrained space, everyone was moving slowly, but nobody seemed to mind. In all, the atmosphere was calm and relaxed. Just north of the promenade, on the broad plaza angling over the water, couples were tango-dancing to soft music.

The promenade along the
northern tip of the Western
Harbour

Strolling along the Sundspromenaden in the late afternoon

Tango dancing at sunset on the platform at the northern end of the Sundspromenaden

The Sundspromenaden illustrates how much can be achieved with a promenade that is relatively narrow and not very long. Key to its success is an abundance of seating that is conducive to social gathering, and the relaxed atmosphere generated by the lack of any nearby vehicle traffic and the moderate amount of commercial activity.

Fewer people promenade along the Ribersborgsstigen path, which is more of an exercise trail than a promenade. On a sunny Sunday morning in May, 357 people per hour were observed moving along it, almost 60 percent on bikes.

The many people who visit the Sundspromenaden and the other new park promenades get there by walking, cycling, or public transit. In keeping with the eco-district objectives, few nearby parking areas have been provided but even though the promenades are at some remove from the rest of the city they are easily accessible via the city's extensive system of connected bicycle and walking paths and two bus lines. The neighborhood adjacent to the promenade is largely pedestrianized and otherwise traffic-calmed so it is not necessary to cross major traffic streets to get to the waterfront. Access to the Ribersborgsstigen path and to the beach can be had at several park entries, serviced by car parking lots, public transit stops, and pedestrian and bicycle paths.

Climate Change and Sea Level Rise Concerns

Like so many other coastal cities, Malmö faces challenges from future sea level rise related to climate change. Sweden's land mass is experiencing uplift, so the relative local sea level rise along Malmö's coast will be less than the global average, but is still projected to be sizable.[11] The Western Harbour District was planned around the assumption that by 2100 the sea level will have risen .22 to .66 meters (.72 to 2.2 feet) above the current level, and that extreme flood heights could reach 3 meters (9.8 feet). The western edge of the Western Harbour district where the Sundspromenaden is located sits above the 3-meter line and the revetment in front of the promenade is designed to protect against wave action, so it is in a position of some safety. However, other parts of the Western Harbour, as well as the beach area to the southwest and parts of the central city just inland, are lower than 3 meters and so some protective action will at some time become necessary. Meanwhile, the city has enacted a policy that requires all new buildings be constructed with ground floors raised above the 3-meter flood zone.[12]

On the one hand, the sea level rise predictions are ominous. On the other hand, the city seems up to the many challenges, given its ecological awareness. Answers to Malmö's specific problems may not be known now but recent history suggests that the city will look for answers and put them into operation as becomes necessary.

HafenCity Promenades, Hamburg, Germany

Since 2002, a major new mixed-use development, HafenCity, has been under construction in Hamburg on former docklands protruding into the Elbe River near the historic city center. A series of innovatively designed promenades, meant to sometimes flood, line the water's edge of areas so far developed, and more floodable promenades will be built in future development phases.

Hamburg, which sprawls along both banks of the Elbe River some 65 miles upstream from the North Sea, is Germany's second largest city and its largest port. HafenCity is replacing just a small part of the port but is a monumental undertaking that will expand Hamburg's city area by 40 percent. The development is being built from west to east in ten different neighborhoods, with completion expected by 2025. In all, it will occupy 388 acres (157 hectares), 20 percent of it water. Plans call for a total gross floor space of 2.32 million square meters, to include housing for 12,000 people and space for 45,000 service and office jobs.[13] Major cultural facilities include a new HafenCity University and a philharmonic concert hall. Recreational facilities include a number of parks and over 10.5 kilometers (6.5 miles) of waterfront promenades.

The particular qualities of the Elbe River have contributed to HafenCity's unique design. The Elbe River is one of Europe's major rivers, draining a catchment area of over 57,000 square miles. From the coast to a weir beyond Hamburg, it has significant twice-daily tidal cycles, with a tidal range of 3.6 meters (12 feet) at Hamburg.[14] Storm surge can elevate the water even higher. While central Hamburg is protected from flooding by a high dike, HafenCity sits outside the dike, occupying a series of layered quays that stretch parallel to the river's edge from a landmass that was originally an island in the river. The self-imposed challenge was how to develop the quays with flood protection and yet allow people to get close to the water. The design solution was to raise habitable spaces above the flood level and create floodable promenades at a lower level.

Throughout HafenCity, roadways and building ground floors are set at 7.3 meters (23.9 feet) above mean sea level (MSL), matching the flood protection benchmark set for the central city, but the promenades along the edges of the quays are at the original quay height of 4.5 to 5.5 meters

Sandtorhafen harbor basin, with the Sandtorkai promenade on the left

Grasbrookhafen harbor basin, looking over the Dalmannkai promenade

(13.1 to 16.4 feet) above MSL. Building basements along the promenades contain parking garages enclosed in "bathtub" containers, some of which are lined with retail spaces and cafés that can be closed off with massive steel panels during very high water, others of which present blank walls to the promenades.

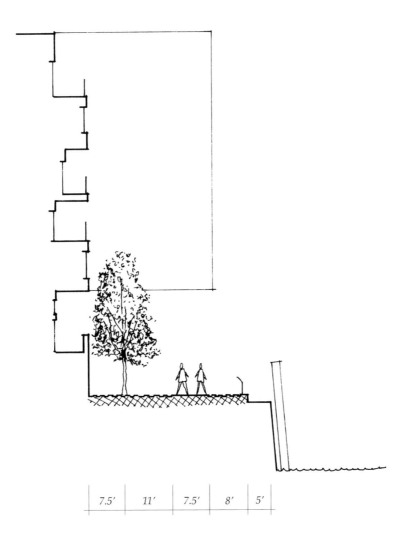

Section: Kaiserkai promenade
Scale: 1" = 20'

| 7.5′ | 11′ | 7.5′ | 8′ | 5′ |

Promenade Design Characteristics

The promenades in the first completed neighborhood, Am Sandtorkai/Dalmannkai, are representative of how the promenades are being designed. The neighborhood is structured around two harbor basins. The inner basin, Sandtorhafen, has promenades along both sides of it, and also another promenade atop a line of pontoons floating on the water, which provide moorage for traditional harbor craft. The outer harbor basin, Grasbrookhafen, has a promenade along its north side.

The promenades lining Sandtorhafen are each different. The one on the south side, Kaiserkai, is 34 feet wide and the one on the north side, Sandtorkai, is 14 feet wide. Neither have any commercial spaces along them, so the walks are along blank facades. Along the latter, cantilevered buildings overhang the walkway some 35 feet overhead, giving a sense of enclosure to the promenade that is not always comfortable. The cobblestone surface has a 6-foot-wide concrete path toward the center. Occasional benches are placed at the building line. Kaiserkai has a more open feel, several small trees along it, and only a handful of benches. The floating pontoon walk is 40 to 65 feet wide and accessible via two gangway ramps from the north side promenade and a third from the plaza at the head of the harbor.

The Dalmannkai promenade along Grasbrookhafen is about 47 feet wide and has commercial uses fronting onto it, including restaurants and cafés whose tables spill onto the promenade, plus a few small shops whose wares also spill out. The promenade is surfaced with cobblestones except for a 7-foot-wide concrete band that is the walking/cycling throughway. There are some benches in the cobblestone areas on both sides of the path and some trees along the inner area that are widely spaced

The blank facades along the Kaiserkai promenade are embellished with art

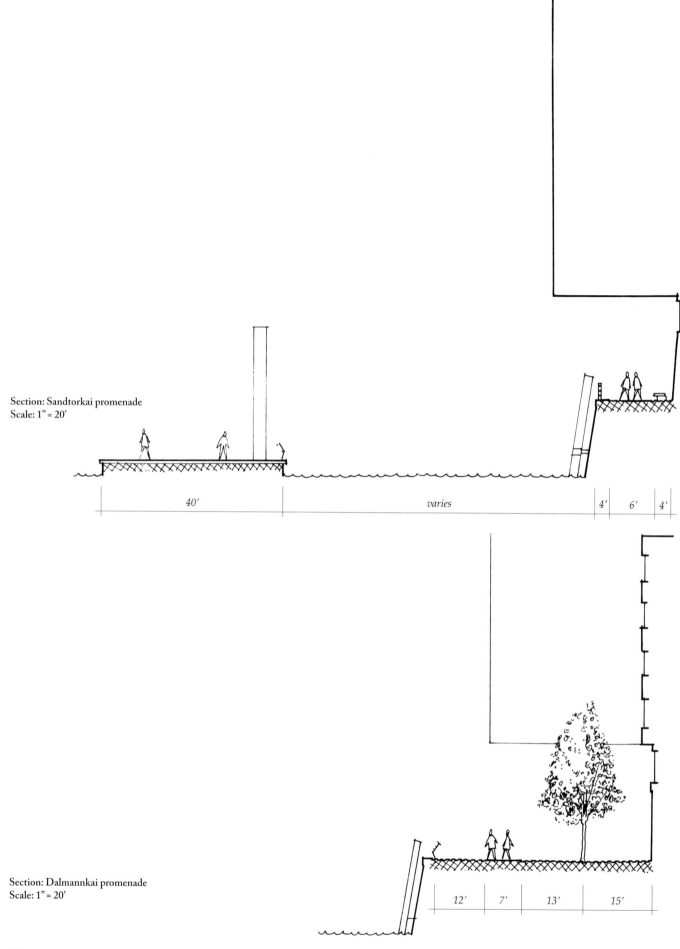

Section: Sandtorkai promenade
Scale: 1" = 20'

40'   varies   4'   6'   4'

Section: Dalmannkai promenade
Scale: 1" = 20'

12'   7'   13'   15'

and as yet small, not offering much shade. A tree-lined linear park lies along the outer edge of the promenade at its western end, and beyond this is a ferry dock.

Promenade Use and Connectivity

From within HafenCity the promenades are easily accessible via broad stairs at the harbor basin heads into which ramps serving both wheelchairs and bicycles have been integrated. The promenades can also be reached mid-block by wide stairs into which sitting places are integrated. However, access to the promenades from the city center is very constrained, limited to four bridges that span the Zollkanal and the historic Speicherstadt district of former warehouses that lie between this part of HafenCity and the city's dike. A new rapid transit line under construction will eventually better connect HafenCity with the rest of the city, making the promenades more accessible.

For now, the lack of easy access to HafenCity from the rest of the city is likely the reason the promenades do not yet see much regular activity. On weekdays, the promenades are most used during the lunch hour, but numbers are not high. Office workers walk along the promenade on the north side of Sandtorhafen going to and from the district's many eating establishments, joined by handfuls of tourists. On an overcast day in late July 2014, 549 people per hour were observed moving along the promenade around noon, only a handful on bikes. Almost as many people were strolling along Grasbrookhafen during the noon hour, many on their way to or from the cafés or the ferry dock or just strolling along enjoying views of the river that this promenade affords. On summer weekends, the open plazas at the quay heads are programmed with special events, such as concerts, which draw people to HafenCity and more people to the promenades. Likely, there will be more activity on the promenades in the future after HafenCity is completely developed and more people are living and working here.

Climate Change and Sea Level Rise Concerns

The Elbe River is going to be impacted by future sea level rise because its fluvial dynamics are closely connected with those of the North Sea. The North Sea has frequent storms and the associated storm

Dalmannkai promenade during lunch hour

Sandtorkai promenade during lunch hour

surge reaches up the Elbe Estuary to Hamburg. With climate change, the frequency and severity of storms is expected to increase and hence Hamburg stands to experience more frequent and larger storm surge events in the future. The city's 7.3-meter-high dike was built following the major flood of 1962 that inundated a large part of city, destroyed over 20,000 buildings, and killed over 300 people.[15] The question is whether this benchmark, which was used to set the ground height in HafenCity, will be adequate to contain flooding in the future. Sea level rise along Germany's coast is expected to be close to the global average, and some of the rise would translate up the Elbe River.[16] The Intergovernmental Panel on Climate Change projects that global sea level might rise by as much as .98 meters (3.2 feet) by 2100.[17] Should this much rise occur, HafenCity's promenades could by overtopped by regular tidal flows, as well as during flood events. Floods have inundated the promenades several times since they were built, most notably in 2013. It is likely that the promenades will be inundated more frequently as time goes on.

The approach taken with the promenades at HafenCity, allowing them to flood periodically, offers a possible approach that could be taken by other cities in adapting their existing promenades to sea level rise as well as in the planning of new ones.

Notes

1 "Hammarby Sjöstad – a New City District with Emphasis on Water and Ecology" (GlashusEtt, 2011; Development Office, Box 8189, SE-104 20 Stockholm, Sweden).
2 Peter Bächtold, *The Space-Economic Transformation of the City: Towards Sustainability* (Dordrecht; New York: Springer, 2013), 98.
3 Ibid., 98–101.
4 L. Phil Graham, Johan Andréasson, and Gunn Persson, "Impacts of Future Climate Change and Sea Level Rise in the Stockholm Region: Part I – The Effect on Water Levels in Lake Mälaren," *Geological Survey of Finland*, no. Special Paper 41 (2006): 131–132.
5 Ibid.
6 Nina Ekelund, "Adapting to Climate Change in Stockholm" (The City of Stockholm, Stockhom's Action Programme on Climate Change, March 2007), 12.

7   Stockholm Stad, "New Slussen – on the Way to a World-Class Stockholm," n.d., 13, accessed September 20, 2015, http://international.stockholm.se/globalassets/ovriga-bilder-och-filer/slussen-broschyr_eng_webb.pdf.

8   Nina Ekelund, "Adapting to Climate Change in Stockholm," 13–15.

9   Anonymous, "Malmö Stad," text, accessed August 22, 2015, http://malmo.se/English.html.

10   "Guide Western Harbour" (The City of Malmö Environment Department, 2012), accessed August 22, 2015, http://malmo.se/download/18.3744cbfb13a77097d879d4e/1383649554922/Guide_Western_Harbour_2012_Web.pdf.

11   "Global and European Sea-Level Rise (CLIM 012) – Assessment Published Sep 2014" (European Environment Agency, 2014), accessed July 22, 2015, www.eea.europa.eu/data-and-maps/indicators/sea-level-rise-2/assessment.

12   "Climate Adaptation Strategy The City of Malmö" (Malmö Stad, n.d.), 18–19.

13   André Stark, ed., "HafenCity Hamburg Essentials Quarters Projects" (HafenCity Hamburg GmbH, March 2014), 67–69, accessed August 10, 2015, www.hafencity.com/upload/files/files/Internet_Projekte_engl_final.pdf.

14   TIDE-Tidal River Development, "Tide Facts: The Elbe River Estuary," n.d., http://tide-project.eu/downloads/0_Elbe_Factsheet.pdf., accessed August 10, 2015.

15   M. V. Mikhailova, "Interaction of Tides and Storm Surges at the Elbe River Mouth," *Water Resources* 38, no. 3 (2011): 283–96.

16   "Global and European Sea-Level Rise (CLIM 012) Assessment Published Sep 2014."

17   J. A. Church et al., "2013: Sea Level Change," in *Climate Change 2013: The Physical Science Basis. Contribution of Working Group I to the Fifth Assessment Report of the Intergovernmental Panel on Climate Change* [Stocker, T.F., D. Qin, G.-K. Plattner, M. Tignor, S.K. Allen, J. Boschung, A. Nauels, Y. Xia, V. Bex, and P.M. Midgley (eds)]. (Cambridge, United Kingdom and New York, NY, USA: Cambridge University Press, 2013), 1182.

Chapter 9

Suburban New Town Promenades

Urban waterfront promenades are usually associated with large cities or beach cities, but some have been built in suburban or otherwise peripheral locations, including in planned New Towns. During the mid-twentieth century, some national governments began programs to build satellite New Towns away from established urban centers. The purpose of many New Towns was to provide housing and employment opportunities for an expanding population while containing the sprawl of central cities. A purpose of others was to stimulate economic development of underdeveloped areas. Some of the planned New Towns have waterfront locations and some of these have waterfront promenades that are quite modest in their design. There is much to be learned from their modesty.

Ma On Shan Promenade, Hong Kong, China

Scale: 1:400,000

Much of the long water's edge of Ma On Shan New Town in Hong Kong's New Territories is lined with a pedestrian promenade and bicycle path. The promenade is new, although the town has been under development since the early 1980s. It has quickly come to symbolize the town's identity and, more important, ties the whole community together.

Ma On Shan is a relatively typical Hong Kong New Town. Hong Kong began building New Towns in the late 1950s to alleviate overcrowding in its central districts on Hong Kong Island and Kowloon.[1] The New Towns are planned to be self-contained communities, where people can both live and work, and are developed at high densities. Most buildings are high-rise residential towers set in superblocks. A high proportion of buildings are public housing estates but there are also many privately developed buildings in which residents own their units.

The Sha Tin New Town District, of which Ma On Shan is a part, dates from 1967.[2] Its development began in a river valley running inland from an inlet of Tolo Harbour. The valley lies on the north side of the Kowloon Peninsula, separated from central Hong Kong by a mountain range, through which a tunnel was bored. Part of the town was built on land reclaimed from the harbour and a straight channel was created through the fill to extend the Shing Mun River from the natural valley to the new coastline. The town was designed to be bicycle friendly and bike paths were built along both sides of the river. The Ma On Shan extension of Sha Tin began in the 1980s and it is now considered to be a separate New Town. Starting east of the mouth of the Shing Mun River, it occupies a narrow strip of mostly reclaimed land that lies between Tolo Harbour and Ma On Shan Mountain. The town covers three and a half square miles (900 hectares)[3] and currently has a population of just about 215,000 people.[4]

Ma On Shan's waterfront promenade was built in 2010 in conjunction with a reconstruction and enlargement of the town's seawall, done in order to provide more community open space.[5] Previously, the water's edge had been lined with a narrow bicycle path, beyond which land sloped steeply down to a seawall, protected with riprap. A new, higher seawall was built terraced back from the first and lined with more riprap, resulting in a tiered edge protection system.[6] The promenade was built on flat land created between the new seawall and the bicycle path. Two miles long and occupying almost 13 acres of land (5.2 hectares),[7] it was achieved at a cost of $220 million Hong Kong dollars (US$28.38 million).[8]

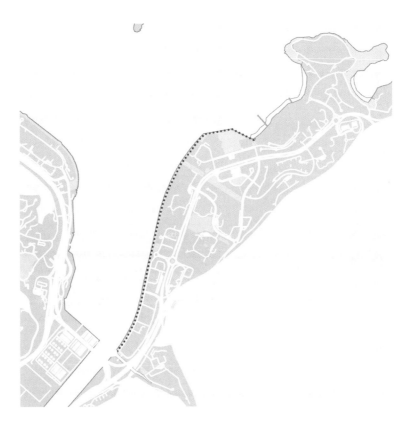

Scale: 1:40,000

The promenade offers bucolic views over the water toward tall mountains on the other side of the harbour. Small fishing boats and small ferries ply the waters. There are no big ships as this is not a commercial harbour. Inland views are of an almost solid line of high-rises, generally 25 to 37 stories high, so densely placed that they completely conceal Ma On Shan Mountain, which lies just behind them.

Promenade Design Characteristics

The promenade is all of a piece in its overall design, but different sections vary in their layout. All along, a 15-foot-wide walkway lines the water's edge and a 9- to 11-foot-wide two-way bicycle track lines the inland edge. The area between the walk and the bicycle path varies in design from place to place. For about two-thirds of the promenade a jogging track marked with directional lanes runs through this zone, winding through heavily planted spaces. A number of fitness stations, some designated for the elderly, are scattered along the track. Elsewhere there are children's play areas, tai chi areas, public toilet facilities, and benches set under shade-giving structures. The water's edge walkway is in full sun for much of the day, only when the sun is low in the sky does it become shaded by the shadows of the adjacent buildings.

The promenade's design details are straightforward and somewhat playful. Ground surfaces are colorful: red for the bicycle lanes, two shades of blue for the jogging track, and swirls of pink, blue, and gray pavers for the walking path. The water's edge is lined with a tall sloping curb (a wave wall) topped with a sturdy metal rail, which is higher than a typical guardrail to discourage people from climbing over it to get to the top of the lower seawall below. Some people climb over it anyway, in order to fish off the lower seawall. The inner edge of the walking path is lined with closely spaced (30 feet on center) 30-foot-tall double-headed light fixtures, which at night illuminate both the walkway and the planted exercise areas. Other lights illuminate the bench pavilions. A goal of the promenade project was to promote environmental consciousness, and so arrayed along it are several hybrid solar and wind lamps, and also three wind turbines that provide some of the electricity used by the other light fixtures.[9]

High-rise buildings line the promenade

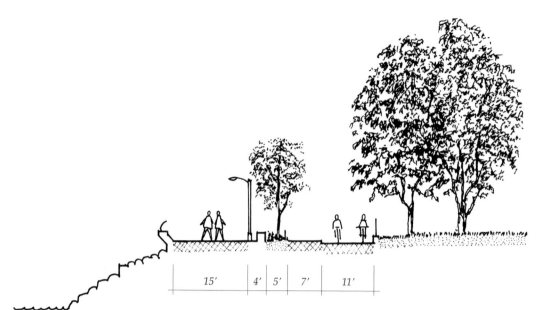

Section: Ma On Shan
Promenade, near Ma On Shan
Park
Scale: 1" = 20'

| 15' | 4' | 5' | 7' | 11' |

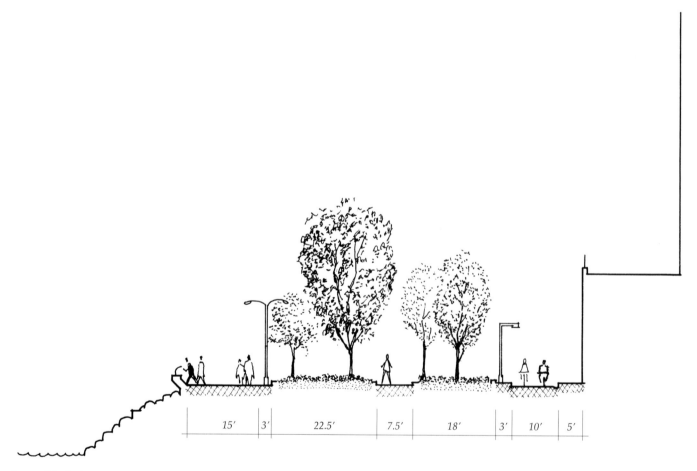

Section: Ma On Shan
Promenade, where fitness trail
occurs
Scale: 1" = 20'

| 15' | 3' | 22.5' | 7.5' | 18' | 3' | 10' | 5' |

The tiered seawall and tall buildings along Ma On Shan Promenade

Promenade Use and Connectivity

People using the Ma On Shan Promenade are mostly local residents or people who live in the greater Sha Tin District. It is not a place that attracts many tourists, because getting to it from Hong Kong Island takes about an hour by rapid transit (MTR) and the ride involves at least three train transfers. Several small beaches lying just east of Ma On Shan arc well celebrated on social media and do attract some visitors from out of the area, but the promenade is not well advertised. For those who do come by rapid transit, there is the option to get off at any of the three stops that serve Ma On Shan, and from them it is relatively easy to get to the waterfront promenade. The easternmost stop, Ma On Shan Station, gives the best access. From this station, people can walk through a popular air-conditioned shopping mall, take overhead walkways across two busy streets, walk down a ramp into a large public park, and then walk through the park to the promenade. Between the elevated MTR tracks and most of the rest of the waterfront are large superblocks built with residential complexes that have towers rising from multi-level podiums. Access from the other stations is via big streets running between the superblocks or pedestrian paths running through them. People can cross the bike lanes to get to the promenade via marked crosswalks at 15 locations.

On a hot and humid Sunday morning in late May, 333 people moved along the promenade in an hour: 50 percent biking, 28 percent strolling, and 22 percent jogging or fast-walking. By mid-afternoon, overall numbers had increased to 582 people per hour with a slightly larger proportion of people strolling, and slightly fewer people biking or jogging. People strolled in groups or on their own, and many seemed to be walking long distances. Bikers included many males on their own, many family groups with small children, and some groups of young people. All day, the park adjacent to the promenade was full of lounging Filipinas, who according to a local resident were domestic servants enjoying their time off. A small handful of them also took walks along the promenade.

Ma On Shan Promenade near Ma On Shan Park

Ma On Shan Promenade fitness trail

Ma On Shan bicycle track where it passes a public housing estate

Hybrid solar and wind light fixtures are are arrayed along the promenade

The Ma On Shan waterfront promenade represents a very large public investment in a non-central and non-tourist-oriented location. The goal was to improve livability for residents already living nearby rather than to spur new development or to draw outsiders and increase economic activity. The promenade is designed to serve local needs, including the exercise needs of people of all ages. Along with the adjacent park, it has become the community's major outdoor public gathering space.

Climate Change and Sea Level Rise Concerns

With its armored, double-tiered seawall, the Ma On Shan promenade seems well protected from coastal flooding and from future sea level rise. However, Hong Kong typically experiences six to seven tropical cyclones every year and Tolo Harbour is particularly susceptible to high storm surge, more so than central Victoria Harbour. Past typhoons, such as Typhoon Hope, which struck in 1979, have caused storm surge in excess of 3 meters.[10] With Hong Kong's local sea level projected to rise as much as 1.07 meters (42 inches) by 2100,[11] and tropical cyclones expected to increase in both frequency and severity,[12] future challenges may be in store.

Waterfront Promenades, Gruissan, France

Scale: 1:400,000

Gruissan, a small town of fewer than 5,000 people on the shore of the Mediterranean Sea in the Languedoc-Roussillon region of southwestern France, has almost 4 miles of waterfront promenades. The promenades were built in the 1970s, when a state-sponsored tourist resort was appended to the tiny fishing village of Gruissan, which dates from the Middle Ages. A mile-long promenade runs along a beachfront facing the sea, another mile-long promenade runs along a protected lagoon, and the rest, connected with the latter, run around the multiple basins of the town's 1,300 berth marina. The promenades are of simple but highly attractive design, reflecting the nature of the town itself, although grander ambitions were once envisioned.

In the early 1960s, the French government embarked on an ambitious program to turn the marshy and windswept 180-kilometer long Languedoc-Roussillon coastline into a beach vacation destination for tourists from France and northern Europe, a plan that has been described as the largest state-sponsored tourist development in Europe.[13] The idea was to strengthen and diversify the economy of this largely underdeveloped area and attract as many tourists as the French Riviera further to the east.[14] The state acquired coastal land and planned five seaside resorts, including Gruissan, to be separated by natural areas.[15] Different architects were appointed to design each town and the initial plans for all of them called for building modernist mega-structures inspired by the work of Le Corbusier.[16]

Several of the towns were built with mega-structures, but existing residents of Gruissan objected to that approach and demanded something that would fit in better with the local Mediterranean context.[17] In response, a plan emerged for low-scale development and an architectural style of rounded rooftops inspired by the shape of waves and sand dunes and partially modeled on traditional buildings of North Africa. In keeping with a mandate to meet growing demands for moderately priced beach vacations, several waterfront areas were set aside as camping spots.[18] Wine growing areas around the town were protected as permanent open space with the establishment of the Massif de la Clape Conservation Area and working salt ponds that had once been Gruissan's main industry were also retained.

Scale: 1:40,000

Gruissan old town

The New Town was built on land created out of the marshy lagoon, the Etang du Grazel, which lay between the old fishing village and the outlying spit of beach fronting the Mediterranean. Part of the pond was dredged to create a marina and lagoon, and spoils from the dredging were used to fill surrounding areas to above sea level.[19] A massive mosquito abatement program was also undertaken and annual spraying continues.

Promenade Design Characteristics

Gruissan now has three distinct parts: the old town, which has a unique circular form centered around a ruined hilltop castle; the new town, which is focused on the marina and the lagoon; and, along a beach spit, a sizable gridded area of modest beach chalets raised on stilts, most of which were built in the 1920s and 1940s and have since been modernized. While the old town has several plazas in it where people gather and where weekly markets are held, the waterfront promenades are the main public open spaces in the other two areas, along with the beaches.

The water's edge of the New Town is almost entirely pedestrianized. Most of the roadways and parking lots serving buildings are held back from the water's edge and most of the waterfront walks have buildings facing directly onto them. Around the central marina basin are three- and four-story buildings with restaurants and shops at the ground floor, and apartment and hotel units above. Here, the promenade consists of a somewhat undefined space at the edge of tables and displays spilling out from the restaurants and shops. Two marina basins beyond the central area are also partially lined with low multi-family residential buildings, without commercial uses. Here the promenade becomes a wide paved walk lined with a row of palm trees running down its middle.

Along the lagoon, which stretches east from the central area, are one- and two-story row houses and single-family dwellings, all with gardens in front. Here the promenade is more designed. It varies in width from 12 to 17 feet and in many places is lined with palm trees, sometimes planted in a grass lawn. Along its length are playfully designed light fixtures with bright blue tops, and occasional wood benches that are also bright blue. A narrow beach lines the lagoon, and the promenade is raised about 6 feet above it. A low wall running between the promenade and the beach protects inland areas against high tides and storm surge. The occasional portals through the wall are designed to be closed off with boards should the need arise. In a few places, simple benches are mounted on top of the wall. The small front yards facing the promenade are all well landscaped with an abundance of flowering plants, often oleander and lavender. Toward its far end, the promenade crosses a small suspension bridge, artfully designed of wood and galvanized steel, which spans a canal feeding into the lagoon. Most of the houses along the promenade are of modest size and similar in their design, but some at the far end are quite large and of custom design.

The beachfront promenade is part of a raised lineal landscape structure built to protect the beach chalets beyond it from the flooding that occurs when the strong easterly winds that often hit

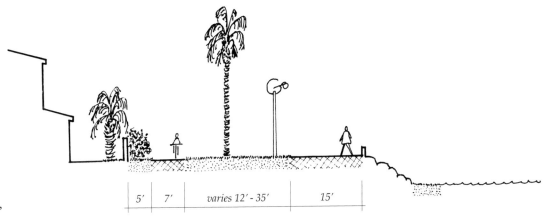

Section: Gruissan Promenade, along the lagoon
Scale: 1" = 20'

5'   7'   varies 12' - 35'   15'

Promenade along the central marina

Promenade along the lagoon

Promenade along the beach

PART 1 An Assembly of Waterfront Promenades

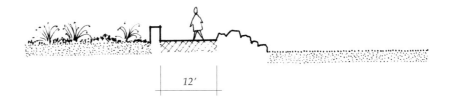

12'

this coast coincide with high tide events. The promenade is raised about 3 feet above beach level and is very simply designed. It is 12 feet wide, surfaced with pink concrete (faded from red), and lined with wide swaths of stone riprap boulders along its beach side and a low wall of rustic construction on its inland side. The promenade follows an irregular path of arcs and tangents as it skirts the saw-toothed edge of the angled grid of streets on which the chalets are built. Most of the streets end in triangular plots of open land that are used as parking areas. Planting strips of varying width mediate between the promenade and the parking areas and this is where occasional benches facing landward rather than the sea are located, an odd placement possibly responding to the heavy winds that blow off the sea.

A recreational vehicle campsite sits at one end of the promenade and here is a line of color-fully decorated carts vending ice cream and beach fare. There is also a small sailing club and a shop that rents stand-up paddleboards, jet skis and open-top dune buggies that can be driven on the beach. At the other end of the promenade, separated from it by a stretch of road, is a working oyster fishery.

Pedestrian bridge along the lagoon promenade, where it crosses a canal

Rustic detailing along the beach promenade

Promenade Use

On summer evenings the walkways around the central marina area are usually full of people, who go there for meals, to get ice cream, and to watch the various entertainments that the town puts on. The other walkways, around the other marina basins and along the lagoon, are understandably less peopled but are used for strolling. A weekly morning market sets up along one section near the marina and many people walk or bike along the promenade on their way to and from it. The beachfront promenade is seldom very active, perhaps because it is often very windy, but some people do stroll or bike along it, usually moving slowly and in small groups.

Gruissan is a town for everyman and its promenades are as well, which is a large part of their charm. In building the New Towns, the state hoped to attract an upper income national and international market to the coastal areas of Languedoc-Roussillon. Gruissan has instead attracted a middle-class largely regional market.[20] Modest evidence of some wealth can be seen in the many large yachts moored in the marina, the several yacht brokerages with more yachts on display and for sale, and the custom-designed houses fronting the water at the far end of the lagoon. However, most of the boats in the marina are not fancy yachts and most of the dwellings are modest.

Climate Change and Sea Level Rise Concerns

All of Gruissan's promenades are relatively low-lying and so will be impacted by sea level rise. The European Environment Agency projects that relative local sea level rise along France's western Mediterranean coast will be similar to the average global sea level rise,[21] which according to recent projections of the Intergovernmental Panel on Climate Change is likely to be between .42 to .98 meters (1.4 to 3.2 feet) by 2100.[22] A sea level rise of even the lower range of the projections would leave very little freeboard along the promenades lining the marina and lagoon. These water bodies are protected from wave action by breakwaters and the beach spit, but are subject to tidal flows, storm surge, and wind-driven high water, and so with sea level rise they are likely to flood. Gruissan's beach sees wave action as well as the other phenomena, and so with sea level rise it may be subject to damage during storm events. As of yet, the town has not developed a sea level rise adaptation plan.

Notes

1 Eddie C. M. Hui and Manfred C. M. Lam, "A Study of Commuting Patterns of New Town Residents in Hong Kong," *Habitat International* 29, no. 3 (September 2005): 421–437, accessed August 12, 2015, doi:10.1016/j.habitatint.2004.01.001.
2 Peter Hills and Anthony G.O. Yeh, "New Town Developments in Hong Kong," *Built Environment (1978–)* 9, no. 3/4 (January 1, 1983): 266.
3 Ibid., 272.
4 "Hong Kong: Districts, Major Cities & Towns – Population Statistics in Maps and Charts," accessed August 15, 2015, www.citypopulation.de/Hongkong.html.
5 "Item for Public Works Subcommittee of Finance Committee, 395RO-Ma On Shan Waterfront Promenade," December 19, 2006, 3, accessed August 14, 2015, www.legco.gov.hk/yr06-07/english/fc/pwsc/papers/p06-53e.pdf.
6 "CEDD Contract No. CV/2006/06," accessed October 12, 2015, www.manking.com.hk/index.php?route=product/product&product_id=3898.
7 Ibid.
8 "Leisure and Cultural Services Department – Press Releases," accessed August 17, 2015, www.lcsd.gov.hk/en/news/press_details.php?id=2830.
9 Ibid.
10 T. C. Lee and C. F. Wong, "Historical Storm Surges and Storm Surge Forecasting in Hong Kong; Hong Kong Observatory Reprint 734" (JCOMM Scientific and Technical Symposium on Storm Surges (SSS), Seoul, Republic of Korea, 2 – 10/6 2007), 2–3, accessed October 11, 2015, www.iwaponline.com/wpt/006/0081/0060081.pdf.
11 "Projections of Hong Kong Climate for the 21st Century – Mean Sea Level Projection," accessed October 6, 2015, www.hko.gov.hk/climate_change/proj_hk_msl_e.htm.
12 B.Y. Lee, W.T. Wong, and W.C. Woo, "Sea-Level Rise and Storm Surge – Impacts of Climate Change on Hong Kong," April 12, 2010, 4, accessed July 29, 2015, www.weather.gov.hk/publica/reprint/r915.pdf.
13 Ellen Furlough, "Vacations and Citizenship in Post-war France," *The Journal of Twentieth-Century/Contemporary French Studies Revue d'Études Français* 5, no. 1 (2001): 125.
14 F. Roy Willis, "The Languedoc Littoral Tourism as an Instrument of Regional Economic Growth," *Growth and Change* 8, no. 2 (April 1, 1977): 44, doi:10.1111/j.1468-2257.1977.tb00328.x.
15 "La Mission Racine – Un Projet Pharaonique," *La Grande Motte*, accessed September 9, 2015, http://www.lagrandemotte-architecture.com/La-Grande-Motte-et-son-histoire/La-Mission-Racine-un-projet-pharaonique.
16 Daniel Leclercq, *L'aventure du balnéaire Port-Gruissan* (Édition valda/saint-roch, 2013), 110–117.
17 "It Was Once the Port of Gruissan," accessed September 7, 2015, www.ville-gruissan.fr/il-etait-une-fois-le-port-de.
18 Furlough, "Vacations and Citizenship in Post-war France," 125.
19 "It Was Once the Port of Gruissan."
20 Furlough, "Vacations and Citizenship in Post-war France," 126.
21 "Global and European Sea-Level Rise (CLIM 012) – Assessment Published Sep 2014" (European Environment Agency, 2014), accessed July 22, 2015, www.eea.europa.eu/data-and-maps/indicators/sea-level-rise-2/assessment.
22 Church, J.A. et al., "2013: Sea Level Change," in *Climate Change 2013: The Physical Science Basis Contribution of Working Group I to the Fifth Assessment Report of the Intergovernmental Panel on Climate Change* [Stocker, T.F., D. Qin, G.-K. Plattner, M. Tignor, S.K. Allen, J. Boschung, A. Nauels, Y. Xia, V. Bex, and P.M. Midgley (eds)] (Cambridge, United Kingdom and New York, NY, USA: Cambridge University Press, n.d.), 1182.

Chapter 10

Promontory Promenades

Some wonderful waterfront promenades are not close to water but instead on promontories high above and overlooking water. There are usually expansive water views from promontory promenades as well as dramatic edge conditions, which is what makes them so special: the experience of being on a promontory promenade can be exhilarating. In places where urban land rises up from the edge of a body of water, whether an ocean, lake, or river, reserving the bluff top for public uses and creating a walk along the edge claims the big view and unique experience for everyone.

The two cases that follow are both long-standing promontory promenades with very different origins and design characteristics. The Brooklyn Heights Promenade tops a double-decked expressway that wraps around a steep bluff lining part of the city's East River waterfront, and is of formal design. Its construction in the 1950s created a public space in front of a previously privatized bluff top. Santa Monica's Palisades Park promenade runs along a cliff edge high above the city's beach within a somewhat informally designed park. It dates from the mid-1880s, when claiming the bluff top for public use was one of the first moves of the city's founders. They illustrate different approaches to making the most of difficult water's edge locations.

Brooklyn Heights Promenade, New York City, New York, USA

The Brooklyn Heights bluff, which lines the southern stretch of Brooklyn's East River waterfront, has long been known for its spectacular views of the East River and its confluence with the Hudson River, and of Manhattan's ever-evolving skyline. In 1864, when the bluff was occupied by the private gardens of well-to-do residents, President Abraham Lincoln is reported to have said: "There may be finer views than this in the world, but I don't believe it."[1] After many proposals over the years to create a promenade along the bluff, it took the construction of the Brooklyn-Queens Expressway in the 1940s and 1950s to make it real.

A project of Robert Moses, the expressway was originally planned to go through the middle of the Brooklyn Heights neighborhood but was moved instead to a double deck configuration along the side of the bluff because of public outcry over not wanting the neighborhood to be torn in two.[2] A platform was placed atop the freeway structure, to shield the adjacent neighborhood from the expressway traffic, and a very thin public park and promenade was built on top of it. The promenade deck is about 60 feet above mean sea level.[3] The two freeway decks terrace out below it, following something of the promontory's original slope, with the lower freeway deck overhanging a surface level roadway. The tiered and cantilevered design makes it feel like the promenade sits on the edge of the bluff, but in reality it sits completely on the expressway structure. The promenade runs just beyond the back gardens of the residential buildings that line the bluff top, and its construction opened up the formerly privatized grand water views to everyone.

Scale: 1:400,000

Promenade Design Characteristics

The Brooklyn Heights Promenade is about a third of a mile long and is wholly for pedestrians. The rear gardens of the brownstone buildings edging the promenade are separated from the walkway

Scale: 1:40,000

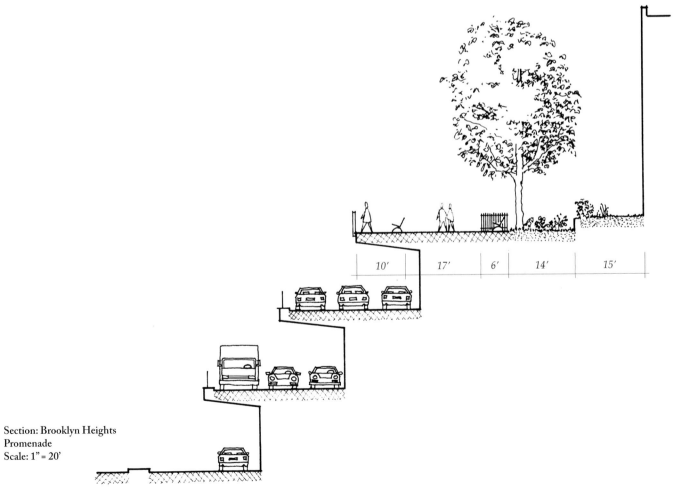

10'   17'   6'   14'   15'

Section: Brooklyn Heights
Promenade
Scale: 1" = 20'

Strolling along the Brooklyn Heights Promenade in the late afternoon

Brownstones and planted areas along the Brooklyn Heights Promenade

View of the Brooklyn Heights Promenade and the Brooklyn–Queens Expressway from an unconstructed part of Brooklyn Bridge Park

by a 21-foot-wide planted area, filled with tall trees, which is lined with an old-fashioned looking wrought-iron picket fence, painted black. The planted area is owned and maintained by the New York City Department of Parks and Recreation, but it is a buffer space rather than an active park space. The promenade itself is 27 feet wide, which includes a 10-foot-wide bench zone along the platform's outer edge and a 17-foot-wide walkway. In places, 6-foot-deep alcoves carved into the planted area create another bench zone on the inland side of the promenade. In both bench areas, wood slat benches are set in long lines, facing the view. A wrought-iron guardrail topped with pointed prongs protects the outer edge of the promenade platform and dissuades people from trying to lean too far over the edge or sit on it. Traditionally designed light fixtures line the promenade's inner edge.

The promenade faces west, so in the morning it is somewhat shaded by the trees in the planted area, but in the afternoon it is in full sun. Trees couldn't be planted along the promenade proper because the freeway deck wasn't designed for them, so the possibility of creating a shaded walk was not available.

The ambience along the promenade is an unusual mix of bucolic and urban. The tall trees and stately brownstone facades fronting the promenade and the distant water views create a graceful, relaxed ambience. At the same time, one can feel the rumble of traffic moving beneath the promenade, hear its noise, and smell its fumes, so the ambience is not completely peaceful.

Close-in views down to the waterfront below the bluff have changed dramatically over the years. When the promenade was built, the immediate waterfront was largely hidden from view by warehouse and shipping buildings. Those buildings are mostly gone and the foreground view now is of an attractive evolving lineal park, the Brooklyn Bridge Park, which is being built on the remaining large pier structures and the narrow foreshore beyond the expressway.

Promenade Use and Connectivity

The Brooklyn Heights Promenade sees only a moderate amount of activity. On a cool Sunday afternoon in early November, some 600 people per hour moved along it, almost all walking but a few jogging. A spectacular waterfront promenade runs through the lush landscaping in Brooklyn Bridge Park down below (see Chapter 5). It has become very popular, and may be drawing people away from the older promontory promenade.

The Brooklyn Heights Promenade is easy to get to from the adjacent Brooklyn Heights neighborhood, but it is difficult to get to from the waterfront. Access to it can be had from the ends of six local streets, and via a steeply inclined street that begins a few blocks away from the waterfront, near the base of the Brooklyn Bridge, and connects to the promenade's northern end. The plan for Brooklyn Bridge Park called for making connections between it and the Brooklyn Heights Promenade, and this process was begun but has stalled. In 2013, a connecting pedestrian bridge was built at a cost of $4.1 million. The upper end of the bridge lands in Squibb Park, which lies two blocks north of the start of the Brooklyn Heights Promenade. This should have made it easy to go between the old promenade and the new one, but hasn't because the bridge was only open for a short time before being closed. The zigzagging bridge is 400 feet long and just 8 feet wide. Constructed of wooden poles, wood planks and wire cables, it snakes high up in the air and was designed to bounce when people walk on it, but the bounce was too pronounced and caused the bridge to tilt dangerously, so it was shut down in summer of 2014. Repairs to the structure will be expensive and the project awaits a final redesign and funding.

People have dreams of wonderful public spaces and these dreams may or may not grab the imagination of others, may or may not ever be built. The dream to create a public promenade along the Brooklyn Heights bluff took a long time to become a reality and surprisingly it was accomplished via the construction of an elevated waterfront freeway, the very kind of project that usually cuts people off from the waterfront. Had people not dreamed of a bluff top promenade and had that idea not been around long enough to be in many people's minds, the freeway might have been built without its top deck, which would have created the usual barrier. The promenade may not be perfect because its ambience is impacted by the traffic running below it, but it is nonetheless a spectacular public space and far better than what might have been had the freeway not been decked.

Palisades Park Promenade, Santa Monica, California, USA

Scale: 1:400,000

Santa Monica's linear Palisades Park, which lies atop a craggy bluff high above the city's famous 400-foot-wide sand beach, provides stunning views of the Pacific Ocean and the long arc of Santa Monica Bay with its headlands at either end. A pedestrian promenade lines the bluff edge of the park and, though there are other promenades closer to the water, it is Santa Monica's best waterfront promenade because of the grand views it provides, the graciousness of the park within which it sits, and its close physical proximity to the city's downtown and residential neighborhoods. Palisades Park is the graceful hinge that connects the city with the Pacific Ocean and the pedestrian promenade that runs along its edge invites people to stroll and take in the views.

Santa Monica's topography somewhat isolates most of the city from its 3-mile-long beach. The steep bluff on which the park sits lines the northern two-thirds of the beach, and a gentler slope lines the rest. Near the dividing point between these topographies, the famous Santa Monica Pier, with its amusements, extends a third of a mile across the beach and over the ocean. The pier does allow one to walk out over the water, but it is more of an entertainment destination than a promenade. South of the pier, a wide sidewalk edges the beach, running along some commercial establishments and small parks but mostly along parking lots. North of the pier, private homes, beach clubs, and public parking lots directly front the beach, backed by the fast-moving Pacific Coast Highway, which lies at the base of the bluff. All along the beach, weaving through the sand, runs a narrow, concrete path that is designated for shared use but understandably is mostly used by cyclists: it would be a stretch to call it a promenade.

Palisades Park, and its promenade, have been a feature of Santa Monica almost since the city's beginning. Santa Monica is a small city, just over 8 square miles in size and with a population of less than 100,000 people, that is carved out of the enormous sprawl of Los Angeles, which surrounds it on three sides. The entrepreneurs who founded it in 1875, Colonel Robert S. Baker and Senator John P. Jones, both of whom had grown rich through mining-related activities, had big industrial dreams for the town. They lobbied for it to become the major Los Angeles area port, but the port went south to

Scale: 1:40,000

San Pedro instead. The new town prospered nonetheless, becoming a resort and summer home enclave for well-to-do people, who were drawn by the beautiful views.[4] Catering to this clientele, a bathhouse featuring hot saltwater baths was built along the beach, backing up to the bluff and connected to the urban area developing above via a wooden stairway.[5] Santa Monica was incorporated as a city in 1886 and shortly thereafter a 14-block stretch of the bluff land west of Ocean Avenue, the western-most street that had been platted, was set aside for a park, with the land gifted by Senator Jones and the Santa Monica Land and Water Company.

From the start, the new park catered to well-to-do-ness, while the city's beachfront, then quite narrow, catered to amusements. Photos from the 1890s show the park as an open expanse with a dirt path rambling along its edge, and Ocean Avenue lined with fine homes and planted with a row of tall trees.[6] Other photos show a large hotel on the bluff, with bathhouses fronted by a boardwalk on the beach below it. Along the base of the bluff north of these bathhouses stood a rambling line of simple wooden and tent structures, described as summer dwellings. By this time, pedestrian connections between the bluffs and the beach included a grand wooden stairway and a ramp across the bluff face, the beginnings of what would become the California Incline, so-called because its upper end connects with the end of California Street, which intersects with Ocean Avenue.

The turn of the twentieth century brought many changes to Santa Monica's waterfront. In early 1913, the parkland on the bluff was developed with rows of trees, wide linear pathways, and green lawns.[7] Historic photos[8] show a two-lane highway, the precursor of today's Pacific Coast Highway, at the base of the bluffs alongside the railroad track. By the 1920s, the rail track had been removed, the highway widened, and a municipal pier and adjacent privately owned amusement pier had been built toward the southern end of the bluffs. Santa Monica was hit hard by the Great Depression, but recovered during World War II as workers moved to Southern California in great numbers to work in industries building military airplanes and other war effort supplies. The city's beach was extended to its present width in the 1930s when extensive nourishment was undertaken of all the beaches along Santa Monica Bay.[9] In the mid-1960s, the Santa Monica freeway was built in the ravine at the southern edge of the bluffs, connecting with the Pacific Coast Highway and filling it with traffic.

Santa Monica's wide beach stretches below the eroding bluff atop which sits Palisades Park

A pedestrian path runs along the edge of the bluff, and a jogging path and bicycle lanes run along the roadway

While changes went on all around it, Palisades Park remained more or less in its early twentieth-century form. The park was given a facelift in the mid-1990s, and drought tolerant native plants were planted along the bluff line, but it retains much of its original design and furnishings.

Promenade Design Characteristics

Agave plants along the bluff edge

The park's design is relatively informal. It ranges from about 30 feet to 180 feet wide, with its inner edge running straight along Ocean Avenue and its outer edge following the craggy edge of the bluff. A pedestrian path, typically 12 to 16 feet wide, runs along the bluff, paved in some sections and unpaved in others. Sometimes the path threads through double rows of tall palm trees and elsewhere it is lined with a single row of palm trees. A concrete post and plank fence lines the bluff edge, usually set back from it 6 to 8 feet. Sometimes the path runs right along this fence and sometimes it is held back from the fence by a buffer of low planting, which includes Agave succulents. People are warned to stay behind the fence, away from the bluff edge. The bluff top path is lined with traditionally designed pedestrian-scale light fixtures. Benches occur along the path, sometimes situated in pairs to the inland side, looking out toward the view, elsewhere grouped perpendicular to the view next to the fence and surrounded by plantings. Inland of the path are grassy lawns. An unpaved jogging path runs adjacent to Ocean Avenue all along the park, lined in some areas by enormous stone pines. Bicycle lanes run on Ocean Avenue.

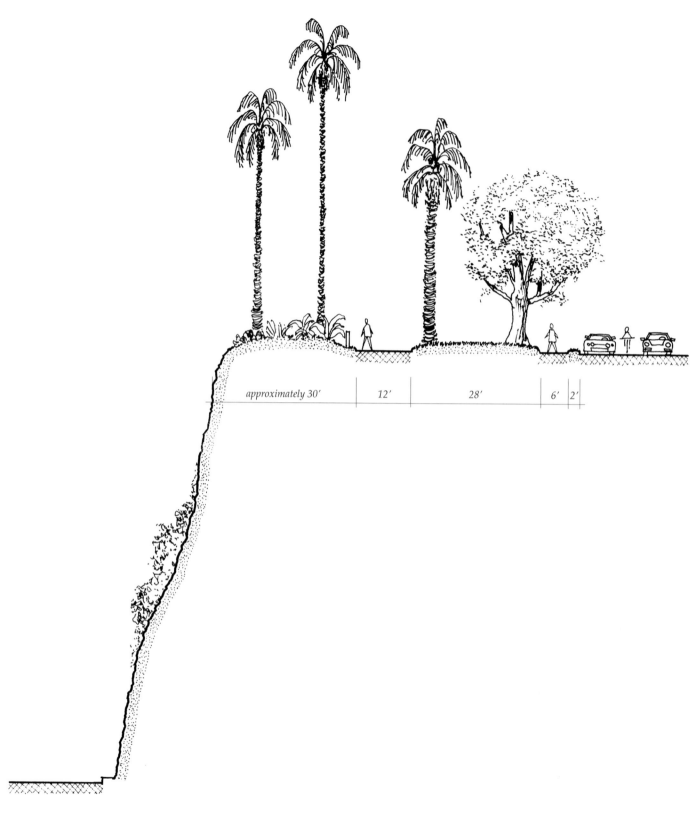

approximately 30'   12'   28'   6' 2'

**Section: Palisades Park
promenade
Scale: 1" = 20'**

Promenade Use and Connectivity

Taking advantage of the calm pleasantness of the park and the grand views from it, close to 800 people per hour were on the promenade on a sunny and warm early Saturday afternoon in July. Overwhelmingly they were strolling, with only a few jogging (10%) and even fewer biking (5%). Most people were in groups, usually in pairs, rather than alone, and most were young or middle-aged. Many more people were moving through the park than were sitting on the occasional benches lining the walks or on the lawns. Several people were exercising or doing yoga on the lawns. The numbers of people on the park promenade can be significantly reduced when the weather isn't as good. On a sunny but cool Monday afternoon in November, only about 100 people per hour were observed using the promenade. People were again overwhelmingly strolling, but most were on their own rather than with others.

It is relatively easy for people to get to Palisades Park and its promenade because some 15 streets feed into Ocean Avenue along the park's length, and there are big zebra crosswalks at every intersection. Ocean Avenue itself is relatively easy to cross. One stretch of it carries one travel lane in each direction, and another carries two lanes in each direction. Traffic is seldom heavy in either area and it usually moves relatively slowly.

Climate Change and Sea Level Rise Concerns

As might be expected, sea level rise is not as pressing an issue for this promenade as it is with so many others, but there are other worrisome environmental issues. With climate change, sea level rise along the Southern California coast is expected to be near the global average by 2100, which according to recent projections of the Intergovernmental Panel on Climate Change could be as much as .98 meters (3.2 feet)[10] and according to recent projections by the National Research Council could be as much as 1.67 meters (5.5 feet).[11] Maps prepared by Climate Central Surging Seas project show that with these amounts of sea level rise much of Santa Monica's beach would still be intact.[12]

A bigger problem for Palisades Park and its promenade is bluff erosion. A recent study by the city's Civil Engineering and Architecture Department notes that the bluffs are "relatively fragile Pleistocene age alluvial deposits with near-vertical slopes and peninsular soil columns" and that they have been constantly receding due to weathering, surface erosion from heavy rain storms, earthquake shaking, groundwater seepage and animal burrowing.[13] Recent and on-going efforts to decrease the rate of deterioration and to maintain the rim of the park include the installation of better surface drainage in the park, horizontal drains drilled hundreds of feet into the toe of the bluff, chemical grouting of the uppermost section of the bluffs to create a thin protective skin, the installation of 20- to 30-foot-long soil nails in key locations along the face of the bluffs, and the planting of native coastal habitat shrubs on the bluffs.[14] In all this there is an effort to maintain the historic look of the bluffs.

Maintaining the bluffs is no small matter for Santa Monica. Much more than the wonderful Palisades Park and its promenade would seem to depend on them because Ocean Avenue is not that far away from the bluff edge. Given the wealth of the community and the pride it has in its bluff top park that has long been a prime community amenity, it is likely that solutions will be found and that keeping the promenade at the edge of the bluff will remain a community priority.

A concrete guardrail protects much of the bluff edge

Sitting area along the bluff

Palm trees of various heights line the promenade

Notes

1   "Historical Sign Listings: NYC Parks," accessed August 20, 2015, www.nycgovparks.org/about/history/historical-signs/listings?id=136.
2   Hilary Ballon and Kenneth T. Jackson, eds., *Robert Moses and the Modern City: The Transformation of New York*, 1st ed (New York: W. W. Norton & Co, 2007), 220–224.

People strolling along the promenade

3   "Article 2 in Series: Determining the Correct Reference Point for Height Measurement," *Save The View Now*, February 19, 2015, accessed June 30, 2016, http://savetheviewnow.org/2015/02/.

4   "History of Santa Monica | Santa Monica Conservancy," accessed November 13, 2015, www.smconservancy.org/historic-places/history-of-santa-monica/.

5   "Water and Power Associates," accessed November 13, 2015, http://waterandpower.org/museum/Early_Views_of_Santa_Monica.html.

6   Ibid.

7   Margarita J. Wuellner and Sonali Gupta-Agarwal, "City Landmark Assessment Report Palisades Park," March 2007, accessed November 13, 2015, www.smgov.net/departments/pcd/agendas/Landmarks-Commission/2007/20070312/Palisades%20Park%20Landmark%20Assessment%20Report.pdf.

8   "Water and Power Associates."

9   Department of Boating and Waterways and State Coastal Conservancy, "California Beach Restoration Study," January 2002, 6.16, accessed November 12, 2015, www.dbw.ca.gov/PDF/Reports/BeachReport/FUll.pdf.

10   Church, J.A. et al., "2013: Sea Level Change," in *Climate Change 2013: The Physical Science Basis Contribution of Working Group I to the Fifth Assessment Report of the Intergovernmental Panel on Climate Change* [Stocker, T.F., D. Qin, G.-K. Plattner, M. Tignor, S.K. Allen, J. Boschung, A. Nauels, Y. Xia, V. Bex, and P.M. Midgley (eds)] (Cambridge, United Kingdom and New York, NY, USA: Cambridge University Press, 2014), 1182.

11   Committee on Sea Level Rise in California, Oregon, and Washington; Board on Earth Sciences and Resources; Ocean Studies Board; Division on Earth and Life Studies; National Research Council, *Sea-Level Rise for the Coasts of California, Oregon, and Washington: Past, Present, and Future* (Washington, D.C.: The National Academies Press, 2012), 107–108.

12   "Sea Level Rise | Climate Central," accessed July 22, 2015, www.climatecentral.org/what-we-do/our-programs/sea-level-rise.

13   City of Santa Monica EPWM Civil Engineering and Architecture Department, "Santa Monica Palisades Bluffs Improvement Project Final Initial Study/Mitigated Negative Declaration SCH# 2007021027," July 2007, 2–1, accessed November 12, 2015, www.smgov.net/uploadedFiles/Departments/Public_Works/Civil_Engineering/SM%20Bluffs%20Final%20ISMND.pdf.

14   Ibid., 2.9–2.18.

Chapter 11

Classic Bridge Promenades

Some major old bridges are iconic masterpieces: beautiful structures, engineering marvels of their times, built high over major water bodies, offering dramatic water and cityscape views. Some of these iconic bridges have pedestrian promenades that were part of their original design, and these classic bridge promenades have things to teach about how spectacular pedestrian-oriented public spaces can coexist with major traffic arteries. New York City's Brooklyn Bridge and San Francisco's Golden Gate Bridge are perhaps the most outstanding classic bridge promenades and these are the subjects here.

Pedestrianized bridges exist in cities around the world, often over rivers. Many such bridges have a unique physical form and offer a special walking experience. Several pedestrian bridges connected with larger waterfront promenades systems are mentioned in other chapters, the rest of the bridge promenades will have to wait for another book.

Scale: 1:400,000

Brooklyn Bridge, New York City, New York, USA

The Brooklyn Bridge, built in 1883 to connect the then separate cities of New York City and Brooklyn, was the first bridge crossing of the East River. It was a major engineering feat of its time because of

Scale: 1:40,000

The walkway is suspended above the roadway

its wide span, the busy river traffic below, and difficult foundation construction challenges.[1] Before the bridge, people took ferries to go back and forth between the two cities; when the bridge opened it offered multiple travel options. Its lower deck held lanes for horses, carriages and horse-drawn trolleys, and tracks for trains, above which, in the center of the bridge, was a wood plank walkway for pedestrians. The lower level was eventually reconfigured to serve motorized vehicles exclusively, but the pedestrian walk today retains much of its original form, and can now also be used by bicyclists.

Promenade Design Characteristics and Connectivity

Walking across the bridge at a leisurely pace takes 20 to 30 minutes, but many people linger longer to enjoy the spectacular views. The bridge span itself has a length of about two-thirds of a mile, but for pedestrians and cyclists the total crossing length is somewhat over a mile because of long approach ramps on either side that climb up to the span. The approaches start some distance away from the water's edge: in Manhattan near City Hall and in Brooklyn at Cadman Plaza. After crossing the bridge, if people do not want to re-cross it to get to where they came from, they have the option of taking either a subway train or a ferry back to the other side.

View of the East River and Manhattan skyline from the walkway

Once on the bridge, walkers and cyclists are about 150 feet above the river, but the walk's location centered over the roadway below does not allow views directly down to the water. Distant views of the water and of the Manhattan and Brooklyn skylines are dramatic, perhaps all the more so because they are filtered through the many crisscrossing cable stays of the bridge itself. Closer up views of the bridge's two massive granite towers, detailed with double gothic arches through which the walkway passes, are also dramatic. In addition, the sheer experience of walking or biking high above the water is exciting, as is the experience of being in a vast open space so different from the dense urban fabrics at both ends of the bridge.

More than 150,000 vehicles cross the Brooklyn Bridge every day, and from the pedestrian walkway one is aware of the vehicles moving below, because traffic noise and fumes drift up,

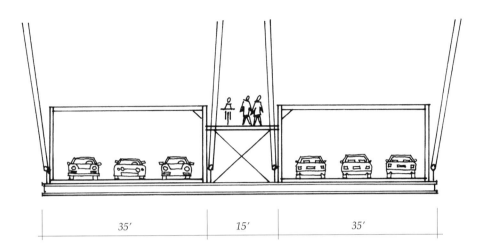

Section: Brooklyn Bridge
Scale: 1" = 20'

35'   15'   35'

but at the same time the traffic doesn't overwhelm the experience because it is largely screened from view by the many steel beams that span across the roadway providing support for the walkway structure. The traffic doesn't feel threatening, as it might if the walkway ran alongside the traffic lanes.

The exhilarating experience offered by the promenade is packed into a narrow and simply designed space. The walkway is a mere 15 feet wide and surfaced with simple wood planks. It is divided down the middle by a painted white line that is supposed to create a pedestrian path on the south side and a bike path on the north side, but is often disregarded. When there are many pedestrians they occupy the whole path, and when there are few pedestrians, bikers do so. Guardrail height metal fences protect the walkway edges and along stretches where the main cables, which loop between the two towers and also between the towers and the bridge's end supports, are at their low points they curve overhead not far above the guardrails. All along the walkway, vertical cables protrude through the decking just inside the guardrails and then soar up to meet the sloping cable. Old-fashioned metal light fixtures hung from the cables provide evening lighting.

Brooklyn Bridge looking toward Manhattan

Promenade Use

Local residents have long commuted across the Brooklyn Bridge on foot and bike. Many tourists also walk and cycle across the bridge; it ranks as a major must-do activity when visiting New York City. On many weekends, group walks organized for one community or national cause or another draw big crowds. Banners and t-shirts publicizing these events are often much in evidence.

The number of people walking across the Brooklyn Bridge during peak times on weekends can greatly exceed the number found on the busiest of European pedestrianized commercial streets. On a late Sunday morning in November, when it was sunny but cool, 5,572 people per hour were counted on the walkway, including many who were part of multiple organized events and only 25 who were on bikes moving very slowly through the crowd. This is the highest volume observed on any of the waterfront promenades in this study. It equates to 6.19 people per minute per foot of walk width (20.32 people per meter per minute), which, according to Allan Jacobs' *Great Streets*, is almost one and a half times as many people as can be found on Copenhagen's main pedestrianized street Stroget.[2]

Walking across the Brooklyn Bridge on a cool Sunday morning

The Brooklyn Bridge was built at a time when people commonly travelled using multiple travel modes, before the advent of the private automobiles that are now so dominant. The pedestrian walkway on the bridge was just one of many possible ways to travel across it. Today, when the whole lower part of the bridge is dedicated to cars, the elevated walkway offers a very special way of being on the bridge without being in a vehicle. It is notable just for being there, but also for the great deal of activity that happens on it within a very constrained space.

Golden Gate Bridge, San Francisco, California, USA

Beyond its role as a civic icon for San Francisco and the Bay Area and its function as a major transportation route connecting San Francisco with Marin and Sonoma Counties and the coastal wilds and communities of Northern California, the Golden Gate Bridge is a major pedestrian and bicycle promenade for local people and tourists alike, who are drawn by the bridge's grandeur. Walks on both sides of the bridge have been there since the bridge was opened in 1937 and people have come to them in droves ever since to experience the thrill of being 220 feet above the dramatic meeting of San Francisco Bay and the Pacific Ocean, and to enjoy the spectacular vistas.

Just as views of the bridge itself are grand, so are the views from it: to the east are views of San Francisco, the bay with its sailboats, Sausalito, the Tiburon peninsula, Angel Island, Alcatraz, Yerba Buena and Treasure Islands, and the distant East Bay hills; to the west are views of the Pacific Ocean, the Marin Headlands, the Point Bonita lighthouse, San Francisco's Sea Cliff area and Baker Beach, and the San Francisco approach buoys and shipping channel. Views of the red bridge towers, looming 50 stories above the roadway, are also striking—witness all the people on the bridge having their pictures taken in front of a tower.

Promenade Design Characteristics and Connectivity

The bridge walkways have a design aesthetic in keeping with the elegant industrial nature of the whole bridge, and are surprisingly modest in size. The walks are raised slightly above the vehicle roadway and protected from traffic by steel curbs and metal railings. They are mostly 10 feet wide, but narrow to 7½ feet around the bridge towers and to 5½ feet at the pylons from which the suspension cables rise. Massive steel railings, integral to the structure and painted the same red as everything else, line the outer edge of the walks. They are at guardrail height, so people can lean out over them if they wish. Every so often, small alcoves cantilever over the water, allowing even more dramatic views to the water below. Along the walks are regularly spaced lights of unique design whose poles are integrated into

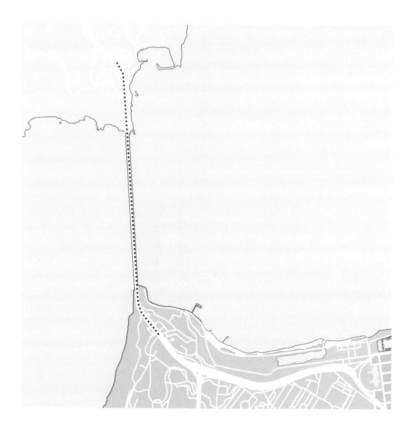

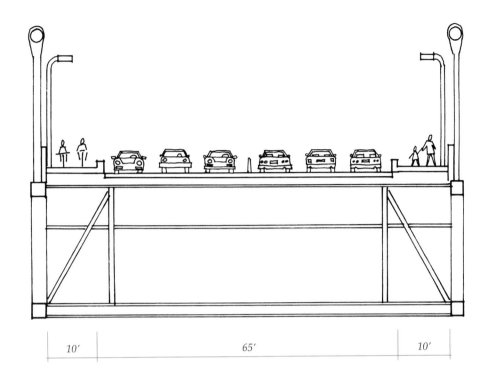

Section: Golden Gate Bridge
Scale: 1" = 20'

| 10' | 65' | 10' |

The view of downtown San Francisco from the Golden Gate Bridge promenade

the railings. At night, high-pressure sodium lights, which arch over the walkway, cast a gentle amber glow.[3]

Walking or biking across the Golden Gate Bridge is almost a rite of passage for tourists, and many local residents use it regularly for exercise, and so the Golden Gate Bridge District has made the bridge easily accessible to walkers and bikers, which is no mean feat considering that the bridge and the vehicle approaches to it are part of the Highway 101 freeway. For people coming by car or tourist bus, there are parking lots on both sides at either end of the bridge, which often overflow. People coming on foot or bike from the San Francisco side can do so via stairs and trails from Crissy Field and Fort Point at bay level. From the Sausalito side, walkers and bikers can get to the bridge through the parking lots. Bikers going to or from Sausalito or the Marin Headlands travel on roadways without marked bike lanes.

Promenade Use

Although getting to the bridge by foot or bike is relatively easy, the flow of bikers and pedestrians is highly regulated. People on foot are restricted to the east walk and can only use it during daylight hours, after which gates close the walks. Bikers must shift from walk to walk depending upon the time of day or day of the week. During weekdays, they must mix with pedestrians on the east walk from 5 am to 3:30 pm, and then shift to the west side until dusk. At night, they must shift back to the east side with security guards giving them access through the gates. On weekends, they must use the west side during daylight hours.[4]

The regulations about who can be where are not without reason, given the numbers: on a summer Sunday afternoon as many as 1,400 pedestrians and 900 cyclists have been counted entering the walks during the peak hour. On the east walk, where 1,500 combined pedestrians and cyclists were counted, this comes to approximately 2.5 people per foot of walk width per minute, which is about half as much as might be seen on a major European pedestrianized street such as Stroget in Copenhagen.[5] At the pylons, the figures rise to over 45 people per foot of walk width per minute. Not everyone walks the whole length of the 1.7-mile-long bridge, perhaps not surprisingly given that by

The Golden Gate Bridge at its Marin County end

Crowds of people walk on the Golden Gate Bridge even when the weather is cold, foggy, and windy

the time you've reached mid-span you've climbed the equivalent of an eight-story building. People might well be tired without even knowing why.

The nighttime closure to pedestrians is linked to a dark reality. Although the walk on the Golden Gate Bridge is a joy for most people, some people have used it to end their lives by jumping. After years of study about how to create a deterrent, in 2014 the Bridge Authority approved building a net below the span,[6] which was completed in 2017.

The grandness of the bridge, its dramatic geographic location, and the views from it combine to draw people to it as a destination, but being on the bridge as a pedestrian or bicyclist is not a peaceful

The walkway is separated from the roadway by a curb and railing

experience. As compelling as being on the bridge is, it is impossible to ignore the constant nearby presence of fast-moving traffic, with its noise, fumes, and rushing speed. There are six travel lanes on the bridge, with the number serving each direction shifted according to traffic flows. An average of more than 100,000 vehicles cross the bridge every day,[7] and while the posted speed is 45 miles per hour, many vehicles often move faster.

Nonetheless, the Golden Gate Bridge is a magnificent waterfront promenade. The experience of walking along the bridge is certainly different now than what it was when it was first built—early photos show much less traffic and no railings between the roadway and the walks—but it remains a remarkable experience. Placing sidewalks on the Golden Gate Bridge was an inspired move. Luckily the bridge was built early in the age of automobiles when people could conceive of putting sidewalks along a major traffic arterial. If the bridge had been built later, like the several other bridges spanning the San Francisco Bay, it may well not have had sidewalks, as those other bridges do not. A recently rebuilt part of the Bay Bridge includes a bike path on one side.

Notes

1   "Brooklyn Bridge Construction and History," accessed August 20, 2015, http://history1800s.about.com/od/bridgebuilding/a/brooklynbrid01.htm.
2   Allan B. Jacobs, *Great Streets* (Cambridge, MA: MIT Press, 1993), 317.
3   "Golden Gate Bridge," accessed August 20, 2015, http://goldengatebridge.org/research/factsGGBLighting.php.
4   Alta Planning + Design, "Bicycle Safety Study for the Golden Gate Bridge," April 15, 2011, accessed August 19, 2015, http://goldengate.org/news/bridge/documents/bikesafetystudy_april2011.pdf.
5   Jacobs, *Great Streets*, 317.
6   "Final Design of Golden Gate Bridge Suicide Barrier Complete, Approved – San Jose Mercury News," accessed August 20, 2015, www.mercurynews.com/crime-courts/ci_27177901/final-design-golden-gate-bridge-suicide-barrier-complete%20accessed%2012%20March,%202015.
7   "Golden Gate Bridge," accessed August 20, 2015, http://goldengatebridge.org/research/crossings_revenues.php.

Chapter 12

Incrementally Built Central Area Promenades

As shipping and maritime-related industrial-central waterfront uses of cities have declined, some cities are working to make their waterfronts more publicly oriented and pedestrian friendly through incremental steps rather than single large development projects. In these cities, change is happening slowly for any number of reasons: waterfront parcels may become available piecemeal, funding for development projects may be hard to secure, funding for public realm improvements may come out of city or port authority budgets and hence only be available in small chunks, or barriers to waterfront access, such as freeways or major roadways, may be difficult to dismantle for political or jurisdictional reasons. Whatever the challenges, the creation of a waterfront promenade along the central waterfront is often a long-range objective of such endeavors. The two incrementally built promenades that follow are very different from each other. San Francisco embarked upon its effort some time ago, spurred by the opportunity to take down its elevated waterfront freeway after it was damaged in an earthquake. Lisbon has just begun.

Ribeira das Naus, Lisbon, Portugal

Scale: 1:400,000

Lisbon has recently begun to create a promenade along its central waterfront where ships for exploring the New World were once built and where industrial docks long held sway. The promenade is an early step in the city's recently adopted ambitious plan to reconnect the city and its people with its long waterfront through strategic removal of industrial uses and the creation of new public spaces. The central waterfront is the first area being transformed, and what will be a lengthy waterfront promenade is being built stretch by stretch, with the first Ribeira das Naus section completed in 2013.

Lisbon sprawls along the western side of the wide Rio Tejo (Tagus River) estuary and its central area lies just above the inlet connecting with the Atlantic Ocean. The central waterfront is marked by a large public square, the Terreiro do Paço (Praça do Comércio), built following the 1755 earthquake and tsunami that destroyed much of Lisbon,[1] behind which lies a fine grid of streets bounded by irregular streets climbing steep hillsides. Stretching along the waterfront for some distance to either side of the square is a narrow strip of flat reclaimed land, created in the latter half of the nineteenth century for port and infrastructure facilities. These facilities effectively cut off much of the city from the waterfront.

The coastal strip is the focus of the city's 2008 Riverfront General Plan, which is directed toward opening up 19 kilometers (11.8 miles) of the city's waterfront for public use.[2] In the city's 1994 masterplan almost all waterfront land was designated for port and industrial uses, with the exception of a few green areas and a site far north of the downtown designated for the Expo98 Parque das Nações (Park of Nations) project (see Chapter 5).[3] The 2012 masterplan, which was adopted following an extensive public participation process, envisions "giving the waterfront back to the people" by creating new public spaces and infrastructure along it.[4] It is notable that the new masterplan was adopted despite Lisbon having been in an era of austerity since the 2008 economic downturn. The city believes that high quality public spaces will attract private development and increase economic prosperity, and that during hard economic times its people, particularly the young, have need of good public spaces so that they'll feel good about the city's future prospects and stay engaged.[5]

Scale: 1:40,000

The vision for the central waterfront articulated in the new masterplan includes a redesign of the Terreiro do Paço, a new park and waterfront promenade to its west, a new state-of-the-art cruise terminal and promenade to its east, and a new bicycle path all along the shore, to be part of an 11-kilometer (6.8-mile) waterfront route.[6] With the exception of the new cruise terminal, the plan doesn't call for major new commercial development along the waterfront, or any residential development.

Projects undertaken so far include renovation of the Terreiro do Paço and construction of some areas west of it, including the park, part of the bicycle route, and a section of the promenade. The Ribeira das Naus promenade begins just west of the square, running in front of the grand old buildings of the naval ministry, one of which has been renovated into a museum that will display replicas of ships that sailed to the New World. The land between these buildings and the waterfront has been cleared and turned into a simply designed park, consisting mostly of lawns. A four-lane street that had cut diagonally through the area was replaced with a traffic-calmed two-lane street that curves through the space and then runs adjacent to the promenade.

The other areas remain largely as they have been, although some pop-up eateries have been established in a few places near the waterfront, and so the overall ambience retains something of a working waterfront feel. At the far end of the Ribeira das Naus, a train station and its tracks lie just back of the waterfront, fronted by a ferry dock and other working docks. This area is slated to become a major transit hub. East of the Terreiro do Paço is a ferry dock, other working docks, an old cruise ship terminal, and industrial warehouses.

Promenade Design Characteristics

The Ribeira das Naus promenade has three distinct sections. It begins on a 200-foot-long wooden bridge that spans a water inlet feeding a small lagoon in front of the museum. The promenade part of the bridge consists of an 8-foot-wide sidewalk along its waterside. The promenade, the roadway, and a sidewalk on the other side of the bridge are all surfaced with wood planks, loosely set in metal frames.

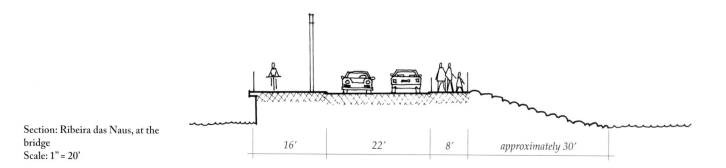

Section: Ribeira das Naus, at the
bridge
Scale: 1" = 20'

| 16' | 22' | 8' | approximately 30' |

Section: Ribeira das Naus, at the
urban beach
Scale: 1" = 20'

| varies | 6' | 10' | 23' | 7' | 20' | 3' | 7' | 7' | 7' | 7' | 7' | 7' | 5' |

It is a simple and handsome design, but the loud rattle created by vehicles traversing the planks leads pedestrians to quicken their pace to get beyond this area.

After the bridge, the second and main section of the promenade runs along an approximately 800-foot-long "urban beach," a set of six broad steps that slope down to the water. The Tagus estuary has large daily tidal flows and several of the lowest steps are regularly inundated at high tide. The promenade walk itself is 20 feet wide. It is lined on the waterside by a 3-foot-wide ledge that starts the steps, and on its other side by a 7-foot-wide slightly raised sidewalk, which runs along the street. The promenade, sidewalk, and street are all surfaced with randomly sized and shaped gray cobbles, as is the paved area on the far side of the street, through which a bicycle path is subtly marked with a strip of black cobblestones. Mixed deciduous trees are staggered along the promenade, roughly in three rows but without defining any continuous paths; people moving on the promenade must either weave through the trees or walk outside of them. The young trees as yet offer little shade, but in the future the promenade will likely be well shaded. At the end of the urban beach, the promenade passes by a small waterside plaza that is filled with tables and chairs serviced from a fanciful food and drink kiosk, which has a tiny public restroom squeezed into its rear side. The favored café seats are the canvas sling-back chairs that line the water's edge of the plaza.

Beyond the plaza, a third promenade section is as yet undeveloped, but people can move along the water to the ferry terminal and train station through a series of undefined spaces. Along the way, the path passes by the site of the future transit hub, where the city has placed a temporary intervention to invite people to gather at the waterfront. Here, the water's edge is lined with a dozen or so large and brightly colored hemispherical fibreglass tree planters with seats indented into their sides.

A pop-up eatery

PART 1 An Assembly of Waterfront Promenades

The bridge section of Ribeira das Naus where it passes by the former naval ministry building, with the Terreiro do Paço in the background

Ribeira das Naus at the urban beach, with the waterside plaza in the distance

Temporary planters and seats along the as yet undeveloped waterfront area near the future transit hub

Bicycle path marking

Strolling and sitting along the urban beach

People relaxing at the water's edge

In all, the Ribeira das Naus has a casual and relaxed feel to it. It is homey, in the best sense of the word, rather than ostentatious, and seems more oriented toward locals than tourists. Materials used are in keeping with local character, in particular the cobblestone paving, which is a subdued version of city tradition. Many of Lisbon's sidewalks and plazas are paved with black and white cobblestones set in geometric, wave-like, or floral designs.

Promenade Use

The urban beach part of the promenade is the most used. On a warm and sunny Sunday in mid-June, 1,053 people per hour were observed walking along it around noon, almost all (86%) walking leisurely. At the same time, bikers were also moving along the on-road bicycle lanes, but in considerably fewer numbers. That same evening, shortly before the traditional late dinnertime, the promenade was somewhat less busy, with 774 people passing in an hour, and more were strolling (95%). During both the afternoon and evening, most people were with others rather than alone, mostly in couples.

The urban beach itself is a popular gathering place. Many people sit or lie on the steps, some on beach towels. People also like to walk along the step closest to the water, whichever one it may be, depending on tidal conditions, and dip their toes into the water, just as one would along a sandy beach. The café at the end of the urban beach is also a favorite gathering place.

Climate Change and Sea Level Rise Concerns

Like other coastal cities, Lisbon faces challenges from sea level rise. The Atlantic coast of Portugal is expected to have a local sea level rise similar to the global average, and this will translate into the Tagus estuary.[7, 8] According to projections of the Intergovernmental Panel on Climate Change, the sea level could rise by as much as .98 meters (3.2 feet) by 2100. High tide events already come very close to the top of the seawall fronting the Terreiro do Paço, and it is predicted that by 2100 the city will see coastal flooding events that go significant distances inland.[9] The Terreiro do Paço's renovation included installation of a new drainage system to handle storm water. The city is in the process of developing climate change adaptation strategies and could be expected to come up with plans and projects that address sea level rise.[10] How these might influence the design of future segments of the central area waterfront promenade, or redesign of already built parts, is not yet known.

Another waterfront challenge, of which local people are well aware, is that the city will no doubt be hit by tsunamis in the future as it has been many times in the past, most notably the 1755 event that inundated the city for 250 meters (820 feet) inland and killed almost 1,000 people.[11] After that event, the city eventually rebuilt itself and re-embraced the waterfront by building the grand Terreiro do Paço. Presumably the city will find ways to continue to embrace its waterfront should another tsunami occur, and as sea levels rise.

The Ribeira das Naus promenade is a significant start to carrying out a major transformation of Lisbon's central waterfront. Sections completed so far have modest designs that are highly compelling. The promenade feels as though it is evolving naturally out of its surrounding context, rather than imposing a new urban design aesthetic. This is a refreshing approach for a big city waterfront. If the remaining work is as thoughtfully well done as the first work, there is every reason to expect that the entire envisioned promenade will be eminently livable and attracts visitors.

Embarcadero Promenade, San Francisco, California, USA

Scale: 1:400,000

San Francisco has a promenade along its northeastern bay waterfront that was built in the 1990s after removal of an elevated freeway but whose character continues to evolve as the many piers along its water's edge, which are owned by the Port of San Francisco, incrementally transition to other uses. Development of the piers is happening slowly because many of them are historic structures subject to preservation requirements, and because there are limitations on how they can be developed. California law requires that Port properties located on reclaimed land, which includes the piers along the Embarcadero, be restricted to maritime, recreational, and commercial uses that bring activity to the waterfront such as restaurants and retail establishments.[12] Residential and office uses are not allowed, except offices directly connected with uses that satisfy the requirement. Proposed projects go through lengthy public review processes and many have failed to find approval, most notably a recent proposal to building a new basketball stadium for the Golden State Warriors on one of the piers. In the meantime, many piers have interim uses on them, including parking lots, or host temporary events, such as the headquarters for the America's Cup defense.

San Francisco's northeastern waterfront, adjacent to the city's downtown, has a storied history. It was a major west coast port for a hundred years, from the 1850s to the 1950s. The port was created on fill incorporating the hulls of ships abandoned during the Gold Rush as people headed inland to the gold fields. The Embarcadero (landing place) along it was built with shipping piers, rail lines, and goods warehouses. By the 1930s, 49 piers and 21 ferry slips were in operation, many with impressive neo-classically designed bulkhead structures, including the large Ferry Building at the foot of Market Street with its landmark clock tower. The port operated at high capacity through World War II,[13] but then went into decline because it could not handle the large container ships that were becoming industry standard.

In the late 1950s, a large wholesale produce market occupying a site west of the Ferry Building, just inland of the waterfront, was shut down and the area around it was turned into a redevelopment project. The Embarcadero Center, an enormous complex containing five high-rise office buildings, a Hyatt Regency Hotel, and multi-level shopping center, was built there, along with a mix of low-rise

Scale: 1:40,000

and high-rise residential buildings. In conjunction with the redevelopment project, an elevated double deck freeway was planned to go all along the city's northern waterfront to the Golden Gate Bridge. The first section of the freeway, opened in 1959, ran between the Bay Bridge and Broadway, the street marking the western boundary of the redevelopment area. The double-decked structure was built directly above the Embarcadero roadway and in front of the iconic Ferry Building and other pier buildings, separating them from the downtown.

San Francisco's famous citizen-led freeway revolt of 1964 stopped construction of the rest of the Embarcadero Freeway, and other planned freeways, but the damage had already been done to the northeastern waterfront. Even though shipping and industry had largely left the waterfront by the late 1960s, and views of the water were opened up as some pier structures were removed, few people went there because the overhead freeway created a harsh and noisy environment. In the 1970s, the Fisherman's Wharf area further west along the waterfront was cleaned up and turned into a tourist attraction with the building of the Cannery and Ghirardelli Square shopping complexes, and Pier 39 was built as a tourist-attracting shopping mall themed as a New England fishing village, but the part of the waterfront with the freeway became increasingly derelict. The area was kept alive only by the activity associated with the ferry service operated from the Ferry Building.

The turning point came with the 1989 Loma Prieta earthquake, which severely damaged the elevated freeway structure. The question was whether to repair it or tear it down, with a groundswell of people calling for its removal. Studies done by the City Planning Department in the 1970s had shown that the freeway was never needed in the first place, that traffic could be handled at grade, and these studies became the basis for the argument that the freeway could come down. Consensus coalesced around the idea, the freeway was demolished, and the Embarcadero was transformed into a grand landscaped boulevard, with transit running in a dedicated space along its central median—a light rail line south of the Ferry Building and refurbished historic streetcar line north of the Ferry Building—and a promenade along the waterfront.

Historic streetcars run along the Embarcadero north of Market Street

Promenade Design Characteristics

The Embarcadero Promenade is a wide sidewalk along the boulevard's waterside. It is 3 miles long, running from Pier 45 at Fisherman's Wharf, past the Ferry Building, to the San Francisco Giants ballpark, built in the 1990s, which lies south of Pier 40. (Even numbered piers run west of the Ferry Building and odd numbered piers run east of it.) It varies from 25 to 35 feet wide, with most sections 25 feet wide. The bay side of the Embarcadero remains lined with many piers and bulkhead buildings, and so along some stretches of the promenade only intermittent water views can be had. The Port has built public walkways around several piers, creating auxiliary promenades that give more direct water views.

The Ferry Building is the promenade's centerpiece. It was renovated in the 1990s to include a public market and continues to serve ferries connecting with East and North Bay cities. Since the early 2000s, a very popular farmers' market has been hosted in front of and alongside the Ferry Building on Saturday mornings, with stands lined up along the edge of the promenade. Every day, chairs and tables line some sections of the promenade, outdoor seating associated with restaurants inside the Ferry Building.

The Embarcadero Promenade has a distinctly different feel to either side of the Ferry Building. To the northwest, leading to Pier 39, the promenade is relatively enclosed, passes many historic bulkhead buildings, looks out toward central San Francisco Bay, and is used very heavily by walkers and bikers, perhaps because there are many destinations along it. Attractions include the recently built Exploratorium, a science museum directed mostly to children, a cruise ship terminal that hosts over 80 cruise ships a year, a fishing pier, and Pier 39.

To the southeast, between the Ferry Building and the ballpark, the promenade is less enclosed by buildings, looks toward the less dramatic South Bay, runs at times along park-like settings, and is normally less used except on game days during the baseball season. This section of the promenade passes under the Bay Bridge, which spans high overhead, giving close views of this impressive structure. The parks and open areas include Rincon Park, which has a giant bow and arrow sculpture in it, Cupid's Span, designed by Claes Oldenburg and Coosje van Bruggen, a large open pier structure used for temporary events such as Cirque du Soleil shows, an elevated green lawn atop the Brannan Street Wharf, and the South Beach Marina.

Section: Embarcadero
Promenade, northwest of the
Ferry Building
Scale: 1" = 20'

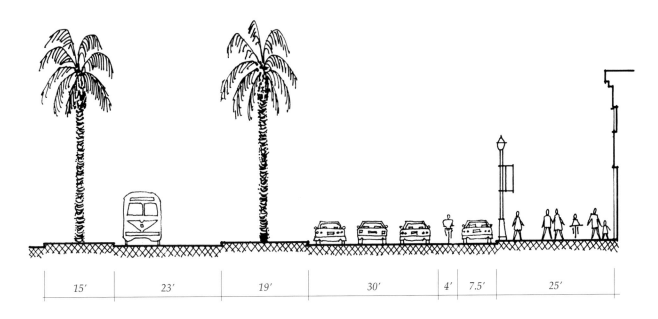

| 15' | 23' | 19' | 30' | 4' | 7.5' | 25' |

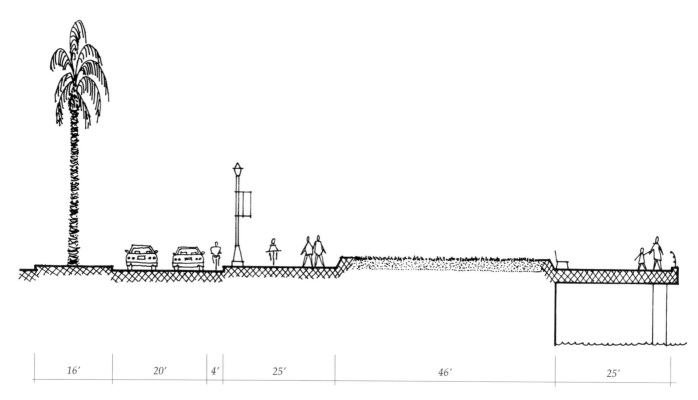

| 16' | 20' | 4' | 25' | 46' | 25' |

Section: Embarcadero
Promenade, southeast of the
Ferry Building at the Brannan
Street Wharf
Scale: 1" = 20'

In spite of the different characters of its east and west parts, some common design elements tie the whole promenade together. A 5-foot-wide concrete strip containing a glass block covered lighting strip runs along most of it, in places embedded in the walk's surface and elsewhere raised to sitting height. Its position within the walk varies because it marks the location of the historic seawall lying hidden below.[14] At the curb runs a line of traditionally designed light fixtures, painted a sea-blue color.

The Embarcadero Promenade
northwest of the Ferry Building,
where the light strip is embedded
in the sidewalk

The Embarcadero Promenade
southeast of the Ferry Building
at Rincon Park

Set within the walking space at widely spaced intervals are black and white striped poles on which are mounted historic photographs of the Embarcadero. There are no trees along the promenade, except for a line of London Plane trees directly in front of the Ferry Building, a design approach intended to give the water's edge an open feel. This means that there is almost no shade along the promenade for most of the day, except in the early morning when some areas are briefly shaded by shadows cast by pier bulkhead buildings or in the late afternoon when some areas are shaded by the long shadows of downtown high-rise buildings.

The Embarcadero roadway is also all of a piece in its design. The roadway carries two or three lanes of traffic in each direction, depending on location, with extra left-turning lanes at some intersections. The transit tracks, running in a dedicated right-of-way in the middle of the roadway, have medians on both sides that provide pedestrian refuges for people crossing the street. These medians are paved with cobblestones and planted with palm trees. The sidewalk on the inland side of the roadway is planted with palm trees for the two blocks to either side of Market Street, and with London Plane trees elsewhere. On-street bike lanes run along both sides of the roadway, and there is curbside parking in some places.

Promenade Use and Connectivity

People sitting along a raised
section of the light ribbon

The promenade section west of the Ferry Building is the most used. It gets particularly crowded on weekends, especially on farmers' market days. On a pleasant, sunny Saturday in early April, 3,396 people passed just north of the Ferry Building during the lunch hour, almost all of them walking, only a few running, biking or on skateboards. That's a lot of people and the 30-foot-wide walk felt very crowded. People on bikes and skateboards mixed with the pedestrians, weaving in and around them and going slowly. A number of bikers were using the on-street bicycle lane, including many pedicabs providing rides to tourists. The number of people dropped off significantly, by about half, at the cruise terminal two-thirds of a mile to the north. One senses that on weekends, with the exception of locals coming to buy produce at the Farmers' Market, most of the people are not San Franciscans but are visitors, either from the Bay Area or afar, come to visit the attractions, rather than to have a leisurely stroll. At the same time that all the activity was happening on the promenade, the

The Embarcadero Promenade
southeast of the Ferry Building
near the base of the Bay Bridge

adjacent Embarcadero roadway was congested with vehicle traffic, so much so that it often stood at a standstill.

On weekdays, there tend to be far fewer people moving on the promenade near the Ferry Building, less than half those of a Saturday. Of the 1,400 people per hour observed passing in an hour on a sunny weekday afternoon in March, most (95%) were strolling. The pace was slower and there was a greater sense of leisurely promenading.

Considerably fewer people use the promenade east of the Ferry Building, even on the weekends. On the same Saturday in April, 400 people per hour were moving along it around the noon hour. Most people were strolling, but here more were running (15%) and biking (6%), perhaps because the less crowded conditions make these activities more enjoyable. People strolling seemed out for a leisurely walk, perhaps choosing this location because of the open water views and the parks. Activity levels are similar on weekdays. On a partly cloudy weekend early afternoon in March, 540 strollers, bikers and runners per hour were observed. On baseball game days or evenings, many more walkers frequent this section of the promenade as people head to or from the ballpark.

People throng the promenade
near the Ferry Building on
Farmer's Market days

The promenade is relatively easy to get to on foot because many streets lead into it, but crossing the wide Embarcadero roadway can be a challenge when traffic is heavy. When the Embarcadero was reconstructed, a large oval plaza was built at the foot of Market Street, in front of the Ferry Building, between the eastbound and westbound lanes. This is the main crossing that connects the promenade with the downtown, including the nearby Embarcadero BART station. Other intersections along the Embarcadero are mostly signalized and have crosswalks. The challenges for pedestrians come from the many vehicles making turning movements onto or off the Embarcadero, the need to keep a close eye out for streetcars when crossing the Embarcadero because transit vehicles pre-empt regular signal phasing and they sometimes seem to come out of nowhere, and drivers who are quick off the mark when they get a green light.

Climate Change and Sea Level Rise Concerns

People strolling and jogging along the Promenade near the Ferry Building on a sunny weekday afternoon

The Embarcadero Promenade is threatened by sea level rise. A recent climate change assessment report prepared by the National Research Council projects that by 2100 San Francisco's sea level will have risen by between .42 and 1.6 meters (1.4 to 5.5 feet).[15] Seasonal king tides already overflow the seawall along the northeastern waterfront, and studies indicate that a 16-inch sea level rise coupled with storm surge could inundate areas back to the original shoreline, some distance inland of the Embarcadero.[16] Notwithstanding this reality, and even though large sections of the existing seawall are in disrepair, no conclusions have been reached about how to address the problem. Small measures to protect against flooding were included in the design of the park recently built atop the Brannan Street Wharf, including elevating the park, using salt-water resistant materials, and placing a 12-inch curb along the edge railing, but most other areas of the Embarcadero remain unprotected.[17]

A more comprehensive approach to sea level rise may be on the horizon. In 2016, the city issued a *Sea Level Rise Action Plan*, which sets objectives for mitigating sea level rise impacts, and it expects to have a citywide sea level rise adaptation plan complete by 2018.[18] The city has also begun to take a serious look at what to do about the aging seawall in response to a recent study that found it could collapse in a major earthquake.[19]

San Francisco has 37 miles of shoreline including the 3 miles of bay shoreline along which the Embarcadero Promenade lies. For certain, some changes, big or small will have to be made to the Embarcadero, but it is a fair bet that San Franciscans are going to want to keep the promenade.

San Franciscans' continuing concern about keeping access to the northeastern waterfront was recently evidenced through political action. In 2013, a developer proposed redeveloping a parcel adjacent to the Embarcadero into a 136-foot-high luxury condominium building, which would have meant raising the zoning height limit, but this proposal was defeated at the ballot box. Citizens became so concerned about what could happen along the city's waterfront that in 2014 voters passed a ballot proposition that maintained existing height limits on all Port-owned property unless a project-specific up-zoning was approved by a vote of the people. This means that development along the Embarcadero will likely continue to happen in incremental, piece-meal fashion, into the future.

Notes

1   João Pedro Teixeira, "Space in the Industrial Riverfront of Lisbon. Processes of Spatial Formation," *On W@terfront* 11 (October 2008): 18, accessed August 5, 2015, www.raco.cat/index.php/Waterfront/article/viewFile/218449/297616.
2   AIVP (Worldwide Network of Port Cities), "Lisbon: A New Relationship with the River," April 2015.
3   "Report / Lisbon: Valuing the Public Realm | The Academy of Urbanism," accessed January 11, 2017, www.academyofurbanism.org.uk/valuing-the-public-realm/.
4   "Site of Lisbon City Council: Master Plan," accessed October 10, 2015, www.cm-lisboa.pt/viver/urbanismo/planeamento-urbano/plano-diretor-municipal.
5   "Report / Lisbon."
6   "Site of Lisbon City Council: Front Riberinha," accessed October 10, 2015, www.cm-lisboa.pt/viver/urbanismo/projetos-obras-e-espaco-publico/espaco-publico/frente-riberinha.
7   "Modelling Sea-Level Rise in the Lisbon City Coastal Area, Using Free and Open Source Technologies," accessed October 10, 2015, www.academia.edu/8018770/Modelling_Sea-Level_Rise_in_the_Lisbon_city_coastal_area_using_Free_and_Open_Source_Technologies.
8   "Global and European Sea-Level Rise (CLIM 012) – Assessment Published Sep 2014" (European Environment Agency, 2014), accessed July 22, 2015, www.eea.europa.eu/data-and-maps/indicators/sea-level-rise-2/assessment.
9   João Miguel Dias, Juliana Marques Valentim, and Magda Catarina Sousa, "A Numerical Study of Local Variations in Tidal Regime of Tagus Estuary, Portugal," *PLoS ONE* 8, no. 12 (December 2, 2013), doi:10.1371/journal.pone.0080450.
10 "26 Municipalities Will Have Climate Change Adaptation Strategies,"

accessed October 11, 2015, www.eeagrants.gov.pt/index.php/en/
en-news/530-26-municipalities-will-have-climate-change-adaptation-strategies.

11 M. A. Baptista et al., "Potential Inundation of Lisbon Downtown by a 1755-like Tsunami," *Nat. Hazards Earth Syst. Sci.* 11, no. 12 (December 16, 2011): 3319, doi:10.5194/nhess-11-3319-2011.

12 Port of San Francisco, San Francisco (Calif.), and Waterfront Urban Design Technical Advisory Committee, eds., "The Port of San Francisco Waterfront Design & Access: An Element of the Waterfront Land Use Plan" (Port of San Francisco, 2004), 4.

13 Ibid., 13.

14 Port of San Francisco, "San Francisco Port Department : Embarcadero Promenade Design Criteria," January 13, 2011, 10, accessed July 20, 2015, www.sfport.com/index.aspx?page=1631.

15 Committee on Sea Level Rise in California, Oregon, and Washington; Board on Earth Sciences and Resources; Ocean Studies Board; Division on Earth and Life Studies; National Research Council, *Sea-Level Rise for the Coasts of California, Oregon, and Washington: Past, Present, and Future* (Washington, D.C.: The National Academies Press, 2012), 107–108.

16 City and County of San Francisco Civil Grand Jury 2013-2014, "Rising Sea Levels. . .At Our Doorstep," June 2014, 5,7, accessed August 19, 2015, http://civilgrandjury.sfgov.org/2013_2014/2014_CGJ_Report_Rising_Sea_Levels_w_correction.pdf.

17 San Francisco Bay Conservation and Development Commission, "Designing Public Shoreline Spaces for a Rising Bay," n.d., 2, accessed August 19, 2015, www.bcdc.ca.gov/planning/climate_change/AdaptPublicAccessSLRcaseStudy.shtml.

18 City and County of San Francisco, "San Francisco Sea Level Rise Action Plan," March 2016, accessed June 9, 2016, http://sf-planning.org/sea-level-rise-action-plan%20.

19 Los Angeles Times, "San Francisco Proposes $8 Million to Find a Fix for Quake-Vulnerable Sea Wall," *Latimes.com*, accessed May 7, 2016, /www.latimes.com/local/lanow/la-me-ln-san-francisco-sea-wall-20160505-story.html.

Part 2 | Patterns of Connectivity and Access

The urban contexts of the waterfront promenades included in this study are as varied as the promenades themselves. The patterns of streets and blocks adjacent to the promenades make them more or less accessible from nearby neighborhoods and can influence their usage. Whether promenades are situated in a traffic-calmed environment or near major roadways impacts not only their accessibility but also what it feels like to be on them.

If areas are drawn to the same scale it is easier to compare their patterns of connectivity and access. Here we have chosen to represent one square mile around select promenades drawn at a scale of one inch to one thousand feet (1″ = 1,000 feet, or 1:12,000) because this is a scale that allows patterns to be seen clearly. All of the square mile maps are oriented so that north is toward the top of the page. Decisions about which promenades to include in this analysis were based upon the availability of detailed spatial data, the desire to show a range of different patterns, and some personal choices.

The whole length of some promenades can be included in a square mile map, but other promenades and promenade systems extend well beyond the square mile. For these, the choice of what area to include in the map was made to show either typical conditions or particularly unusual conditions, as seemed appropriate.

Public parks are shown so that the patterns of parks around and near the promenades in different cities can be compared. Building footprints are shown to give a sense of the coverage of buildings near the promenades, an idea of the surrounding density, and a sense of whether there are many or few buildings. In places where public ferries connect promenade segments, their routes are shown with dashed lines.

Hong Kong (Kwun Tong), China

Scale: 1:12,000

- The elevated freeway running alongside the promenade limits access to it.

- Entries under the freeway are widely spaced.

- Streets giving access to the promenade are typically widely spaced, as much as 1,000 to 1,200 feet apart.

- Two large traffic circles one block inland of the promenade are difficult for pedestrians to navigate.

Hong Kong (Ma On Shan), China

Scale: 1:12,000

- The promenade is lined with large superblocks filled with high-rise buildings, except at Ma On Shan Park (toward the top), and so access except from the nearby housing estates is difficult.

- Streets giving access to the promenade are widely spaced, typically 700 to 1,000 feet apart.

- Pedestrians must cross the bicycle path to get to the promenade, which can only be accomplished at widely spaced crosswalks.

Gruissan, France

Scale: 1:12,000

- The promenades running along both the lagoon (toward the top) and the beach (lower right) can be frequently accessed from traffic-calmed neighborhood streets.

- Along the lagoon streets lead into the promenade at intervals of about 100 to 500 feet.

- Along the beach streets lead into the promenade at intervals of about 400 feet.

Lisbon (Passeio das Tágides and Passeio do Tejo), Portugal

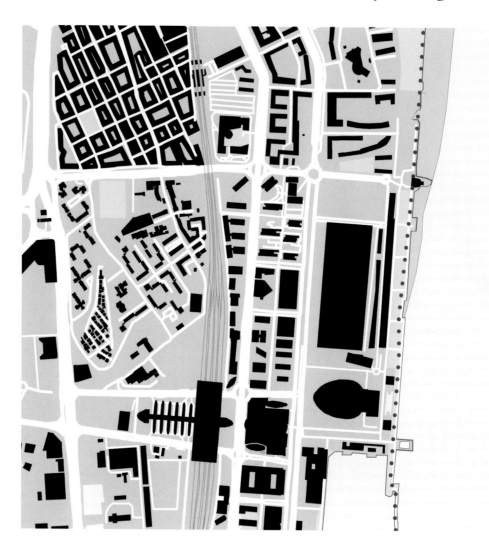

Scale: 1:12,000

- The Passeio das Tágides and Passeio do Tejo promenades (which connect at the one building situated to their waterside, toward the top) both run through narrow linear parks lined with large superblocks. Access to the Passeio das Tágides through the former Expo site, which has large footprint buildings in it, is particularly limited.

- A railroad track parallels the waterfront about a third of a mile inland, cutting off access to the promenades from older lower-income neighborhoods to the northwest.

Malmö (Western Harbour), Sweden

Scale: 1:12,000

- The promenades in the Western Harbour District (toward the top) are lined with small residential blocks and woonerf streets, making pedestrian access easy. They are also easy to get to by public transit because there are several bus stops on the nearby larger streets.

- The Ribersborgsstigen path along the beach (lower left) is more difficult to get to because access points to it are widely spaced.

New York City (Hudson River), USA

Scale: 1:12,000

- The Hudson River Park promenade, within its narrow linear park, is separated from adjacent neighborhoods by West Street, a wide arterial street. Many neighborhood streets lead into West Street, but only some intersections are signalized and have crosswalks.

- The Battery Park City Esplanade (lower left) can be easily accessed from the traffic-calmed streets of the immediate neighborhood, but getting to it from neighborhoods beyond West Street, which widens in this area, is difficult. Elevated walkway bridges are provided, but they require a climb.

Portland (Central Waterfront), USA

Scale: 1:12,000

- The westbank Esplanade (to the left) is relatively easy to get to. Streets lead to the waterfront at 260-foot intervals, but some climb to bridge approaches and don't give waterfront access. Crossing the wide street running along the park in which the Esplanade is situated can be a mild challenge.

- The eastbank Esplanade (to the right) is difficult to get to because a freeway closely parallels it and access points under the freeway are infrequent.

Rio de Janeiro (Leblon and Ipanema Neighborhoods), Brazil

Scale: 1:12,000

- Access to the beachfront promenade is restricted by the wide and heavily trafficked arterial street running adjacent to it.

- Streets in the Leblon neighborhood (to the left) lead to the waterfront at intervals of approximately 250 feet, giving good connectivity to the promenade.

- Streets in the Ipanema neighborhood (to the right) lead to the waterfront at intervals of approximately 750 feet, giving poorer connectivity to the promenade.

San Antonio (Downtown), USA

Scale: 1:12,000

- The downtown loop of the River Walk is a full level below street level. Main surface level streets cross it on bridges, and most bridges have stairs that connect with it.

- The River Walk segment that connects with the Convention Center built for the 1969 Hemisfair (lower right) can be accessed from street level via mid-block stairs.

- Many city blocks near the River Walk are filled with parking lots, and so density around it is low.

San Francisco (Embarcadero near downtown), USA

Scale: 1:12,000

- The wide and heavily trafficked Embarcadero roadway, with its central streetcar tracks, makes reaching the waterside promenade difficult, except at the plaza in front of the Ferry Building at the foot of Market Street (the diagonal street that separates the two different grids).

- North of Market Street, streets lead toward the water at intervals of about 350 feet but many don't cross the Embarcadero.

- South of Market Street, streets lead toward the water at intervals of about 750 feet.

Seoul (Cheonggyecheon near downtown), South Korea

Scale: 1:12,000

- Major arterial streets cross the recessed stream corridor at intervals of 1,300 to 1,600 feet.

- East of the downtown superblocks, small streets connect into the streets running along the stream corridor at intervals of 220 to 400 feet. Here, many buildings face the stream.

- The stream corridor is somewhat difficult to get to because the stairs or ramps down into it are widely spaced, at intervals ranging from 860 to 1,400 feet, near bridge crossings.

Stockholm (Hammarby Sjöstad), Sweden

Scale: 1:12,000

- Neighborhood streets connect with all the promenades at regular close intervals.

- The promenades on the north side of the lake are connected to those on the south side via a free public ferry.

- Along the south side of the lake, a streetcar line runs along the main roadway that parallels the waterfront two blocks inland, giving easy access to the promenades to those coming from afar.

Toronto (Beach Neighborhood), Canada

Scale: 1:12,000

- Neighborhood streets lead to the waterfront at intervals of 250 to 350 feet, giving easy local access to the boardwalk. The block orientation of many short ends fronting the boardwalk increases the sense of neighborhood connection with it.

- A streetcar line runs along the main commercial street that parallels the waterfront one long block inland. The streetcar connects with the downtown, making the promenade easily accessible to people coming from elsewhere in the city.

Vancouver (North and South False Creek Neighborhoods), Canada

Scale: 1:12,000

- The promenade along the north side of False Creek (toward the top) is easily accessible via narrow neighborhood streets, pedestrian walkways, and parks. The large street paralleling the waterfront has been traffic calmed with tree-lined medians.

- The promenade along the south side of the creek (toward the bottom) is easily accessible from immediately adjacent residential areas, but cut off from other neighborhoods by a wide arterial street.

- Ferries connect the promenades on each side of the creek.

Venice Beach, USA

Scale: 1:12,000

- Neighborhood streets lead to the waterfront at intervals of 250 feet, giving easy local access to the promenade. North of the Venice Pier, mid-block alleys also lead toward the waterfront.

- North of the pier, the main street paralleling the waterfront two blocks inland is relatively narrow but carries considerable traffic and has few crossings, creating a barrier.

- Many inland streets are interrupted from reaching the waterfront by canals, but walkways along the canals give connectivity for pedestrians.

Part 3 | Designing Waterfront Promenades

Chapter 13

Designing for People and Place

Communities have developed promenades for many different reasons and within widely varying circumstances. Some were built as part of economic development strategies, some were conceived as amenities within bucolic parks, and some were conceptualized foremost as entertainment venues. Some are oriented toward local residents, some toward tourists, and some toward both. All are to take advantage of a water setting with a public amenity.

Communities contemplating a new waterfront promenade or redesigning an existing one would do well to first determine the objectives of the project and contemplate the design approach that will best meet community needs and aspirations. There are many possibilities, and ultimate decisions will derive from local circumstances, community values, and cultural practices. Looking at what has been done elsewhere helps give a sense of the opportunities.

Promenades are of many different designs. Some are grand and others modest. Some are formally designed with a regular pattern of repeating elements and others are informally designed with a looser pattern and differentiated elements. Some are all of a piece in their design and others have multiple segments of varied design. Some are heavily landscaped and others mostly hardscape. Some have traditionally designed benches, light fixtures, and railings, and others have furniture elements of modern design. The design possibilities are endless.

We have seen different processes used to create promenades. Some were conceived by community groups and designed through participatory planning processes, and others created more autocratically through the actions of an entrepreneur, government official, or government agency. Some were achieved rapidly and others were built incrementally over time, or are still in the process of being built. The process through which a promenade comes into being has an impact on its character, its integration with or separation from its surrounding context, and how the community embraces it.

What follows are observations about design opportunities and planning approaches that derive from analysis of the many urban waterfront promenades studied.

Design Characteristics of the Best

Whatever the overarching project objectives and preferred design aesthetics, the best urban waterfront promenades have qualities that make them welcoming places for people and the unfolding of public life. They are inviting places that attract people in groups, in couples, and on their own to participate in the social life of the city. They are places where women feel safe. They invite people of all ages and abilities, including the elderly and differently abled people, by incorporating universal design features and elements attractive to people of all ages. Perhaps most important, the best promenades invite use by people of varied socio-economic status by providing free places to sit, by having land uses along them that are inclusive rather than exclusive, and by being accessible by public transit.

The best waterfront promenades are also designed to take advantage of two unique opportunities offered by a water's edge location: the possibility of creating a linear pedestrian way uninterrupted by vehicle crossings and the possibility of contributing to the ecological wellbeing of the water-to-land interface.

Certain physical characteristics contribute to making waterfront promenades inviting and inclusive community social spaces. Other characteristics contribute to taking advantage of an edge location.

A Place for Moving with Leisure

San Antonio River Walk

There are no precise rules for how much width is needed for a waterfront promenade. Engineering standards for roadways generally base recommended widths on calculations meant to maximize throughput and capacity, but more qualitative criteria are appropriate for waterfront promenades because people are drawn to them for other than their functional characteristics. Some people may use them for getting from one place to another, but most people use them for simply moving back and forth. For the most part, they are destinations rather than the functional means to get to some other destination. People value them for the experience of being on them while amongst others, rather than for the ability to move along them quickly, and so their nature is slow-paced. The Oxford Dictionary defines the word promenade as "a leisurely walk, ride, or drive, typically in a public place so as to meet or be seen by others."[1] Indeed, a sense of leisure lies at the heart of what a promenade is, and so the best criterion for determining the width of a promenade is that it should be sized to allow people to walk along it with leisure. If a promenade is also for bicyclists, then it should sized so that people can bike along it with leisure.

Different communities will need to determine what a sense of leisure means for their urban and social contexts, but some numbers may be helpful to understand how people walk and bike along existing promenades and the sense of leisure or excessive crowdedness associated with different promenade widths and usage numbers. The highly commercialized pedestrian-only downtown section of San Antonio's River Walk is in most places configured with 8-foot-wide walks on both sides of the streambed. On a typical Saturday evening in mid-March, each walk was observed to carry similar large numbers: 1,752 people per hour on the north side and 1,698 on the south side. These are high numbers in comparison with other promenades, particularly in light of the narrow walks. People could only move slowly rather than at a normal strolling pace, and the flow bunched up in places, sometimes even coming to a momentary stop. To put it simply, the walks felt uncomfortably crowded. Considering just the north side, a measure of its crowdedness that considers the number of people and the width of the walk calculates as 3.65 people per minute per foot of width (11.97 people per minute per meter of width). Considering both sides together, the crowdedness calculates to 3.59 people per minute per foot of width (11.78 people per minute per meter of width). This measure is at the outer edge of what is desirable, perhaps even beyond it.

The Brooklyn Bridge promenade at times gets even more crowded. On a sunny Sunday morning in November, the 15-foot-wide walkway was observed to handle 5,572 people per hour, including 25 frustrated bicyclists. Although the path is striped to indicate half is for pedestrians and half for bikers, pedestrians had taken over the whole width. People were walking at a slower than normal strolling pace and were almost touching each other as they walked. If someone paused to look at the view they were likely to be bumped into. The measure of crowdedness that day calculates as 6.19 people per minute per foot of width (20.32 people per minute per meter of width), the most crowded conditions observed on any of the promenades studied. For comparison, this figure is much greater than that found on two well-known European pedestrian-only shopping streets: the highly used Via dei Giubbonari in Rome (16.8 people per minute per meter) and Copenhagen's famous Stroget (13.1 people per minute per meter).[2]

San Sebastián's Paseo de La Concha also sees a particularly high number of users but doesn't feel crowded because people are distributed over a wider area. On a warm Thursday afternoon in June, 3,000 people per hour were observed moving along the 68-foot-wide promenade inclusive of the bicycle path, which some people used for walking because it was in shade, which amounts to 0.73 people per minute per foot of width (2.4 people per minute per meter).

In Barcelona, the promenade along San Sebastia Beach is particularly well used in the early evening. On a typical summer evening the 28-foot-wide walking path was observed to comfortably handle the 1,179 walkers and joggers per hour, which amounts to 0.70 people per minute per foot of width (2.3 people per minute per meter). The many walkers could stroll at whatever pace they wanted and the far fewer joggers could easily weave around them and maintain whatever pace they wanted. At the same time, the adjacent 10-foot-wide two-way bicycle path comfortably handled the 582 people per hour moving on bicycles, skateboards, and segways: 0.97 people per minute per foot of width (3.18 people per minute per meter). The bikers moved at a leisurely pace and those moving slightly

Paseo de La Concha, in San
Sebastián

faster than others were able to overtake the slower riders with ease by slipping momentarily into the opposing direction side of the path when it was clear.

Most of Vancouver's waterfront promenades allow leisurely strolling and biking even at their busiest times. The Coal Harbour promenade tends to be most used by walkers around noontime on weekdays, when people from nearby offices are taking a lunch break. On a typical summer weekday, 942 people per hour were observed walking or jogging along the 20-foot-wide pedestrian path, which amounts to 0.78 people per minute per foot of width (2.57 people per minute per meter). At the same time, 144 bikers per hour were observed moving along the 13-foot-wide two-way bicycle path, which amounts to only 0.18 people per minute per foot (0.24 people per minute per meter).

The waterfront promenades in Southeast False Creek tend to be most used by pedestrians and bikers alike on weekend and weekday afternoons. On a typical weekend afternoon in early September, 663 people per hour were observed walking or jogging along the 16-foot-wide pedestrian path near Hinge Park. This amounts to 0.69 people per minute per foot of width (2.26 people per minute per meter of width). At the same time, 399 people per minute were observed biking along the 15-foot-wide biking path, which amounts to 0.44 people per minute per foot of width (1.46 people per minute per meter). On a Tuesday late afternoon that same week, 432 people per hour were observed walking or jogging along the 15-foot-wide pedestrian path near the community center (1.58 people per minute per meter) and 356 people were observed biking along the 15-foot-wide bicycle path (2.58 people per minute per meter). At both times, pedestrians were strolling leisurely, joggers were moving at a range of paces, and bicyclists were moving at different speeds, though none were moving very fast, and were able pass each other with ease.

When waterfront promenades are meant to accommodate people on both foot and bicycle, an important consideration becomes whether both movement modes can happen on a single path or whether separated paths should be provided. It comes down to numbers and desired character. When both modes move on a single path, safety requires both walkers and bikers to act with awareness.

The Golden Gate Promenade at
Crissy Field, in San Francisco

A busy mixed path requires constant vigilance and can lead to conflicts and unsafe situations. For a mixed path to have a leisurely feel and be safe it is essential that bicyclists slow their movement to be amenable with the pace of pedestrians, and so the cultural norms of bicyclists should be taken into account. Observation suggests that bicyclists in some cultures are more willing to slow for pedestrians than in others.

In San Francisco, pedestrians and bicyclists mingle on the Golden Gate Promenade at Crissy Field and this works reasonably well because it doesn't get too crowded, most people follow the unwritten "rules of the road" of staying toward the right in the direction they are going in, and the dirt surface of the path works to slow the bikers. On a Saturday afternoon in March, 945 people per hour were observed moving along the path where it was 35 feet wide, with somewhat less than one quarter of the people on bikes. In all, this amounts to a total of 0.45 people per minute per foot of width (1.48 people per minute per meter), including both pedestrians and bikers.

The shared path arrangement doesn't work as well on San Francisco's Embarcadero Promenade, where pedestrian numbers can get very high and the handful of bikers who brave the crowd must constantly weave around walkers and are sometimes forced to stop because they have no room to maneuver. The measure of crowdedness observed just north of the Ferry Building on a typical Saturday around noon was 1.89 people per minute per foot of width (6.19 people per minute per meter). Cyclists do have the option of using the bicycles lanes striped at the edges of the Embarcadero roadway, but these lanes feel somewhat treacherous because they are narrow, heavy traffic is constantly moving next to them, and cars are often double parked in them: they are not places to bike with leisure.

In general, separated walking and bicycling paths is the better solution and helps make a promenade feel and be safer, especially for older people, young children, and differently abled people. The question is how much separation. If just a painted line or a rolled curb separates the paths then people may unconsciously or carelessly stray from their designed path and this can lead to conflicts.

Separated walking and biking places on the Southeast False Creek waterfront promenade, in Vancouver

The one-way bike path on Vancouver's Stanley Park seawall is a case in point. Bikers sometimes back up on it and when this happens more aggressive bikers, typically teenagers, will jump the rolled curb that distinguishes the bike path from the directly adjacent walking path and ride among the pedestrians. Walkers can be scared when these maneuvers happen abruptly and some serious accidents have occurred.[3] A stronger separation is usually a good idea, but experience suggests it doesn't have to be too wide. All of Vancouver's recently built waterfront promenades have a similar separated path design: a 15- to 20-foot-wide pedestrian walkway runs close to the water's edge, then comes a planted median that ranges from 4 to 7½ feet wide, and next comes a 12- to 15-foot-wide bicycle path. The medians are designed with regular breaks in them so that walkers entering the promenade can easily

Charleston Waterfront Park offers a good mix of sun and shade along its promenades

cross the bicycle path to get to the walking path. Each promenade segment has a different median planting design, some with trees and some without, which helps give them different identities.

Physical Comfort

If people are going to walk or bike for any distance along a waterfront promenade then it needs to be a physically comfortable place to be. For daytime use, perhaps the most important aspect of physical comfort has to do with there being both sun and shade, but there are no absolutes. The variables include climate, local culture, and visitor expectations. For instance, people on a beach boardwalk may be particularly seeking sun and people in cold northern climates may also be looking for as much sun as possible, and so perhaps providing areas of shade along promenades in these contexts is less necessary. In general, however, the best waterfront promenades offer a mix of sun and shade so that people can choose which they prefer, can get out of the sun when they need to or can be in the sun if they wish.

Spending considerable time on a waterfront promenade is facilitated if there are nearby public restrooms. Vancouver has integrated public restrooms into all of its promenades, including modestly designed facilities along its older promenades and elegantly designed ones along its newer promenades. Public restrooms are fitted under a grand staircase leading down to the Coal Harbour promenade, and a cascading waterfall abuts a facility along the False Creek North promenade. Public restrooms are also available in the several community centers facing onto or located near the promenades. At Charleston Waterfront Park, public restrooms can be found in the city-built and -run art gallery that overlooks the park and in two nearby parking garages. The restrooms are always open when the park is open (6 am to 11 or 12 pm), even those in the gallery when the gallery itself is closed. The location of these restrooms is noted on the several signs that describe park usage rules. All of Hong Kong's recently built promenades—the Ma On Shan Promenade, Kwun Tong Promenade, and Central and Western District Promenade—have multiple public restroom facilities integrated into their design. Public restrooms are also available along all of New York City's waterfront promenades or are planned, including one that will be housed in a pavilion under the freeway at the East River Waterfront Esplanade.

A promenade's surface has an impact on comfort. For pedestrians, walking on a soft surface, such as decomposed granite, may be more comfortable than walking on a paved surface, but some people may not like dirt paths if they are dusty. In Tiburon, California, where a locally oriented promenade built along a former rail corridor lines a stretch of San Francisco Bay, the solution was to build a central paved path flanked by narrow dirt paths on either side. This gives people a choice of which surface they prefer to walk on, even those walking side by side. Biking is most comfortable on a smooth paved surface, and so most bicycle promenades are designed this way. Exceptions include the bicycle paths along Lisbon's Passeio das Tágides and Ribeira das Naus, both of which are paved with cobblestones, and a segment of the older South False Creek promenade in Vancouver, which is paved with rough flagstones that are loose and wobbly in a few places. These rough surfaces generate vibrations when biking over them, making for an uncomfortable biking experience.

The landside frontage of a promenade can also affect people's comfort. Promenades directly bordered by high traffic roadways can be noisy and have bad air quality, and the moving vehicles can be an annoying visual presence, but variables like promenade width and edge buffering can make a difference. The central part of the Promenade des Anglais in Nice is used for leisurely promenading in spite of the adjacent high traffic roadway because its 50-foot width allows walkers to be far removed from the traffic. Busy West Street borders New York City's Hudson River Park but the waterfront promenade in the park is well buffered from the traffic by berms, trees, and high plantings. Conversely, the relatively narrow 13-foot-wide promenades along the Ipanema and Leblon beaches in Rio de Janeiro feel less than leisurely because of the relentlessness of the heavy traffic flowing by on the closely adjacent roadway, especially the constant flow of buses on the lane nearest the promenade. The 10-foot-wide two-way bicycle track that directly borders the roadway, with only a 2-foot-wide separating concrete curb, feels dangerous to ride on when moving west, and thereby closest to the traffic, because of the sense that you could be clipped by a bus, be forced to suddenly veer to avoid hitting passengers disembarking from buses onto the narrow curb, or that if you were to wobble you could fall into traffic. This is not a bicycle path for older people, small children, or the faint of heart.

Places to Sit

Seating along a waterfront promenade is important for comfort and also for enjoyment, because promenades are as much about taking in the scene as they are about linear movement. The best waterfront promenades offer many places where people can sit and have direct water views or watch the parade of people moving by. Seating may take the form of benches or sitting height ledges, although seats with backs may be most comfortable for most people. Relatively close spacing of seats both encourages lingering and makes the promenade more welcoming to seniors and people with mobility difficulties. Ideally, some seats should be placed where they will often be in shade and others should be placed where they will often be in sun, so that people will have choice.

Some promenades have seating arrangements that strongly invite lingering. The more than 700-foot-long raised wooden seat along Malmö's Sundspromenaden is a spectacular example. True, none of the seat is shaded, but local people flock to it in the summer when the populace of this far northern city seems intent on soaking up every bit of sunshine possible. In Charleston, copious benches line both the full-sun and the shaded walking paths. Along the Paseo de la Concha in San Sebastián, which is lined with two rows of closely spaced tamarind trees, two-sided benches sit between each tree in both rows. From them, people can look out toward the water and also watch the people strolling by on the main promenade path, or they can look in the other direction and

The promenade along Southeast False Creek, in Vancouver, is designed with fun places to sit

The Ipanema promenade, in Rio de Janeiro, offers only limited public seating

watch bikers moving on the bicycle path. While most benches offer full sun, many offer some spots of shade.

Some promenades have particularly creatively designed seating options. Along New York City's East River Waterfront Esplanade, barstool-like seats attached to the guardrail, which has a counter-like top cap, offer a place where people can seat and eat lunch or enjoy an evening drink. Regularly spaced benches sheltered by vine-covered trellises are to be found along Hong Kong's Kwun Tong Promenade. Along with benches, a variety of alternative seating options are to be had along Vancouver's Southeast False Creek promenade, including swiveling chairs, sculptural chaises longues, and undulating wood-decked seating walls.

Some waterfront promenades, even very famous ones, do not provide adequate public seating. The only free places to sit along Rio de Janeiro's promenades are widely spaced concrete benches, low concrete walls found near the restroom and changing structures that accompany most of the widely spaced lifeguard stations, and the steps that edge some sections of beach. These perches are in high demand and usually hard to get. Seating is available at the café kiosks that line the Copacabana and Leme promenades and are scattered along the Ipanema and Leblon promenades, but one must buy something to occupy one of these seats. These "rented" seats usually offer a choice of sitting in the sun or sitting in the shade because most kiosks have café umbrellas. The Venice Beach Boardwalk also has very little seating, just occasional benches of rustic wood and concrete construction. Of course, in both Rio and Venice the wide beaches next to the promenade offer a multitude of places to sit or lie down on the sand, and this is what many people do.

Ease of Access

The best urban waterfront promenades are easy to reach. They are well connected with the city's street system, have many access points, have nearby public transit stops, and are without major pedestrian barriers to be overcome, such as nearby wide arterial streets. The classic beachfront boardwalks in

Venice, California, and Hollywood, Florida, are perhaps the most connected to their immediately surrounding neighborhoods, with streets leading into them at intervals of roughly 250 and 200 feet respectively along their entire lengths, most of them small neighborhood streets. However, the beach strips of both the communities are somewhat isolated from neighborhoods further inland. In Venice, a parallel arterial street and canal combine to create a barrier. In Hollywood, the narrow beach strip lies on a barrier island separated from the mainland by an inland waterway. The access characteristics of a number of other promenades are discussed in Part 2.

Lack of easy access doesn't mean that a promenade will not be used. Some spectacular waterfront promenades have been built in poorly connected contexts but still attract people because they are in cities where open space is in high demand. The Brooklyn Bridge Park waterfront promenade is not at all well connected with the city street system, lying as it does at the base of a steep promontory alongside of which runs a double-decked freeway, and can only be accessed at its ends. And yet, the promenade draws many people because it runs through a wonderfully designed park that offers respite from the dense crush of the city and is one of the few large open spaces anywhere nearby. Likewise, the 2-mile-long Ma On Shan Promenade, in suburban Hong Kong, has only a handful of access points because it is fronted by superblocks, but people from the surrounding community come to it, if in smaller number than in Brooklyn, because it is the community's main open public space along with a park that itself fronts the promenade. What can be learned from these examples is that whether or not a disconnected promenade is well used will likely have to do with the density of people nearby, the availability of other open space alternatives, and whether or not the promenade offers a truly special experience.

Safety

For waterfront promenades to attract many people they must feel safe. One of the most important qualities that can contribute to a sense of safety is the quality of openness. Paths configured so that people using them will have open sight lines rather than narrow or constricted sight lines provide a sense of openness.

Light fixtures along the promenade running next to the lagoon, in Gruissan

Light fixtures along the Battery
Park City Esplanade

Low lighting in a seating area along the
Central District Promenade, in Hong Kong

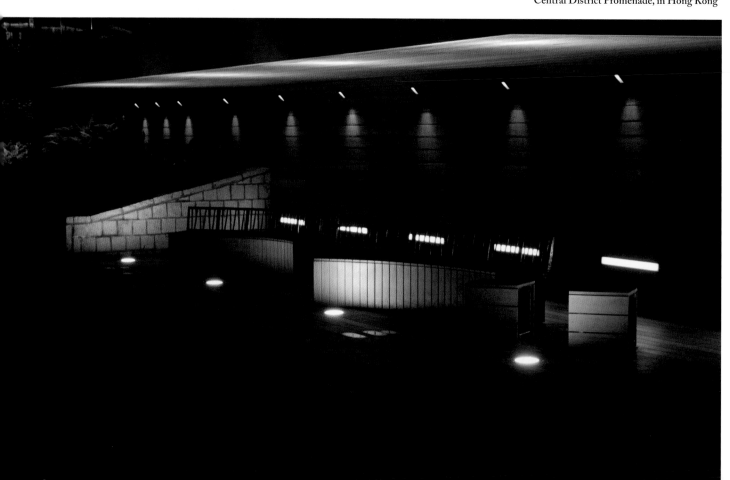

In addition to openness, perhaps the best way to ensure that a promenade will feel and hopefully be safe for all users is to design it so that there will usually be many eyes upon it. Foremost, this means designing the promenade to attract many users. In most cultures, the presence within eyesight of multiple diverse others on a promenade, people of different ages, both sexes, and representing a range of socio-economic groups, will likely contribute a sense of safety to users who might feel vulnerable in more isolated public situations. A sense of eyes on the promenade can also be provided by the fronting land uses: cafés along the promenade with people sitting at outside tables, parks along the promenade with people lounging or playing in them, dwelling units immediately on the promenade with windows overlooking it, or better yet with front doors, entry terraces, and windows overlooking it.

If promenades are to be used after dark then lighting is essential for safety. Many waterfront promenades are lit with pedestrian-scale light fixtures set along the walking path at regular intervals of typically 50 to 80 feet, sometimes within a line of trees, but some promenades are lit more strategically. In Rio de Janeiro, where there is concern to discourage illicit activity, the Copacabana promenade and beach are illuminated by floodlights mounted on tall posts located in the center median of the adjacent roadway. In Barcelona, the Barceloneta segments of the Passeig Marìtim and adjacent beaches, which see considerable nighttime use, are illuminated by tall floodlights located right on the walkway.

The newly constructed Central District Promenade in Hong Kong, where the after dark emphasis is on providing good viewing of the nightly Symphony of Lights show, is only dimly lit by various uplights and downlights mounted near seating areas and within low bollards. This promenade is not well frequented at night, has no residential buildings directly overlooking it, and has no cafés or commercial spaces along it. In combination with these things, the low lighting level makes the promenade feel unsafe at night. Sightlines along the promenade and within the adjacent park are relatively open, which helps somewhat counteract the sense of possible danger.

Good Maintenance and Quality Materials

Cleanliness generally helps make public spaces attractive and inviting, and so it is with waterfront promenades. On weekend mornings, the waterfront promenade along San Francisco's Ocean Beach is often marred by large piles of trash spilling out from and stacked around trashcans. Nighttime beachgoing partiers leave the trash. The trashcans are clearly too small or too few in number to contain all the trash generated. Until it is picked up, which usually happens late morning, the ambience of the promenade is largely ruined. Although relatively frequently located and regularly emptied trash containers are important for maintaining the cleanliness of a promenade, experience suggests that placing trash containers directly next to seating can be problematic because it is unpleasant to sit near smelly trash.

As important as cleanliness are well-maintained walking and biking paths. In Lisbon, the main path of the Passeio das Tágides promenade is surfaced with a mix of concrete aggregate pavers and cobblestones that have settled differentially. This makes walking challenging for people with balance or mobility problems.

Fine materials and fine or elaborate detailing can certainly help make a waterfront promenade attractive and memorable, but simpler materials and detailing can also be appealing as long as good materials and craftsmanship are used. More important is keeping the physical elements in good condition. The benches, railings, and light fixtures that attend promenades don't have to be fancy but they should be kept in good repair. Likewise, the trees and planted areas that attend many promenades don't need to be elaborate in their design but should be well maintained.

Complementing and Inclusive Frontage

A promenade's landside frontage has a big impact on its ambience. We have seen promenades fronted by parallel roadways, lineal parks, housing, restaurants, stores, industrial uses, and parking lots—the gamut of urban uses of land. In some places the frontage was planned and built in conjunction with the promenade, and elsewhere the promenade was inserted into an existing context and inherited the existing frontage. Communities will have different preferences for the ambience of their promenade, but in general the frontage should complement the promenade, not overwhelm it, and be inclusive rather than exclusive.

In this regard, San Francisco's Crissy Field promenade is a gem, running through open space, with many places to sit and grand views of San Francisco Bay and the Golden Gate Bridge, and with just enough modest commercial space along it to create activity and options for people but not distract from the promenade experience. At the western end of the promenade is the Warming Hut, a small wooden building adaptively restored from its previous industrial use, where people can buy food and drink, or souvenirs. At the promenade's eastern end is the Crissy Field Center, a structure of more modern design that also serves food. Auto parking near the Warming Hut is hidden from view by mounded earth berms, contributing to the bucolic atmosphere. The much larger auto parking area near the Crissy Field Center is not screened but much of the parking takes place on grass and there are interspersed picnic areas, so although the atmosphere is less bucolic it is not harsh.

The commercial uses along the recently built Marina Bay Promenade in Singapore, which include a casino, a large upscale shopping mall, a luxury hotel, and expensive eateries, are anything but modest and their attractions tend to overshadow the promenade itself. One reason is that Singapore's hot and humid climate helps make the air-conditioned commercial spaces more attractive than the promenade. Misters meant to moderate the temperature are a feature of one promenade segment, solar powered fans create breezes along another segment, and trees shade many areas, but these elements aren't enough to compete with indoor air-conditioning. The promenade is only lightly used except for short evening periods when people spill out of the shopping mall, sit on a part of the promenade that converts into a temporary amphitheater, and watch video, light, and water spectacles. After the shows, people quickly disperse and retreat back inside. In addition, the commercial spaces are so high-end that they give an air of exclusivity to the promenade, making it feel like a place only for the well-heeled.

Some American waterfront promenades are highly commercialized in a way that overwhelms the promenade but at the same time gives it an inclusive feel. Along the downtown section of San Antonio's River Walk, people's ability to walk with leisure is compromised because of the crowds

Commercial spaces line the
Venice Beach Boardwalk

generated by the many eateries and drinking establishments, and the atmosphere is jarring in places because of blaring music. And yet, there is a wide choice of eating establishments, some expensive and some inexpensive, and so all types of people frequent this promenade. Along the Venice Beach, Hollywood, Fort Lauderdale, and Coney Island boardwalks, taking in water views seems less of a focus for many people than partaking of the pleasures of sidewalk cafés, eateries, and drinking establishments, or, at Coney Island, riding the amusement rides, or, at Venice, interacting with sidewalk vendors. In the evening, loud music emanates from some venues along these promenades, creating a party-like atmosphere. Along all of these promenades, some stretches are less commercialized than others, giving people who desire it the choice of a less chaotic place to be.

How very different are the Western Harbour promenades in Malmö and the Hammarby Sjöstad promenades in Stockholm, where residential uses in mid-rise buildings, with or without occasional ground floor cafés, border the walks. These promenades have a peaceful neighborhood ambience to them and yet also feel inclusive because they are so welcoming. Malmö's Sundspromenaden serves as a major outdoor living room for the city, drawing people from afar, but the predominantly residential land uses along it keep things calm. Similarly, the small-scale cafés, restaurants, shops, hotels, and housing along Portland's RiverPlace Boardwalk create an ambience that is active but also peaceful.

For overall balance of adjacent uses that complement waterfront promenades, it is hard to do better than what is found in Vancouver at False Creek North, Southeast False Creek, and Coal Harbour. These walks run through linear parks or at the edge of larger parks and are only rarely bounded by roadways, though street ends, often pedestrianized, regularly meet them. The promenades pass residential buildings in the form of either point towers over podium bases or mid-rise blocks. Vancouver mandates that all ground floor residential units have direct street-facing entries, so those units facing the promenades look like townhouses, with front entry doors and terraces. There are small commercial areas near each promenade, and also community centers with cafés in them that offer outdoor seating.

Townhouses line the False Creek
North promenades, in Vancouver

Uninterrupted Movement

Along with water views, the other characteristic common to all waterfront promenades is their edge location. This means that promenades can be designed to allow people on foot or on bicycles to move for some distance without crossing a vehicle roadway. What a welcome relief this can be! What an encouragement for getting physical activity! The possibility of uninterrupted linear movement in an attractive waterfront setting may encourage people to engage in physical exercise, long walks, or runs, or bike rides, especially when they see others doing so. It may also contribute to people's mental health by providing a place to walk and bike free of the stresses of interacting with motorized vehicles.

In Vancouver, it is possible to start walking or biking at Granville Island, go all around False Creek, along English Bay, around Stanley Park, along Coal Harbor and then retrace one's route back again to Granville Island, a total distance of more than 13.5 miles (22 kilometers), without ever crossing a vehicle roadway. Vehicle roadways do not interrupt most promenades but driveways do cross some, and in those places where many vehicles use the driveways it makes the promenade experience less pleasant than it otherwise would be. Notable places where driveway conflicts occur are along San Francisco's Embarcadero Promenade, where piers to the waterside of the promenade have parking lots on them, and along the Venice Beach Boardwalk, where large parking lots are carved out of the beach beyond the promenade.

A seemingly playful pedestrian path design used on some promenades can frustrate continuous pedestrian movement. Along central area portions of the promenades in Fort Lauderdale and Lisbon, lines of trees are planted in a random staggered pattern across the walking path, which forces walkers to constantly change their course along what would otherwise be a straight walking path. Doing this for much of a distance is annoying.

Places to Get Close to the Water

All waterfront promenades provide substantial water views, with the exception of promenades nestled in beach dunes or wetland grasses that give only water glimpses, and many promenades are configured to allow people to look directly down into the water. Some of the best are also designed to allow people to get close enough to the water to actually touch it if they want. Clearly this opportunity isn't available for all promenades, such as beach fronting boardwalks (where the beach gives water access) or promontory promenades, but is a good option for promenades in other contexts.

We have seen several promenades designed to provide direct water access. Malmö's Western Harbour Promenade is situated atop a high riprap armored seawall, but at several locations broad steps lead down to large bathing platforms or onto long piers from which people can jump and dive into the ocean water. Modest, individually sized sunbathing platforms attach in places to the wooden boardwalk that snakes through Hammarby Sjöstad's constructed wetland area. These platforms are a step or two down from the boardwalk and allow people sitting on them to dangle their feet in the water if they wish. Part of Lisbon's Ribeira das Naus promenade is designed with broad steps that slope down to the water, and is configured so that the lower steps become inundated when the Tagus River is at high tide. People like to walk along whichever step is closest to the water at a given time and may sometimes dip a foot into the water. Along the section of Portland's Eastbank Esplanade that runs atop floating pontoons, people can sit at the pontoon's edge and dangle their feet toward the water several feet below. A bench-lined finger dock extending from the main walkway offers the best place for this activity.

Vancouver's various promenade segments offer multiple possibilities for getting close to the water. In numerous places around Stanley Park, steps lead down from the seawall to mudflats that are exposed at low tide and inundated at high tide. Along one stretch of the North False Creek seawall, a second walkway situated at a lower level than the main walkway and accessible only to pedestrians is lined with seats along its inland side and with various steps leading into the water on its waterside.

Ecological Services

Most waterfront promenades, with the exception of bridge and promontory promenades, are situated at or near the important ecological seam that occurs where land and water meet. In natural environments, this seam is often occupied by wetland plant species and is a rich habitat zone for sea life and bird life. In urban areas, the natural seam between land and water has in most places been disrupted, whether by land reclamation, the building of bulkheads or seawalls, or by beach "nourishment." Creating a waterfront promenade offers the opportunity to re-introduce nature at the water's edge, or at least to design the promenade so that it provides ecological services. Options range from planting trees along a promenade to contribute to the urban forest, designing the promenade with water catchment and infiltration areas that contribute to storm water management, or creating wetlands at the promenade's edge.

Of all the promenades studied, those at Hammarby Sjöstad, Brooklyn Bridge Park, and Crissy Field stand out for their ecological features. Hammarby Sjöstad was designed as an eco-district, and so ecological design features abound throughout the neighborhood. The promenades that ring the lake around which the district is built all do their part by contributing to neighborhood walkability, and the boardwalk through the constructed wetland offers people the opportunity to get close to this rich habitat zone without disturbing natural processes. At Brooklyn Bridge Park, the water's edge of the promenade is in many places a living shoreline, with wetlands and habitat. At Crissy Field, the promenade runs adjacent to reconstructed beach dunes and a constructed marsh. The inlet to the marsh changes shape and location in response to tidal flows, making natural processes visible. The shoreline design is such that the beach along Crissy Field may actually enlarge over time as sea level rise occurs, although it was not intended as an adaptive waterfront.[4]

Particularly important for the current era, waterfront promenades can be designed to make urban water edges resilient to sea level rise, where there is a need to do so. This topic will be explored in the following chapter.

Hammarby Sjöstad wetland
boardwalk bathing platform

Brooklyn Bridge Park living
shoreline

Key Planning Concepts

Beyond giving an understanding of the design characteristics that contribute to making waterfront promenades inviting and inclusive social places that take full advantage of the opportunities presented by their edge location, the promenades that have been studied suggest some key planning concepts.

A Simple Idea Implemented Over the Long Term Can Add Up to a Lot

The Vancouver waterfront promenade achievement speaks volumes about what can be accomplished when a city embraces the idea of preserving its waterfront for public use and prioritizing pedestrian and bicycle movement at the water's edge, hangs on to the vision for a long time, and implements it with determination and creativity whenever opportunities arise. In Vancouver, the vision was first articulated in the city's comprehensive plan of 1929, prepared at the behest of a citizens' group. It built upon the success of the Stanley Park seawall promenade begun some years earlier. Over the next 50 years the city built promenades along the English Bay, Kitsilano and Point Grey beaches in conjunction with waterfront parks. In the 1970s, the city seized the opportunity to build a waterfront promenade along South False Creek in conjunction with city-led redevelopment of former industrial land near Granville Island. Since the early 1990s, the city has been crafting planning policies and design guidance to structure the redevelopment of the rest of the former industrial land around False Creek, and also former industrial land along the Coal Harbour and Fraser River waterfronts, into dense, mixed-use residential neighborhoods. These policies mandate that developers of the waterfront land build generous pedestrian and bicycle promenades at the water's edge, running through linear parks. Landscape architects are free to design the promenades with different detailing, furniture, and planting patterns and palates, as long as the general guidelines set by the city are met.

Through this sustained almost 90-year-long planning effort—longer if the first Stanley Park seawall is included—Vancouver has built a waterfront promenade system second to none. These promenades function as the city's primary public open space and are highly valued by residents and visitors alike. Granted, Vancouver had the advantage of never having built freeways along its waterfronts, or anywhere in the city for that matter, a decision influenced by its vision of a leisure-oriented public waterfront, so it didn't have to dismantle freeways to build promenades. Also, the industrial lands around False Creek and Coal Harbour were under government control and so their development could be undertaken as large projects with single developers, as opposed to the more incremental development that would likely have occurred if many separate owners had held the waterfront land.

New York City has since 1975 envisioned a continuous shared-use bicycle and pedestrian greenway path all around Manhattan Island, and has been incrementally implementing this vision in spite of freeway obstacles and without benefit of large waterfront neighborhood redevelopment projects. The idea was first articulated in a proposal prepared by the City Planning Department and subsequently refined in a multitude of reports and master plans. Various greenway segments had been built by 2002 when, under the direction of Mayor Bloomberg, the City committed to completing the route by summer 2003.[5] The greenway is now 32 miles long, running mostly along the waterfront except for some gaps where it is routed on city streets away from the waterfront.

Lisbon recently embraced the vision of opening its largely industrialized and largely government controlled waterfront for public use, a concept first articulated in the city's 2008 Riverfront General Plan. The plan calls for opening up almost 12 miles of the waterfront and building an almost 7-mile-long waterfront biking and walking promenade. A first segment has been built along the city's central waterfront and plans are being prepared for other segments. It will be interesting to see how the city proceeds in the future and what kind of a waterfront promenade network is eventually realized.

Participatory Planning Processes Help Create Locally Oriented Promenades

When local people participate in planning and designing promenades, perhaps also spearheading the initial idea to create them, the promenade is likely to better meet community needs and desires and be more responsive to the local context. New York City's Hudson River Park Promenade, Brooklyn Bridge Park Promenade, and East River Waterfront Esplanade were created through very participatory planning processes, and their designs are the richer for it.

Conversely, some promenades were accomplished with little community participation or through processes that paid little heed to local input. Of promenades created recently, Hong Kong's Central and Western District Promenade and Kwun Tong Promenade, Singapore's Marina Bay Promenade, and Seoul's Cheonggyecheon Stream Walk come particularly to mind, but it is important to remember that there is less tradition of participatory planning in these countries than there is in the United States. Nonetheless, the lack of citizen participation in the planning and design of these promenades may be a reason the first three of these are so little used.

It is Possible to Overcome Freeway Barriers

All too many cities are cut off from their waterfronts by freeways but this does not mean it is impossible to create a waterfront promenade. Where there is a will, there is a way.

Several cities have removed waterfront freeways and built promenades in their place. San Francisco took down the elevated double-decked Embarcadero Freeway that marred its downtown waterfront for 30 years until it was damaged in the 1989 Loma Prieta Earthquake and residents voted to take it down. A surface boulevard with a streetcar line in its center and a waterfront promenade along its edge was built in its stead, creating a right-of-way that still accommodates cars (perhaps too many of them) but also prioritizes movement by transit, bike, and foot. In 1974, Portland removed its Harbor Drive Freeway, which had for almost 30 years separated the city's downtown from the Willamette River, replacing it with a wide park and waterfront promenade backed by a relatively narrow through traffic street. The park and promenade have become Portland's outdoor living room. In the 1980s, New York City removed the elevated West Side Highway, which ran along a long stretch of the Hudson River waterfront for almost 50 years, replacing it with a surface street. In 1988, the waterfront foreshore and a number of derelict piers beyond

Kwun Tong Promenade

the new roadway were dedicated as the Hudson River Park, and park improvements including promenades have been happening incrementally ever since, funded through a unique public–private partnership.

In Seoul, the Cheonggyecheon Stream, around which the ancient city first developed, had by the 1950s been turned into a sewer and decked with an arterial road, which in the 1970s was itself covered by an elevated freeway. In 2002, through the quick action of the city's newly elected mayor, the freeway and arterial street were removed, the stream was uncovered and augmented with pumped water, and a recessed linear park with promenades was created along it. At street level, frontage roads give access to the buildings that previously fronted the arterial street.

We have also seen examples of cities that have retained their waterfront freeways but have inserted promenades under and next to them, using creative design strategies to make the promenades attractive despite the presence of the freeway structure and the noise and noxious fumes generated by the traffic on it. New York City has done this in several places. Since 2005, the city has been planning and building the East River Waterfront Esplanade under the elevated section of the FDR Drive freeway between the Battery and the East River Park. In Brooklyn, the Brooklyn Heights Promenade was placed atop the double-decked Brooklyn-Queens Expressway that was built along the promontory edge of the Brooklyn Heights neighborhood in the late 1940s and early 1950s. The promenade was meant to mollify the concerns of residents protesting against the freeway's construction, and its inclusion greatly helps mitigate the impact of the freeway. Since 2009, the industrial waterfront land and derelict shipping piers lying at the base of the promontory have been developed into the Brooklyn Bridge Park. A waterfront promenade snakes through the naturalistically designed park and views of the elevated freeway are screened by a tall berm.

In Hong Kong, the Kwun Tong Promenade was built next to an elevated freeway running along an industrial section of the East Kowloon waterfront. The government built it as an early step in a massive public sector led redevelopment project that envisions the adjacent area transformed into a major business district. The promenade is relatively modest in its design and fitted with exercise facilities to attract local residents, but it is also designed to attract tourists as it features unusual artworks

Temporary connection between the Southeast False Creek and South False Creek promenades, in Vancouver

that are illuminated and emit steam at night. The promenade is not yet well used, in part because it is hard to reach since nearby streets are auto dominated.

Portland has overcome the barrier posed by the Interstate 5 freeway, which runs along the east bank of the Willamette River very close to the water, by creating a very attractive waterfront promenade running parallel to the freeway atop pontoons floating on the river.

Simple Connections Are Better Than None

From the Vancouver, Barcelona, Manhattan, Portland, San Antonio, and Hammarby Sjöstad case studies, as well as others, we have learned that having a long continuous promenade system makes for a truly special community amenity. The first three of these also teach that creating connections between separated promenade segments is important even if those connections are very simple in their design.

Vancouver has been working for several decades to create a promenade loop around its False Creek waterway, relying on the developers who are turning the large parcels of de-industrialized land around the creek into residential neighborhoods to build the promenade segment by segment according to the city's design guidelines. Neighborhood development has proceeded in stages, resulting in gaps between promenade segments, most notably between the Southeast False Creek and South False Creek promenades and between the North False Creek promenade and the promenade near Science World at the eastern end of the creek. Rather than leaving the segments disconnected, the city has built simple connectors between them, which in some places are just narrow concrete paths lined with chain link fences.

The northern part of Barcelona's 3-mile-long Passeig Marítim is less developed than the southern part because construction money for the promenade dried up shortly after completion of the 1992

The promenade along the waterfront in Zihuatanejo is created through a series of simply designed segments

Olympic Games. Some stretches toward the very northern end are no more than simple sidewalks running past parking lots and in one location the promenade runs through the middle of a parking lot. It is worth pushing past these stretches because beyond them the promenade connects with the Forum sports park, which has a jetty protected aquatic center and large-scale sculpturally shaped outdoor rooms.

In New York City, the waterfront segments of the Manhattan Greenway that circles Manhattan Island are connected to each other by marked walking and biking paths running on city streets. Northern stretches of the East River Waterfront Esplanade, which constitutes a considerable length of the East River facing greenway, have not yet been built in their planned final form but have been indicated in a temporary way by simply striping walking and biking paths under the elevated freeway beneath which the esplanade runs.

Creating any connection at all between promenade segments, no matter how simple, is much better than having none. The longer and more connected waterfront promenades are, the more they will connect people with urban waterfronts, and the more people will use them.

Promenade connection through a parking lot toward the northern end of the Passeig Maritim, in Barcelona

Notes

1 Judy Pearsall, ed., *The Concise Oxford Dictionary*, Tenth Edition (Oxford; New York: Oxford University Press, 1999).
2 Allan B. Jacobs, *Great Streets* (Cambridge, MA: MIT Press, 1995), 316–317.
3 "Stanley Park Seawall Collision Leads to Lawsuit," accessed May 23, 2016, www.cbc.ca/news/canada/british-columbia/vancouver-visitor-sues-over-cycling-accident-on-stanley-park-seawall-1.3206986.
4 Kristina Hill, "Personal Correspondence Regarding Sea Level Rise and Waterfronts," June 23, 2014.
5 City of New York, "Manhattan Waterfront Greenway Master Plan," November 2004, 1–3.

Chapter 14

Meeting the Challenge of Rising Water

Climate change is threatening urban waterfronts the world over and the challenges will only get greater. Coastal communities face increased flooding from rising seas combined with more frequent and severe storm events that bring storm surge. Riverfront communities face increased flooding as rivers swell with storm water runoff from more frequent and severe storm events, combined in some places with elevated tidal flows. At risk are countless acres of urban waterfront land, countless homes, countless industrial and commercial buildings, and enormous amounts of public infrastructure.

The rising water will also challenge existing waterfront promenades and present challenges for building new ones. In the face of the enormity of the climate change and sea level rise problems it may seem that concern for the placement and design of waterfront promenades for the communal enjoyment of today's and tomorrow's citizens is a relatively small matter, even inconsequential. But these are related matters. People will continue to be attracted to urban waterfronts and will want access to them. Communities with waterfront promenades will want to keep them, rebuilding them as necessary. Communities will also want to build new waterfront promenades and will want them to last awhile, even generations. As urban waterfronts around the world are adapted to the rising water, there will be opportunities to create innovatively designed waterfront promenades as integral parts of adaptation strategies.

Many coastal communities with waterfront promenades have not yet addressed the sea level rise problem, but some have and much can be learned from their example. Here, we first review current sea level rise projections and possible adaptation responses, and then explore the approaches communities are taking to adapt to rising water and also preserve or create waterfront promenades.

Challenges and Adaptation Strategies

The majority of the scientific community agrees that global sea levels have been rising over the past century from human-induced causes and will continue to rise into the future, but there is considerable uncertainty about what may be expected and when. Global sea level rise is tied to global warming stemming from the build-up of atmospheric greenhouse gases that has been occurring since the industrial revolution. Trapped greenhouse gases cause the Earth's surface temperature to rise and the oceans absorb 80 percent of this heat. Seawater expands as it warms, contributing to sea level rise. Warmer temperatures also cause glaciers and the Greenland and Antarctica ice sheets to melt, contributing to further sea level rise. There is uncertainty about future amounts and rates of greenhouse gas emissions, how much and at what rate global warming will occur, and how different levels of global warming will impact ocean water thermal expansion and ice melt, and hence sea level rise.

For many coastal communities there is also uncertainty about how local sea level rise will differ from global sea level rise because relative local sea level rise will be influenced by regional variables including changes in vertical land movement and ocean dynamics. Some regions have long been experiencing gradual coastal land uplift in response to the melting of ice sheets at the end of the last ice age, while other areas are experiencing coastal subduction due to tectonic plate movement or subsidence from groundwater pumping and other causes. Natural climate variability, such as El Niño weather patterns, periodically cause regional sea level changes because they affect water temperature, winds, and ocean currents. Complexities then abound.

Researchers around the world are working to find answers to the many questions related to how much sea levels will rise and when. Many researchers are creating models that use physical scientific evidence in conjunction with assumptions about future greenhouse gas emissions to create projections of future sea level rise. As might be expected, the projections from different models vary based upon the scientific evidence included and what assumptions are used. Some entities are trying to synthesize the whole body of international research and to make sea level rise projections based upon the findings around which consensus has coalesced. Even so, there are differences.

The Intergovernmental Panel on Climate Change (IPCC), established by the United Nations in 1988, is the leading international body working on climate change assessment. The IPCC regularly reviews and assesses the latest scientific, technical and socio-economic information produced around the world relevant to climate change and then prepares reports that synthesize the information and make future projections from it. Thousands of scientists around the world contribute to the IPCC's work and to authoring its reports, and so its projections are widely referenced.

IPCC's most recent Fifth Assessment Report (AR5) was published in a series of reports authored by various working groups in 2013 and 2014, culminating in a synthesis report published in 2014. The report establishes four different scenarios of possible atmospheric greenhouse gas concentrations that may occur by 2100 as the result of different possible emission trajectories, and then makes projections about the global temperature rise and other impacts associated with each, including sea level rise.[1] The scenarios, called Representative Concentration Pathways (RCPs), include a high "business as usual" scenario that assumes continued greenhouse gas emissions (RCP 8.5), a low scenario that assumes aggressive greenhouse gas reduction and sequestration (RCP 2.6), and two medium scenarios that assume in turn stabilization of greenhouse gas emissions by 2050 and sharp reductions thereafter (RCP 4.5) or that greenhouse emissions continue to increase gradually until the last decades of the twenty-first century and then stabilize (RCP 6.0). The name of each scenario refers to the radiative forcing (change in energy in the atmosphere due to greenhouse gas emissions) associated with it, expressed in watts per square meter (W/m^2) of the earth's surface. The likely global sea level rise by 2100 projected from the scenarios ranges from .28 meters to .98 meters (11 inches to 3.2 feet).[2] The report states unequivocally that during the twenty-first century sea levels will rise in more than 95 percent of ocean areas and that most areas will be within 20 percent of the global average.[3]

Some researchers argue that the possible contribution to sea level rise from Antarctic ice melt is grossly underestimated in the IPCC scenarios. The IPCC elected to not include within its scenarios much contribution from Antarctica ice melt because it felt there wasn't enough scientific consensus on that subject. A 2016 study published in *Nature*, which incorporates previously underappreciated ice melt processes, projects that Antarctica ice melt could itself contribute an additional meter of sea level rise to the IPCC high emission scenario RCP 8.5, which would bring the high end projection of sea level rise by 2100 to almost 2 meters.[4]

Some researchers are using an alternative approach to projecting sea level rise known as semi-empirical modeling (SEM). Instead of trying to model all the various processes that give rise to greenhouse gases and all the various effects that rising global temperatures have on sea level rise, which is the approach favored by the IPCC, SEMs take the simpler approach of analyzing historic relationships between sea levels and global temperatures.[5] Some SEM researchers suggest that if findings correlating historic ice sheet configurations with global temperature were to be incorporated into the IPCC scenarios, the upper end projection of sea level rise by 2100 would be to 1.5 meters instead of .98 meters.[6]

Along with the uncertainties about what sea level rise to expect by 2100 there are further uncertainties about what to expect after that. The IPCC report states that it is virtually certain that global mean sea level rise will continue beyond 2100 due to continued seawater thermal expansion, and projects that global sea level may rise by as much as 6.63 meters by 2500, driven mostly by thermal expansion plus substantial melting of the Greenland ice sheet and a small amount of melting of the Antarctica ice sheet.[7] It also finds that evidence suggests sustained global warming of between 2°C to 4°C above pre-industrial global temperatures would likely lead to the eventual near complete loss of the Greenland ice sheet, resulting in a sea level rise of about 7 meters.[8] Meanwhile, SEM researchers suggest that under a high emissions scenario melting of the Antarctica ice sheet could contribute as much as 15 meters (49 feet) of sea level rise by 2500.[9]

Several entities in the United States also conduct climate change assessment and their sea level rise projections differ from the IPCC projections and from each other. The U.S. Global Change Research Program (USGCRP), established in 1989, regularly synthesizes climate change research, publishing a National Climate Assessment (NCA) report every four years. The National Oceanic and Atmospheric Administration (NOAA) was asked to assess the scientific literature on sea level rise for the most recent report and established four global sea level rise scenarios, labeled as Highest, Intermediate High, Intermediate Low, and Lowest.[10] The Highest scenario, which includes estimated global warming from the earlier IPCC AR4 report (in which sea level rise by 2100 was projected to be between .18 and .59 meters) plus a calculation of glacier and sea ice melt that derives from SEM research, projects a sea level rise of 2 meters by 2100.

The National Research Council, a private non-profit institute that acts as the research arm of and is jointly administered by the National Academy of Sciences, the National Academy of Engineering, and the Institute of Medicine, has in recent years provided some climate change assessment. Its 2012 report entitled *Sea-Level Rise for the Coasts of California, Oregon, and Washington: Past, Present, and Future*, which was commissioned by a consortium of west coast state agencies, projects that global sea level will rise between .5 to 1.4 meters (1.6 to 4.6 feet) by 2100, and projects relative west coast sea level rise from this.[11]

Other entities around the world also conduct climate change assessment and their findings and projections differ as well.

Adaptation Strategies

How to plan for the future in the face of so much uncertainty? If both the Greenland and Antarctica ice sheets are lost to global warming the associated sea level rise will be so large that trying to plan now for adapting urban coastlines, let alone planning for adapted waterfront promenades, seems a futile exercise, especially since there is no scientific consensus about what the timeframe for this worst case scenario might be. As alarming as the very long-term prospects seem to be, if the collective global community is unable to find a way to reduce future greenhouse gas emissions, it is perhaps more useful for today's planners to plan for the nearer long term future. Planning for sea level rise adaptation based on projections for 2100 seems a plausible thing to do. Communities will have to decide which projections they wish to plan around, though as NOAA suggests it may be wise to take high range projections into account in situations where there is little tolerance for risk, including new public infrastructure with a long anticipated life cycle.[12] Of course, sea level rise projections are likely to keep changing as the collection and assessment of scientific evidence continues, and so adaptation plans will likely need to keep changing as well.

Communities will want to analyze how their particular waterfronts will be impacted. Beyond determining what the relative local sea level rise is likely to be, based on regional tectonic and weather variations, the vulnerabilities of different waterfront areas can be analyzed. Coastal areas will be subject to gradual hazards such as increased erosion and high tide flooding, and also sudden and severe hazards from coastal storm events, including sudden erosion, storm surge flooding, and wave action. In many coastal communities, sea level rise will gradually lead to increased flooding of low-lying areas during daily or monthly high tide events and to increased erosion of beaches and marshes. The greatest coastal damage will occur when storm surge and high waves coincide with high tides. Different coastlines will be more or less subject to these various hazards depending on their geomorphology, and will be subject to different levels of risk depending on their built form characteristics. Both coastal communities and communities on inland rivers will face more frequent storm event flooding and these floods will impact larger areas than they have in the past.

A 2014 study prepared by the New York City Planning Department entitled *Urban Waterfront Adaptive Strategies* offers a roadmap for how communities might assess their coastal conditions and discusses appropriate adaptation strategies for different situations.[13] The study analyzed New York City coastal areas and categorized them into different geomorphology types and different land use types, which were combined into a matrix to produce a classification of coastal area types: oceanfront beaches/low-density residential; hardened sheltered bay plains/medium density residential; and the like. The study also provides an inventory of the potential adaptive strategies available to address the problem of rising water, the geomorphological situations for which each is most appropriate, and particularly relevant to our concerns here hints at the possibilities for waterfront promenades associated with some.

The adaptive strategies identified in the report include both site-centered approaches that can be used to protect individual buildings from flooding and neighborhood- and district-scale strategies that can be used to protect large swaths of coastal land from flooding, through measures taken upland of the shoreline, at the shoreline, or in the water. Site-scale adaptive strategies include dry or wet flood proofing of buildings, elevating habitable parts of buildings above flood levels, and floating structures. Upland strategies include elevated land and streets, permanent or deployable floodwalls, waterfront parks, and strategic retreat of developed areas away from the water's edge. Shoreline strategies include bulkheads, seawalls, revetments, living shorelines, beaches with dune systems, and levees. In-water strategies include groins, constructed wetlands, breakwaters, artificial reefs, floating islands, constructed breakwater islands, surge barriers, altering coastal terrain, or constructed polders. The study explores the purpose and functions of each strategy, the hazards addressed, the contexts in which different approaches are suitable, the costs, and the co-benefits beyond flood protection that are possible.

Linear public open space and waterfront walking and biking paths are mentioned as co-benefits of a number of the shoreline strategies, in particular bulkheads, seawalls, and levees. Although the study doesn't stress it, waterfront walking and biking paths could also be co-benefits of waterfront parks, and perhaps also of some of the in-water adaptive strategies.

What Communities Are Doing

As we have seen, the reality is that many communities with waterfront promenades have not yet begun to grapple in a serious way with sea level rise and the impacts of climate change. Many long-standing promenades and some recently built ones are vulnerable to rising water but no plans have been prepared or actions taken to address the problem. It may be that community decision-makers have blinders on or are in denial and think that other people will handle things, later, that the political will to acknowledge and plan for climate change impacts has not been marshaled, or that the economic and social costs of dealing with sea level rise are so daunting that the community doesn't know where to start.

We have also seen that some communities with waterfront promenades have started to plan for how their waterfronts might be adapted to deal with rising water and that a few have designed or redesigned their waterfront promenades to incorporate adaptive strategies. Here we review some of the more comprehensive planning approaches being taken and some of the more innovative design strategies that have been implemented.

Planning for Sea Level Rise

New York City is ahead of most communities in planning for sea level rise. Its efforts were underway before Hurricane Sandy wrought devastation on the city in 2012 and have been ramped up since then. In 2007, the city issued *PlaNYC*, a long-term sustainability plan that includes coastal resiliency initiatives. In 2011, the city issued *Vision 2020, the New York City Comprehensive Waterfront Plan*, which recognized risks from climate change and sea level rise.[14] The city was at work on a sea level rise study when Hurricane Sandy hit the city on October 29, 2012, and shortly thereafter Mayor Bloomberg launched his *Special Initiative for Rebuilding and Resiliency*. Seven months later, in June 2013, the city issued a plan intended to protect the city against the impacts of climate change. *A Stronger, More Resilient New York* is a 445-page document that analyzes the city's existing public infrastructure and built environment and also presents community rebuilding and resiliency plans for the parts of the city most impacted by the hurricane.[15] The same month, the city issued its *Urban Waterfronts Adaptive Strategies* study and a companion document *Designing for Flood Risk*.[16] In 2014, Mayor Bill de Blasio established the Office of Recovery and Resiliency to implement recommendations laid out in *A Stronger, More Resilient New York*.[17]

New York City has also benefited from the *Rebuild by Design* ideas competition organized by the U.S. Department of Housing and Urban Development (HUD) in the wake of Hurricane Sandy to elicit ideas for improving the coastal resilience of areas impacted by the storm. In 2014, six competition winners were announced and $920 million were awarded for their implementation.[18] One of the winning projects was the Big U, which envisions a 10-mile-long protective system of new waterfront berms and storm barriers ringing Lower Manhattan. This project received $335 million to begin implementation of its first phase, but the entire project will cost considerably more.

San Francisco has begun to address sea level rise but doesn't yet have an adaptation plan. The San Francisco Bay Conservation and Development Commission (BCDC), the regional agency that has jurisdiction over a 100-foot-wide band along the San Francisco Bay shoreline, did the first studies of how sea level rise might impact San Francisco.[19] In 2007, BCDC published maps showing how Bay Area shorelines would be altered by a 55-inch rise in sea level—using projections that integrated SEMS research with IPCC AR4 projections—and in 2009 it held an international *Rising Tides* competition to solicit response ideas. The six winners of this competition shared a prize of $25,000 but no implementation of any of the ideas has moved forward, and BCDC's 2011 update of its *Bay Plan* does not take much of a proactive stance on sea level rise.[20] However, in 2010 BCDC partnered with NOAA's Office of Coastal Management to create the *Adapting to Rising Tides* project, which brings together local, regional, state, and federal agencies and non-profit groups with the purpose of building Bay Area capacity to plan for and implement adaptation, and this project makes a wealth of information available to concerned citizens and community decision-makers.[21]

In 2016, the city stepped up to the plate and issued the *San Francisco Sea Level Rise Action Plan*, which presents a vision and a set of objectives for planning and mitigating sea level rise and coastal flooding.[22] The plan, which was funded through the Rockefeller Foundation's *100 Resilient Cities Initiative* and developed by an interagency task force co-led by the public works and planning departments, has been touted as a first step toward development of a Citywide Sea Level Rise Adaptation Plan, expected to be complete by 2018.

Meanwhile, San Francisco is grappling with the reality that the aging seawall protecting its northern waterfront, on top of which runs the Embarcadero Promenade, could collapse in an earthquake and is starting to look at reconstruction options and financing possibilities.[23] To what extent a reconstructed seawall would be designed to protect against future sea level rise is an open question, but it is hard to imagine the city not addressing the issue in some manner.

Vancouver has long been concerned with sustainability and to this end has built a great public transit system and encouraged the development of high density, walkable, mixed-use neighborhoods in and around its downtown. The city has also recently begun to address future sea level rise. In 2014, the city remapped its flood zones to reflect the reach of a 500-year storm coupled with one meter of sea level rise and adopted new planning regulations requiring that any new development in the flood zones set the ground floor of buildings above the flood height. These new ground-floor-elevation heights will apply to some as yet un-built areas around False Creek and may impact the elevations at which future waterfront promenades in those areas are set.

Implemented Waterfront Promenade Adaptive Designs

Hamburg is using multiple adaptation strategies to build a large new district, HafenCity, in a flood prone area along its riverfront and create within it a network of waterfront promenades. The objectives were to protect new development on former docklands from flooding by the Elbe River, which sees dramatic daily tidal flows and seasonal flooding, while also allowing people to get close to the water during non-flood times. To accomplish both objectives, the streets and the ground floors of buildings are raised above flood level, set atop flood-proofed basements containing mostly parking garages, while the water's edge of the district's many quays are lined with promenades that sit well below street level, within the flood zone. The inland sides of the promenades are lined with the walls of building basements. In some areas, these walls are punctuated with promenade-facing cafés, restaurants, and retail shops equipped with deployable floodwalls in the form of heavy metal doors. Other communities considering waterfront promenades in conjunction with major new waterfront development projects could

HafenCity floodable promenade, in Hamburg

Berges en Seine floodable promenade, in Paris

use this combination of adaptive strategies. Although the HafenCity design doesn't include adaptive features directed at improving ecological functioning, such as living shorelines, there is no reason why such strategies couldn't be also incorporated into this integrated package of adaptive strategies.

Paris is building floodable waterfront promenades on quays fronting the Seine River where it passes through the city center. The quays, though considerably below street level, are well above normal water levels, but the Seine sometimes floods and when it does it overtops the quays and has even been known to overtop bulkhead walls and flood city streets, such as happened in the summer of 2016. To address this reality, and also to create fun public spaces quickly and inexpensively, the promenades are being created with simple but playful designs and mostly rustic materials. They have the feel of pop-up public spaces and are activated with pop-up cafés, which serve out of repurposed shipping containers or from boats tied up alongside the quay. One such pop-up promenade, the 2.3-kilometer-long Berges en Seine,[24] occupies the river's left bank from Pont de l'Alma to just beyond the Passerelle de Solferino, a pedestrian bridge that links the promenade to the Tuileries Garden near the Louvre Museum, and plans are underway to create another section on the opposite right bank. Along the promenade are floating gardens, private garden rooms that can be rented by the hour, a fruit tree garden, heavy timber beams laid on their side for seating, and areas marked off for games, including hopscotch and sprinting contests.

A better known Parisian pop-up waterfront promenade is the one the city has since 2002 created every summer on a right bank quay of the Seine River through a program called Paris Plages (Paris beaches). At other times of the year the quay is occupied by vehicle traffic, but during July and August it is temporarily converted into a pedestrian and bicycle path with sand beaches along it, where people can play beach sports or sit on beach chairs. Since 2006, Paris Plages has also operated on a stretch of left bank quay, and since 2007 it has also occupied a stretch of the Canal Saint-Martin near Parc de la Villette. Temporary installations such as these are a way of creating public spaces in flood zones during non-flood times.

The "urban beach" section of Lisbon's central area Ribeira das Naus promenade has a unique floodable design. Steps sloping down to the water's edge are regularly inundated when the Tagus River is at high tide, but offer a place for people to sit or recline near the water at low tide. The design is a creative way to allow people to get to the water's edge in a context with sizable daily tidal flows. A park just inland of the promenade has grass berms that could protect some areas from flooding, but since the berms are not continuous they do not appear to be part of an adaptation strategy.

The promenades along Seoul's recessed Cheonggyecheon stream are designed to be floodable when heavy rains overwhelm the city's storm sewer system. Most of the time the stream is shallow but floodgates along the walls of the recessed channel allow storm water to fill the entire channel when necessary, temporarily inundating the promenades.

A thesis project developed by University of California at Berkeley Master of Urban Design student Rohit Tak proposes building floodable waterfront promenades as a way of connecting the people of Pune, India, with its river. The Mutha River runs through a wide channel that bisects the city. The river is normally shallow and occupies only a small part of the channel, but during the monsoon season the river swells to fill much of the channel and during major floods it fills the whole channel. The design proposal reconfigures the river channel and tiers its edge so that during normal conditions parts of it can be used for public activities, including play fields, community gardens, and promenades.

Some areas of Malmö's recently built Western Harbour District incorporate the adaptive strategy of raising streets and buildings above extreme flood zones mapped to reflect projected local sea level rise by 2100 of .66 meters (2.2 feet). The waterfront promenade lining the neighborhood was built atop a tall riprap-reinforced seawall. Along its length various steps lead down to bathing platforms, giving people the opportunity to interact directly with the water.

Several communities have built promenades within adaptively designed upland parks. Charleston's elegant Waterfront Park, which faces onto the Cooper River at the mouth of Charleston Bay, is approximately 3 feet higher in elevation than the streets of the adjacent neighborhood, a design move intended to protect the inland areas from the regular flooding much of the city experiences. The grade change is handled subtly rather than abruptly, so that it is almost unnoticeable. The water's edge promenade sits atop a seawall that rises from a small constructed wetland. The wetland area is probably not large enough to slow down storm surges or reduce their height, but it does provide ecological habitat.

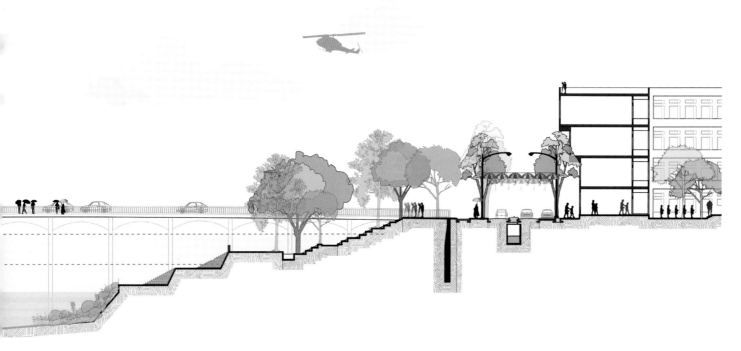

Rohit Tak's proposal for
floodable promenades and other
community open spaces in Pune,
India
Source: Rohit Tak

San Francisco's Golden Gate Promenade is set within the Crissy Field park area, whose overall design incorporates multiple adaptive strategies. These elements include a reconstructed system of low beachfront dunes, a constructed wetland lagoon, and grass covered upland berms. For much of its length, the promenade runs between the dunes and the berms.

New York City's Brooklyn Bridge Park incorporates a number of adaptive features. A living shoreline lines much of its water's edge, in some places combined with revetments. Key portions of the park are elevated above flood zones mapped with sea level rise taken into account. The park both slopes up and steps up from the water's edge and the main promenade is set back from the edge on the higher ground. The idea is that the lowest areas of the park can flood at times while the rest of the park and the promenade do not.

Along the East River in Manhattan, the northern section of the East River Waterfront Esplanade that runs through East River Park will eventually be routed along the top of a tall berm. This idea, known as the bridging berm because it will bridge across an at-grade section of FDR Drive, is one part of the Big U sea level rise adaptation vision for lower Manhattan Island. The Bridging Berm received federal funding in 2014 and its implementation is on the drawing boards.

A deployable floodwall is being considered for another section of the East River Waterfront Esplanade, the part that runs under the elevated part of the FDR Drive freeway. The floodwall would consist of steel panels that would be tucked under the freeway structure at normal times and lowered before a flood event.

An adaptive strategy available for beaches is to reinforce existing dunes, or to create a new dune system. Miami's long boardwalk runs behind a line of dunes that the city has reinforced by planting them with native dune species. The boardwalk itself consists of a newer paved at-grade section from which glimpses of the water can only be had at widely spaced beach access points, and an older wooden elevated section that offers views over the dunes. Unfortunately, Miami faces dire problems from sea level rise because it sits on a low-lying barrier island and local sea level rise is expected to be much greater than the global average, and so this adaptive strategy may protect the boardwalk but will not do much to protect the larger city. Rising seawater will intrude from inland waterways and percolate up through the porous limestone on which the city is built.

In Fort Lauderdale, a new dune system and walkway has been constructed along the part of its beachfront promenade destroyed by storm surge associated with Hurricane Sandy. The roadway

Chenggyecheon floodable
promenade, in Seoul

Miami Beach dunes

adjacent to the promenade was narrowed to give room for the new dune system. The promenade runs back of the dunes as a wide sidewalk along the roadway, and is protected from wave scour by a corrugated metal floodwall that extends far below grade and is topped with a low wall. Fort Lauderdale also sits on a low-lying barrier island and faces the same sea level rise challenges as Miami, and so this adaptive strategy may not protect the city's coastal areas for long.

On Long Island, the 5½-mile-long Rockaway Boardwalk that was largely destroyed by Hurricane Sandy is being rebuilt with a resilient design. Formerly an elevated wooden boardwalk, the new boardwalk will be a paved walk, running atop various coastal protection structures, including a sand retaining wall and elevated and reinforced dunes.[25, 26]

Most of Hong Kong's waterfront is on reclaimed land and all land reclamation projects undertaken since 1990 have been designed to assume that sea levels will rise 10 millimeters per year. Much of Hong Kong's coastline is subject to wave action and the city has constructed wave-deflecting seawalls in places, including along its central waterfront where the Central District Promenade is being built.

In Singapore, an in-water barrier was used to protect the Marina Bay Promenade and other areas along the Singapore River from flooding. The Marina Bay Barrage also creates a large new freshwater reservoir for the city.

The city of Blackpool in the United Kingdom has recently reconstructed its seawall and promenade with a design intended to withstand erosion from the considerable wave action its coast is regularly subjected to.[27] The curving promenade is lined on its ocean facing side with a continuous set of steps that lead down to a beach, and on its inland side by an inwardly curved wave wall through which occasional stairs give access to various public open spaces at street level.

Multi-purpose levees have been proposed as a strategy to upgrade Rotterdam's existing river dike system. It is envisioned that a wide levee would form a foundation for waterfront public spaces, including promenades, integrated with roadways and public transit systems.[28] In 2016, urban design students at the University of California, Berkeley, proposed a multi-purpose levee for San Francisco's central waterfront as a replacement for the city's aging seawall. The design that they prepared included an underground public transit route within the levee and public spaces atop it.

All of these adaptation strategies represent thoughtful responses to sea level rise. Waterfront communities face very real threats from climate change, but these examples illustrate the possibilities for new and innovative protection schemes that include public spaces and waterfront promenades.

Notes

1   J. A. Church et al., "2013: Sea Level Change," in *Climate Change 2013: The Physical Science Basis. Contribution of Working Group I to the Fifth Assessment Report of the Intergovernmental Panel on Climate Change* [Stocker, T.F., D. Qin, G.-K. Plattner, M. Tignor, S.K. Allen, J. Boschung, A. Nauels, Y. Xia, V. Bex, and P.M. Midgley (eds)]. (Cambridge, United Kingdom and New York, NY, USA: Cambridge University Press, 2013), 1137–1216.

2   Ibid., 1182.

3   Ibid., 1140.

4   Robert M. DeConto and David Pollard, "Contribution of Antarctica to Past and Future Sea-Level Rise," *Nature* 531, no. 7596 (March 31, 2016): 591–597.

5   Stefan Rahmstorf, Mahé Perrette, and Martin Vermeer, "Testing the Robustness of Semi-Empirical Sea Level Projections," *Climate Dynamics* 39, no. 3 (2012): 861–875, doi:10.1007/s00382-011-1226-7.

6   M. Perrette et al., "A Scaling Approach to Project Regional Sea Level Rise and Its Uncertainties," *Earth System Dynamics* 4, no. 1 (January 23, 2013): 11–29, doi:10.5194/esd-4-11-2013.

7   J. A. Church et al., "2013: Sea Level Change," 1191.

8   Ibid., 1140.

9   DeConto and Pollard, "Contribution of Antarctica to Past and Future Sea-Level Rise," 591.

10   National Oceanic and Atmospheric Administration, "Global Sea Level Rise Scenarios for the United States National Climate Assessment," NOAA Technical Report, (December 6, 2012), accessed June 2, 2016, http://scenarios.globalchange.gov/sites/default/files/NOAA_SLR_r3_0.pdf.

11   Committee on Sea Level Rise in California, Oregon, and Washington; Board on Earth Sciences and Resources; Ocean Studies Board; Division on Earth and Life Studies; National Research Council, *Sea-Level Rise for the Coasts of California, Oregon, and Washington: Past, Present, and Future* (Washington, D.C.: The National Academies Press, 2012).

12   National Oceanic and Atmospheric Administration, "Global Sea Level Rise Scenarios for the United States National Climate Assessment," 2.

13   The City of New York, Mayor Michael R. Bloomberg; Department of City Planning, Amanda M. Burden, FAICP, Commissioner, "Coastal Climate Resilience: Urban Waterfront Adaptive Strategies," June 2013.

14   Ibid., ii.

15   The City of New York, "A Stronger, More Resilient New York" (Office of the Mayor, 2013), accessed July 28, 2015, www.nyc.gov/html/sirr/html/report/report.shtml.

16   The City of New York, Mayor Michael R. Bloomberg; Department of City Planning, Amanda M. Burden, FAICP, Commissioner, "Coastal Climate Resilience: Designing for Flood Risk," June 2013.

17   "PlaNYC – Resiliency," accessed June 10, 2016, www.nyc.gov/html/planyc/html/resiliency/resiliency.shtml.

18   "Rebuild by Design Finalists," n.d., accessed June 9, 2016, www.rebuildbydesign.org/winners-and-finalists/.

19   San Francisco Bay Conservation and Development Commission, "Living with a Rising Bay: Vulnerability and Adaptation in San Francisco Bay and on Its Shoreline," October 6, 2011.

20   "SFBCDC – New Sea Level Rise Policies Fact Sheet," accessed June 10, 2016, www.bcdc.ca.gov/BPA/SLRfactSheet.html.

21   "Adapting to Rising Tides," accessed June 10, 2016, www.adaptingtorisingtides.org/.

22   City and County of San Francisco, "San Francisco Sea Level Rise Action Plan," March 2016, accessed June 9, 2016, http://sf-planning.org/sea-level-rise-action-plan%20.

23   Rong-Gong Lin II, "It Could Cost $3 Billion to Prevent Disastrous Earthquake Damage along San Francisco's Embarcadero," *Los Angeles Times*, accessed June 10, 2016, www.latimes.com/local/california/la-me-sf-earthquake-20160418-snap-htmlstory.html.

24   "Welcome to the New Seine Quaysides - Paris.fr," accessed July 5, 2016, http://next.paris.fr/english/english/welcome-to-the-new-seine-quaysides/rub_8118_actu_132293_port_19237.

25   New York City Economic Development Corporation, "Rockaway Parks Conceptual Plan," Spring 2014.

26   Nathan Kensinger, "Rockaway Boardwalk Re-Emerges With a New Identity," *Curbed NY*, August 13, 2015, http://ny.curbed.com/2015/8/13/9931108/rockaway-boardwalk-re-emerges-with-a-new-identity.

27   "Sea Defences Protected 600 from Flooding," accessed July 6, 2016, www.blackpool.gov.uk/News/2014/April/Sea-defences-protected-600-from-flooding.aspx.

28   "DE URBANISTEN," accessed July 6, 2016, www.urbanisten.nl/wp/?portfolio=riverdike-part-2.

Chapter 15

Reflections

Waterfront promenades have a role to play in creating connected urban open space systems. There is a long history of thinking that urban parks ought to be connected into citywide park systems rather than standing alone as isolated places, in order to connect more people with parks and extend park-like experiences into the city. In the late 1800s, Frederick Law Olmsted envisioned creating park linkages with parkways. His vision was realized in some cities, but parkways evolved into scenic byways on the outskirts of cities after the advent of the automobile, and then into landscaped urban highways, and so the urban open space and park networks that might have been possible with them were largely denied. Linear waterfront promenades present another opportunity to link open spaces with each other and also connect neighborhoods. Once achieved, waterfront promenades are likely to be long lasting because when a public open space is created it is difficult to erase it with other uses. This was not the case with parkways because their purpose was to serve vehicles as well as link parks, and so in some cities those that had been built were later turned into arterial streets. Once cities have claimed their waterfronts for people and built promenades, the linear park connection is likely to remain.

Beyond their role as linear open space connectors, waterfront promenades offer the opportunity for creating neighborhood park space. We have seen examples of them being built as main open spaces for new waterfront neighborhoods and also examples of them being built to provide much needed open space for existing neighborhoods. Within many built-up cities there is a lack of enough neighborhood park space. As cities become denser this deficit often gets worse because new parks can be difficult to achieve. On the other hand, when water edges become available through de-industrialization or other processes, the opportunity arises to create public open space serving neighborhood needs as well as citywide needs. Witness the basketball courts along the Hudson River Park Promenade, in New York City, and the exercise facilities along Ma On Shan Promenade in Hong Kong.

Seeing and experiencing many waterfront promenades leads to an understanding of the enormous amount of public life that takes place on them, and therefore their value. Where else in most cities, except maybe in big parks, do you see so many people gathered together in a public place on a daily basis for leisure, recreation, and social activity? The pedestrianized linear open space afforded by waterfront promenades creates a place for public life, especially in cities where most of the public open space, which is in streets, serves motorized vehicles, such as in American cities. Put another way, waterfront promenades serve the social role that streets could play if they were not so auto-dominated. Anecdotally, when the Golden Gate Promenade at Crissy Field was created, one wondered if there might be fewer people using Golden Gate Park because they'd go to Crissy instead. That does not seem to have been the case. The promenade seems instead to have created more opportunity for more people to participate in public life.

Waterfront promenades are inviting places to stroll and bike because they abound with interesting things to look at. Just as walkable streets have many things along them that catch and hold people's visual interest, so do waterfront promenades. The water itself, with its constant internal movement and the movement of light upon it, catches people's eyes, and does so in a special, relaxed way. Urban streets may be exciting and pleasurable, but they are seldom relaxing. Most waterfront promenades are all about relaxation. On the streets in many cities these days, many people move around plugged into their mobile phones or other computerized devices. This happens less often on waterfront promenades, probably because the water views are so tantalizing that people are more interested in remaining engaged with the immediate environment. Those waterfront promenades on which a number of people are plugged in tend to be ones directly adjacent to major traffic streets, where listening to music on ones' phone can help drown out the traffic noise.

We have seen that public waterfronts do not need to be created all at one time or through a single large redevelopment project. The examples of Vancouver and New York City, as well as others, show what can be achieved when the idea of creating a public waterfront and prioritizing pedestrians and bicyclists along it is embraced, held onto, and implemented over a long period of time. The idea and hanging onto it is what is important.

It is clear that climate change and sea level rise pose threats to many waterfront promenades, but we have also seen that there are possibilities for adaptation. Waterfront promenades can be designed to help make city shorelines resilient to sea level rise, at least for the near term. They can be part of the solution to the problem that so many cities face. Of course, if the worst projections for sea level rise come true, those that incorporate massive melting of the Greenland and Antarctica ice sheets, then coastal communities will need major reconfiguration. Nonetheless, it seems likely that people will want to remain connected to waterfronts in some way no matter what the sea level rise and so in all likelihood waterfront walks will continue to be built, perhaps in entirely new forms.

Finally, we have seen that design matters with waterfront promenades. Design impacts their ambience, their physical comfort, and how inviting and inclusive they are. A key understanding that comes from having studied many promenades is that they do not need to be made with expensive materials or have flashy designs. Simply designed promenades, such as those in Gruissan, Ma On Shan, on the right bank of the river in Bilbao, can be just as compelling as more elaborately designed ones.

Appendix | People Volumes on Selected Promenades

Promenade	Date/time	Effective path width	Path type	People per hour	People per minute per meter	Notes
Barcelona						
Passeig Maritìm, Sant Sebastia Beach	June 2015 Monday evening	8.54 m 3.05 m	Pedestrian Bicycle	1,179 582	2.3 3.18	Hot and sunny.
Passeig Maritìm, Barceloneta Beach, upper level only	June 2015 Saturday afternoon	12.12 m 3.2 m	Pedestrian Bicycle	753 423	1.04 2.2	Hot and sunny.
Passeig Maritìm, Barceloneta Beach, upper level only	June 2015 Monday evening	12.12 m 3.2 m	Pedestrian Bicycle	1,428 450	1.96 2.35	Hot and sunny.
Passeig Maritìm, Port Olimpic	June 2015 Saturday afternoon	14.94 m	Shared	1,828	2.04	Hot and sunny.
Passeig Maritìm, Nova Icària Beach	June 2015 Saturday afternoon	16.12 m	Shared	942	0.97	Hot and sunny.
Bilbao						
Abandoibarra Promenade, upper level only	June 2015 Thursday evening	6.10 m	Shared	274	0.75	Warm and sunny.
Abandoibarra Promenade, lower level only	June 2015 Thursday evening	6.71 m	Shared	224	0.56	Warm and sunny.
Deusto Promenade	June 2015 Thursday evening	3.66 m 2.29 m	Pedestrian Bicycle	570 126	2.60 0.92	Warm and sunny. An aroma of linden trees.
Charleston						
Water's edge path	May 2014 Saturday morning	6.10 m	Pedestrian	94	0.26	Warm and humid.
Tree-shaded path	May 2014 Saturday morning	3.66 m	Pedestrian	90	0.41	Warm and humid.
Pier	May 2014 Saturday morning	4.57 m	Pedestrian	480	1.75	Warm and humid.

Promenade	Date/time	Effective path width	Path type	People per hour	People per minute per meter	Notes
Fort Lauderdale						
Beachfront Promenade	May 2015 Saturday morning	6.71 m 1.52 m	Pedestrian Bicycle	300 45	0.75 0.49	1,326 vehicles were passing on the roadway during the same time.
Hamburg						
HafenCity, Sandtorkai	July 2014 Wednesday noon	4.88 m	Shared	549	1.88	Warm and overcast.
Hollywood						
Hollywood Beach Boardwalk	May 2015 Saturday afternoon	6.71 m 2.44 m	Pedestrian Bicycle	270 150	0.67 1.02	Hot, sunny, and humid.
Hong Kong						
Tsim Sha Tsui Promenade, Avenue of Stars	May 2015 Friday evening	7.62 m	Pedestrian	2,712	5.93	Hot and humid with light breeze.
Ma On Shan Promenade	May 2015 Sunday afternoon	6.86 m 3.05 m	Pedestrian Bicycle	303 279	0.74 1.52	Hot and humid.
Lisbon						
Passeio das Tágides	June 2015 Monday evening	15.24 m	Shared	422	0.46	Cool and sunny.
Ribeira das Naus	June 2015 Sunday afternoon	15.6	Shared	1,053	1.13	Includes the top three steps of the urban beach, the rest were under water. Sunny, warm and breezy.
Los Angeles						
Venice Beach Ocean Front Walk	November 2015 Sunday morning	6.10 m	Shared	1,245	3.40	Additional people were biking on the separated bike path during the same time.
Venice Beach Ocean Front Walk	November 2015 Sunday evening	6.10 m	Shared	3,225	2.69	Additional people were biking on the separated bike path during the same time.
Malmö						
Sundspromenaden	July 2014 Saturday evening	3.05 m	Shared	1,299	7.10	Warm, at sunset time.
Ribersborgsstigen	July 2014 Sunday morning	3.81 m 3.81 m	Pedestrian Bicycle	144 213	0.63 0.93	Warm, sunny, and humid.
New York City						
Battery Park City Esplanade	November 2014 Saturday afternoon	6.10 m	Shared	408	1.11	Cool and overcast.
Hudson River Park Promenade	November 2014 Saturday noon	6.10 m 6.10 m	Pedestrian Bicycle	900 414	2.46 1.13	Cold and sunny, with a mild breeze. Almost 22% of walkers and joggers were listening to music on headphones.
Brooklyn Bridge Park Promenade	November 2014 Sunday afternoon	7.62 m	Shared	1,212	2.65	Cool and overcast.

Promenade	Date/time	Effective path width	Path type	People per hour	People per minute per meter	Notes
Brooklyn Bridge	November 2014 Sunday morning	4.57 m	Shared	5,572	20.32	Cool and overcast.
Portland						
Westbank Esplanade	September 2014 Saturday Morning	5.49 m	Shared	1,176	3.57	Warm and sunny.
Eastbank Esplanade	September 2014 Saturday Morning	6.10 m	Shared	714	1.95	Warm and sunny.
RiverPlace Boardwalk	September 2014 Friday evening	6.10 m	Shared	552	1.51	Warm.
Rio de Janeiro						
Copacabana Promenade	August 2014 Wednesday afternoon	7.93 m / 2.74 m	Pedestrian / Bicycle	594 / 246	1.25 / 1.5	Hot and sunny.
Ipanema Promenade	August 2014 Wednesday morning	3.96 m / 2.74 m	Pedestrian / Bicycle	704 / 256	2.96 / 1.56	Hot and sunny. Almost 15% of people were listening to music on headphones or talking on phones.
Leblon Promenade	August 2014 Tuesday evening	3.96 m / 2.74 m	Pedestrian / Bicycle	414 / 147	1.74 / 0.89	Hot and sunny. More than 20% of people were listening to music on headphones or talking on phones.
Leblon Promenade	August 2014 Thursday morning	3.96 m / 2.74 m	Pedestrian / Bicycle	696 / 232	2.93 / 1.41	Hot and sunny. More than 20% of people were listening to music on headphones or talking on phones.
San Antonio						
San Antonio River Walk, downtown	March 2014 Saturday evening	4.88 m (both sides combined)	Pedestrian	3,450	11.78	Hot.
San Francisco						
Golden Gate Promenade at Crissy Field	March 2015 Saturday afternoon	10.67 m	Shared	945	1.48	Cool, sunny, and windy.
Embarcadero Promenade, just north of the Ferry Building	April 2015 Saturday noon	9.15 m	Shared	3,396	6.19	Additional bikers were moving along the on-street bicycle lanes during the same time.
San Sebastián						
Paseo de la Concha	June 2015 Thursday afternoon	20.73 m	Shared	3,000	2.4	Warm and sunny.
Seoul						
Chenggyecheon stream walk	May 2015 Thursday noon	4.57 m	Pedestrian	2,208	8.05	Warm and sunny.
Singapore						
Marina Bay Waterfront Promenade, at shopping mall and casino, upper level only	May 2015 Sunday afternoon	11.43 m	Shared	384	0.56	Hot and humid.

Promenade	Date/time	Effective path width	Path type	People per hour	People per minute per meter	Notes
Stockholm						
Hammarby Sjöstad, wetland boardwalk	July 2014 Wednesday evening	3.66 m	Pedestrian	354	1.61	Warm, with a nice breeze and setting sun.
Vancouver						
Southeast False Creek, near Hinge Park	September 2013 Sunday afternoon	4.88 m 4.57 m	Pedestrian Bicycle	663 399	2.26 1.46	Warm and sunny.
Southeast False Creek, at the community center	September 2013 Tuesday late afternoon	4.57 m 4.57 m	Pedestrian Bicycle	432 356	1.58 1.30	Warm and sunny.
Kitsilano Point, near the picnic area	April 2013 Friday late afternoon	3 m	Shared	474	2.63	Warm and sunny.
Coal Harbour	September 2014 Monday noon	6.10 m 3.96 m	Pedestrian Bicycle	942 144	2.57 0.24	Hot and sunny.
Stanley Park seawall	September 2013 Monday afternoon	3.05 m 3.05 m	Pedestrian Bicycle	261 234	1.43 1.28	Warm and sunny.

Note: The counts listed above include both counts mentioned in the text and other counts.

Index

Page numbers in *italics* refer to photographs.

Ma On Shan Promenade, Hong Kong 196–201; climate change and sea level rise concerns 201; connectivity and access 242, 267; connectivity and use 199–201; design characteristics 197–9; history and development 196–7

map sources 3–4

Marina Bay Waterfront Promenade, Singapore 157–64; climate change and sea level rise concerns 164, 287; design characteristics 159–63, 270; history and development 157–9; use and connectivity 163–4

Miami Beach Boardwalk, Florida 68, *71*; climate change and sea level rise concerns 70, 286, 287; design characteristics and connectivity 68–9; use 69

Moses, R. 208

National Climate Assessment (NCA) 117, 281

National Geodetic Vertical Datum (NGVD) 63

National Oceanic and Atmospheric Administration (NOAA) 281, 283

National Research Council 52–3, 59, 140–1, 237, 281

Nervión River *see* Central Waterfront Promenades, Bilbao

New York City: connectivity 278; Department of Parks and Recreation 43–4; freeways 275–6; long-term plan 275; Panel on Climate Change 46, 125; Planning Department 144–6, 281–2; planning for sea level rise 282–3; *Urban Waterfront Adaptive Strategies* 281–2; *see also* Battery Park City Esplanade; Brooklyn Bridge; Brooklyn Bridge Park promenades; Brooklyn Heights Promenade; Coney Island Boardwalk; Hudson River Park Promenade

Nice *see* Promenade des Anglais

Oregon *see* Central Waterfront Promenades, Portland

Palisades Park Promenade, Santa Monica 213–17; climate change and sea level rise concerns 217; design characteristics 215–16; history and development 213–15; use and connectivity 217

Paris waterfronts *284*, 285

participatory planning 275

Paseo de la Concha, San Sebastian 35–40; climate change and sea level rise concerns 39; design characteristics 35–8, 265–6; use 38–9, 260, *261*

Passeig Maritim, Barcelona 72–9; climate change and sea level rise concerns 78–9; connectivity 277–8; connectivity and use 77–8; design characteristics 73–7, 269; history and development 72–3; San Sebastia Beach 78, 260–1

Passeio das Tágides and Passeio do Tejo, Lisbon 131–5; climate change and sea level rise concerns 136; connectivity and access 244; connectivity and use 135–6; criticisms 135–6, 269; design characteristics 131–4, 269; development 131–2

planning: and adaptive designs 282–7; key concepts 274–8

Portland, Oregon *see* Central Waterfront Promenades, Portland

Portugal: Lisbon Riverfront General Plan 226, 275; *see also* Passeio das Tágides and Passeio do Tejo, Lisbon; Ribeira das Naus, Lisbon

promenade, definition of 1–2

Promenade des Anglais, Nice 24–8; climate change and sea level rise concerns 28; design characteristics 24–7; history and development 24; use and connectivity 28

promontory promenades 208–18

protests: Brooklyn–Queens Expressway 276; Coney Island Boardwalk 44, 46; Hong Kong 150, 169; Passeig Maritim, Barcelona 78

Pune, India 285, *286*

restrooms 264

Ribeira das Naus, Lisbon 226–30; climate change and sea level rise concerns 230, 285; design characteristics 227–30, 272; history and development 226–7; use 230

Rio de Janeiro 29–34; climate change and sea level rise concerns 34; connectivity and access 248; connectivity and use 32–3; design characteristics 30–2, 266, 269; traffic flow and noise 32, 33, 264–5

riverfront promenade loops 82–111

Rockefeller Foundation: *100 Resilient Cities Initiative* 283

safety 267–9

San Antonio River Walk, San Antonio, Texas 97–103; connectivity and access 249; design characteristics and use 97–103, 270–1; history and development 97

San Francisco: Bay Conservation and Development Commission (BCDC) *283*; multi-purpose levee design 287; *see also* Embarcadero Promenade; Golden Gate Bridge; Golden Gate Promenade at Crissy Field

San Sebastian *see* Paseo de la Concha

Santa Monica *see* Palisades Park Promenade

sea level rises *see* climate change and sea level rise concerns; *specific promenades*

seating 265–6

semi-empirical modeling (SEM) 280

Seoul, South Korea *see* Cheonggyecheon Stream Walk

shared use 260–4

Singapore *see* Marina Bay Waterfront Promenade

South Carolina *see* Charleston Waterfront Park

Spain *see* Central Waterfront Promenades, Bilbao; Paseo de la Concha, San Sebastian; Passeig Maritim, Barcelona

spatial data 3–4

spectacle promenades 157–75